LANDS OF THE M

A

𝕹𝖆𝖗𝖗𝖆𝖙𝖎𝖛𝖊 𝖔𝖋 𝕺𝖗𝖎𝖊𝖓𝖙𝖆𝖑 𝕿𝖗𝖆𝖛𝖊𝖑.

BY EL-MUKATTEM.

HOC EST VIVERE BIS
VITA POSSE PRIORE FRUI.—*Martial.*

NEW-YORK:
ROBERT CARTER AND BROTHERS,
No. 285 Broadway.
1851.

Entered, according to Act of Congress, in the year 1851, by
ROBERT CARTER AND BROTHERS,
in the Clerk's Office of the District Court for the Southern District of New-York.

In the interest of creating a more extensive selection of rare historical book reprints, we have chosen to reproduce this title even though it may possibly have occasional imperfections such as missing and blurred pages, missing text, poor pictures, markings, dark backgrounds and other reproduction issues beyond our control. Because this work is culturally important, we have made it available as a part of our commitment to protecting, preserving and promoting the world's literature. Thank you for your understanding.

Contents.

FIRST VIEW OF EGYPT,	5
CAIRO AND ITS ENVIRONS,	21, 38
THE NILE,	49, 64
THEBES,	77
THE NILE,	95, 118
THE DESERTS OF SUEZ AND SHUR,	134
THE DESERTS OF SIN AND SINAI,	152
THE DESERT OF SINAI,	171
THE DESERT OF PARAN AND AKABAH,	189
EDOM,	205
EDOM AND THE "SOUTH COUNTRY,"	229
JUDEA,	239
JERUSALEM,	262
JUDAH—BENJAMIN—EPHRAIM,	276
SAMARIA AND GALILEE,	293
GALILEE AND SYRO-PHŒNICIA,	316
LEBANON,	337
THE MEDITERRANEAN,	352
APPENDIX,	369

# First View of Egypt.

ALEXANDRIA—MAHMOUDIYEH CANAL—THE NILE—CAIRO.

On the first day of February, 1849, commenced my personal acquaintance with Egypt. Though a northwest gale was urging our steamer into all the gymnastic accomplishments of which a vessel is capable, and though our strained vision could only rest on low sandy shores, apparently scarce raised above the sea, yet there was a decided satisfaction in the moment, as proclaiming the *beginning* of our initiation in Oriental mysteries and the *end* of a tedious voyage. A few hours after, we were entering the Eunostus, or western harbor of Alexandria. Windmills innumerable, with their eight gigantic arms whirling in the gale, were stationed as sentinels along the coast; mud villages clustered about them, as timid children hanging to their mothers; clouds of sand filled the air, and a fleet of vessels, from the three-decked man-of-war to the fisherman's cockle-shell, were tossing at anchor in the exposed harbour. On our left, and forming the sea-side of the port, was the Island of Pharos, which for more than 2,000 years has been married to the mainland, Ptolemy Philadelphus having officiated at the ceremony. It was at the eastern extremity of this island, and, consequently, upon the eastern harbour that the celebrated Pharos stood, which ranked among the seven wonders of the world. Winding among the shipping, whose blood-red flags, bearing the star and crescent, reminded us of our Mussulman neighborhood, the "Lycurgue" cast anchor before the town. Straightway Arab boatmen, with flowing garments and huge turbans, were vociferating around us, their myriad boats dancing wildly on the troubled waters. We were soon in their midst, and having selected a crazy skiff, among peals of inimitable jabber, only to be likened to a perpetual fire of musketry, we were pulled to the shore. Here was a scene of unparalleled noise and confusion—sore-eyed, half naked Arabs, in the various capacities of boatmen, porters, guides, and spectators, all lavishly indulging in their gutturals, and adding tenfold to the mystification with which we had ever regarded the land of mummies. Summoning a good looking dragoman, who had hailed us in tolerable English, we elbowed our way out of this bedlam, slipped a "backsheesh" into the ready hands of a squalid customs officer, and formed a procession through the unpaved streets to the Frank quarter at the other end of the town. The streets or lanes were crowded with donkeys, camels, and humans, the houses were low, meanly built, and filthy, and the inhabitants ragged to a uniformity—but we were relieved by the Frank Square, which, surrounded by hotels and consulates, wore an air of comfort and cleanliness. The hotel d'Orient received us, where we sat down and tried to believe our presence in Egypt.

And now a word regarding Alexandria's history. Three hundred and twenty-three years before Christ, Alexander had seen the advantages possessed by the site of the village of Racotis, as a station in the transit from Europe to Asia—the Mediterranean connecting it with the extended coast of Spain, Gaul, and Italy, and the Nile and Red Sea uniting it with the wealth of Arabia and India. The mind to design and the power to execute were found in the same person, and Alexander laid the foundations of a city whose fame has already been worthy of the name it bears, and whose future glory is yet to be written. For more than a thousand years it was the capital of Egypt, under the Ptolemies and the Roman emperors, when the Saracen conqueror almost destroyed it through fear of a re-conquest by the Romans. It however partially recovered from this blow, and prospered with varying fortune until the discovery of the Cape of Good Hope in 1499, and the conquest of Egypt by the Turks in 1517, which two events again palsied the enterprise of this commercial city, so that its population fifty years ago had dwindled to 6,000. Mohammed Ali, however, has revived the spirit of the decayed city, the British transit has assisted in the revival, and Alexandria now holds nearly 100,000 souls, and under proper government would regain the glory of its halcyon days. But whether this result will be obtained under Moslem rule, or will need the energies of European spirits, is a problem for the future to solve.

The modern town is built on the Heptastadium, or causeway, that connects Pharos Island and the mainland, while the remains of the old city are to be seen to the south, between the Mahmoudiyeh Canal and the sea.

We sat at our windows and looked curiously down on the novelties that attracted our attention in the square. Women in sombre blue garments which concealed the entire person except the eyes, the *yashmak*, or long covering for the mouth and chin, hanging down, and reminding forcibly of an elephant's trunk—men in the flowing and slovenly garments of the Egyptian, in many cases mere bundles of rags—here and there a lordly Turk in braided-cloth jacket and full pantaloons, with his inseparable pipe in his hands, or borne by a servant—meagre-looking donkeys, with half-naked urchins propelling—long lines of camels, with the halter of each tied to his predecessor's tail—such were some of the new sights witnessed from our windows. But we had small time for gazing and meditation. The canal boat for Atfeh and Cairo was to start the next morning, and we must consequently make the most of our day in Alexandria. As soon, therefore, as our letters could be finished and ourselves put in some order, we perambulated the labyrinthine ways of the city, drinking in large draughts of Orientalism at every turn; and, before the day was completed, we were fully familiar with tarbooshes, turbans, yashmaks, kefiyehs, and a hundred other Eastern improvements on the original fig-leaves. The next morning we made a rapid survey of the principal objects of interest, regretting not a little our limited time. Pompey's Pillar and Cleopatra's Needles always appear to our minds on thoughts of Alexandria, and they are almost all that is left of the ancient city. Pompey's Pillar has been supposed to be the work of Pompey, of Julius Cæsar, and of Severus, and some have considered it the only remnant of the famous Sarapeum—but the truth is known by the Greek inscription upon it, deciphered by Salt and Wilkinson, to this effect:—

"PUBLIUS, PREFECT OF EGYPT, ERECTS [OR DEDICATES] THIS TO THE MOST HONORED SOVEREIGN AND PROTECTOR OF ALEXANDRIA—THE INVINCIBLE DIOCLETIAN."

It is most probable that the shaft (which is one piece of red granite, 73 feet in length,) is the work of the Grecian era, but the capital and pedestal are the works of Diocletian's period, when the whole was put together in honour of that emperor. That it is a patch-work affair, the fragments of old Egyptian buildings in the base amply testify. Wilkinson very wisely supposes that its erection records the capture of Alexandria by Diocletian in A. D. 296. The column stands on a slight elevation, and, by its height of nearly 100 feet, forms a conspicuous object from all directions. Its imposing shaft is miserably disfigured by travellers with little minds and great ambition, who have recorded their names thereon with staring hugeness. I must treat my readers to a quaint description of this monument, given by a worthy, named Joseph Pitts, who visited Alexandria and other parts of the East about the year 1680: —"There are several Pillars in the Ruins of Old Alexandria, of a vast bigness and height; one, especially, I did much admire, for it is as big about as three or four Men can fathom, and higher than I could throw a stone; it shines like Glass, and the Color of it is much like Porphyrian Marble; it looks as if it were one entire Piece, with some curious Stone-work on the Top of it; but I am persuaded it is artificially made, and consists of several Parts, though so well done that the Joinings are not discernible; for I can't see how it would otherwise be possible to mount it, and place it in its present Position. 'Tis called Pompey's Pillar." The same writer also sagely remarks that "No doubt this (Alexandria) was a very famous city in former times." History must be very grateful to Mr. Joseph Pitts for his support. The so-called Cleopatra's Needles are now known to have been brought from Heliopolis by one of the Cæsars, to adorn the entrance of an Alexandrian palace, the obelisks having been originally erected by an ancient Pharaoh, Thothmes III. They are situated near the border of the Eastern port, among the desolate mounds of the old city. One is fallen, while the other retains its erect position.

A fragment of a beautiful mosaic floor has been lately found in the neighbourhood of the city, and is probably a relic of the Cæsarean provincial capital. The subject is Medusa's head, and reminds one of the finished examples of this art in the deserted houses of Pompeii. We rode along an avenue of acacias to Said Pacha's palace, and there, for the first time, obtained some idea of oriental magnificence and luxury: spacious divans, exquisite siesta chambers, and other soft effeminacies so well understood by our Shemitic brethren.

We were forced to give up the catacombs, as our time was fast expiring, and hurry back to our hotel, where the mysteries of packing and preparing were performed with most undignified and unoriental alacrity. By 10 A. M., we were riding in an omnibus to the canal boat on the Mahmoudiyeh Canal, having formed but a slight breakfast on the ruins of Alexandria, and thus not injuring our appetites for the greater glories of the past that awaited us at the Pyramids and in Upper Egypt.

The Mahmoudiyeh Canal deserves some notice. It was cut by Mohammed Ali, in 1819, to facilitate commercial intercourse between his capital and the sea, as the old route down the Nile past Rosetta was dangerous, from the sand-bars at the mouth of the river. In true Eastern style, therefore, some 300,000 men, women, and children were driven to the scene of operations, and whipped to the work of digging out a canal of forty miles in length, seven and a half feet in depth, and two hundred and twenty feet in width. A sufficient supply of provisions for this immense multitude was not prepared, the requisite implements for the work were not at hand, and there were no pumps to keep the water out of the trench: and the natural consequence ensued. Between 20,000 and 30,000 of the miserable labourers fell by disease, and were buried, sometimes, before life had entirely left their bodies; but what was that to the Egyptian Pacha? The canal was completed in seven months, and he was satisfied. The canal commences at Alexandria, and runs easterly to Atfeh, on the Rosetta branch of the Nile. It is rudely constructed, as might be imagined; and from the constant filling of its bed by the debris from the sides, will doubtless, ere many years, require another offering of 20,000 Egyptians to continue its utility.

Our canal-boat was a tolerable specimen, towed by a puffing steamer of diminutive dimensions and corresponding power. A gale was blowing, and we had not proceeded far upon the tortuous stream, when our gallant tug gently drew us into the branches of an overhanging tree, from whose embraces it had not the ability to extricate us. Our Arab crew were instantly everywhere,—in the water and on the boat, in the tree and on the shore, scattering most prodigally their lung-exhausting, ear-splitting yells, as if by incantation to give us release from our stationary position; ropes were cast in all directions, and the sage sons of Mohammed pulled east, west, north and south, as each one found a hawser to handle. Matters thus remained for a half hour, in which we had ample amusement in witnessing the Saracenic homœopathic method of removing a difficulty by increasing its entanglement; until, when our amusement began to give way to impatience, by an unforeseen and unexpected concurrence of events, we found ourselves again in the stream, cast loose upon the "raging canal." Our crew, not burdened by useless garments, swam out to rejoin us, and the excitement of our wreck was fast abating under the influence of new scenes in the "land of Ham."

The banks of the Mahmoudiyeh Canal are certainly not picturesque, but they possess interest enough to set off this deficiency. For upon our right was the wide Lake Mareotis, upon whose borders grew anciently the celebrated wine,

"Mentemque lymphatam Mareotico"
Hor. Od. 1, 37, 14.

whose former existence present appearances would almost make us doubt. Farther on, we look over the Bay of Aboukir, by which stood the Egyptian Nicopolis, built in commemoration of the victory gained by Augustus over Antony. This spot has obtained additional celebrity by the modern victory of Lord Nelson over the navy of France. It was in this vicinity we were for the first time spectators of a mirage. The nothingness of the lake and verdure beyond was scarcely to be credited, and gave us experimental acquaintance with the fact that our senses are not always to be trusted. This natural phenomenon is the effect of different strata of air of different density, in the present instance the lower stratum being the warmer, and consequently the more dense. There is a grand moral lesson illustrated by the mirage—"We must walk by faith, not by sight."

Our canal trip gave us a more intimate knowledge of things in Egypt. In the missing fingers, eyes, and teeth, that should have had place in the persons of our crew, we saw the effects of Mohammed Ali's system of conscription, the dread of which causes thousands thus to mutilate themselves and their children, to avoid a compulsory patriotism. The cunning tyrant had met their evasions by organizing a regiment of these self-disabled subjects, wherein the eyeless was compelled to aim with his left eye (for their fears had never driven them to *total* blindness as a refuge), the toothless was shown a new method of opening a cartridge, and the fingerless was forced to bring one of his surviving digits to perform the duty of its departed brother in the service of the trigger. We were not a little astonished by the Paradisical indifference with which the unclothed human figure is considered in Egypt, a bodily frankness rather amazing to the ladies of our party, who, like Joseph's brethren, could protest that they had not come into Egypt to spy out the nakedness of the land.

For more than ten hours we were travelling on Mohammed Ali's great canal, passing numberless mud villages, that strongly resembled rude ant-hills, until, under a brilliant moon, we reached the villanous village of Atfeh, the termination of the canal, and the place of our embarkation upon the Nile. We here had our first view of the great river; but, not being in condition for rhapsodies, regarded it with no more astonished gaze than if it had been the Croton or the Spuytenduyvil. The truth is, ten hours in our cramped quarters on the canal-boat had rendered us proof against any sensation save that of sleep; and the barking dogs of Atfeh could avail little to put us in a better frame of mind. We therefore, as speedily as possible, transferred ourselves from the canal-boat to the neat little steamer that awaited us; and while turbaned Arabs were making all the noise possible in transferring the luggage and freight, we hastened to the cabin and laid ourselves out upon a table for the night, philosophically banishing all Nilotic thoughts until morning. This steamer was one belonging to the Transit Company (formerly an English, but now an Egyptian enterprise, as far as the passage through Egypt is concerned), and is one of the very few that have ever paddled in the waters of the river of the Pharaohs.

Refreshed by sleep, we rose from our beds (1 should say, tables), ready to feel all the inspiration that the Nile could impart. We were opposite the mounds of Sais, once capital of Lower Egypt. An unsatisfactory gaze, and we were past them, hastening on to the Pyramids and Grand Cairo. The banks were flat and sandy: here and there the white tomb of a sheikh, like a detached oven, caught the eye—then one of the queer ant-hill villages rose on its mound sufficiently high to escape drowning in the inundation—then a line of camels paced with measured tread along the shores; and at various points the black tents of the Bedawin formed a resting-place for the eye in the midst of the dreary scene. In general, a strip of cultivated soil bordered the sacred river, but often the desert had asserted its power, and carried its sandy triumph to the water's edge. A point of great interest upon the Nile, is the junction of the Rosetta and Damietta mouths, about ten or fifteen miles north of Cairo; for near this is in progress the great work of damming the Nile—a work which, if completed, might give Mohammed Ali a rank with the Rameses of antiquity. Myriads of toiling Egyptians, like bees around a hive, were swarming about the erection, and their numbers, with the already accomplished portion of the work, gave token of the greatness of the undertaking. Some time before reaching this point, we had descried the Pyramids, and for an hour we were traversing the boat from side to side, and from corner to corner, to keep them in view as the windings of the river altered the direction of our progress. At two P. M. we halted among a crowd of small craft at Boulac, the port of Cairo. This town contains 5,000 inhabitants, and is a slight improvement upon the villages we had passed on the river. Its minarets give it an air of importance, and a busy crowd upon the steep banks show its claims to commercial consideration. We experienced as warm a reception as. at Alexandria, all Boulac shouting in salutation, and excessively obliging boys were earnest in offering their donkeys for our use—but there was an *omnibus* there —and what power an omnibus has upon the movements of a New Yorker! Though we listened in vain for —" Broadway—ride up ?"—the bait was tempting, and, with the majority, donkeys had to yield to their long yellow rival. Individually, however, I remained; and having seen my luggage safely deposited on a truck, a spirited donkey was selected, and I took the road to Cairo, followed by an Arab boy, by way of spur; the fellow doubtless knew me to be a neophyte at donkey-riding, and this was sufficient reason for his exertions in calling out my embryo ability. The obstinate beast turned as many corners as a tacking ship, and, in spite of my utmost endeavours, kept under full sail, dashing headlong among the groups of pedestrians, now bringing my head against a hanging branch, and then bruising my leg against another rider, until, to crown the measure of his iniquities, he carried me fiercely into the centre of a muffled *harem*, who were taking the air on horseback. Several bamboo rods, wielded by the attendant slaves, put me and my donkey in the right way, while the persecuting boy followed with redoubled shouts till we gained the gate of Cairo. Passing through the beautiful Ezbekiyeh—the large park of the city—I was obliged to tear mself away from Donkey & Co., to enter the Hotel d'Orient, an offshoot of the Alexandrian House.

Cairo, called by the Arabs "Musr-el-Kahirah," is now the capital of Egypt, and contains a population of 200,000 souls. It is a vast collection of narrow lanes and dingy low houses; but yet, in its extreme orientalism, from its mosques and minarets, from its balconies and bazaars, from its camels and costumes, from its gardens and gayety, and especially from the lovely Ezbekiyeh, has an inexpressible charm for the traveller's heart. High over the extended city rises the citadel, which contains within its wide precincts the palace of Mohammed Ali, the courts of justice, and, above all, the new mosque, built of Egyptian alabaster and possessed of the most exquisite minarets conceivable. From this point, not only all Cairo, but its vicinity (green towards the Nile, and arid towards the east), lies before you: the great river flows beyond, and still farther stand the Pyramids—the voices of the olden time. Behind are the Mukattem rocky hills and mountains, beyond whose desolate barrier is the way to the howling wilderness, whose plains and valleys must ere long become familiar to our footsteps.

Cairo was founded in the year 969, under El Moez, the first Fatemite Caliph of Egypt, and four years thereafter became the capital of the country, an honour which it has continued to retain—so that the mosque of Tooloon, of large dimensions and imposing architecture, which now stands within the southern wall of the city, was originally built in the open fields, having been erected in 879 by the usurper Ahmed ebn e' Tooloon. The Fatemites ruled at Cairo for 200 years;

the Aioobite Sultans followed, of whom the first monarch was the famous Saláh-e'deen, commonly known as Saladin, who was probably the original to the numerous Saracens' Heads that are painted on the sign-boards of village inns in England. The Aioobites held the sovereignty about 80 years, when the Memlooks succeeded to a throne, which they held independently until the conquest of Egypt by the Turks in 1517. After that they retained a dependent authority until, in 1811, Mohammed Ali, by a startling exercise of power, completed their overthrow. This act of the Pacha has been severely censured, and doubtless it deserves reproach; but when we contemplate how great an obstacle the Memlooks had been to the consolidation of Mohammed Ali's power, and how great opposition they ever evinced to the mental and moral improvement of Egypt, we are led to temper our censure by the excuses which the knowledge of these facts brings forward.

The Hotel d'Orient is one of the three European hotels that face the Ezbekiyeh. It has many Frank comforts, and thus renders more easy the traveller's transition from European system to the desultory life of the East. The waiters are a mingling of Italian, Maltese, and Egyptian, and are summoned by the primitive method of clapping the hands, bells not having been introduced as yet into Saladin's capital. We actually found a Yankee steward at this hotel, as much at home among the tarbouches, as if he had never known the land of wooden nutmegs. He had come from Marblehead, and, in direct opposition to the tide of emigration, had struck Eastward for a new home. Who knows but this may be the germ of Annexation !— the first dawning of the established series of three stages for the extension of empire, unknown to Alexander, but left to the invention of a later day—viz: Colonization—Declaration of Independence—Annexation!

The population of Cairo (as before said) is 200,000, being about one-tenth of that of all Egypt. Of this, probably 160,000 are Mohammedans, 8,000 Copts, 2,500 Jews, and the rest strangers from the different parts of Europe, Asia, and Africa. The prevailing costume is the turban and flowing robes, though among the higher classes (who are mostly Turks) the European dress is introduced in some cases. However picturesque may be the Oriental garments, they certainly impede the active movements of the body, and conduce to that luxurious lounging habit so characteristic of the East. A man in petticoats is decidedly more ornamental than useful, and seems out of place unless reclining in the bazaar, or calmly smoking his *shebook* in a *dahabiyeh*.

When "the schoolmaster is abroad," he should by all means visit Cairo. He would learn principles of teaching which he had never dreamed of in his philosophy. Forty or fifty boys are collected in a bare-walled room, and there seated on the floor with their legs bent beneath them; a diminutive desk or frame of palmwood is put before each, on which the book (generally the Koran) is placed, and before these the pupils roll themselves backward and forward, accompanying the motion with a loud rehearsal of their task. This method is supposed to give the matter readier access to the brain. The stillness of a school-room cannot, therefore, be proverbial among the Cairenes.

We happened to arrive in Cairo just after the return of the great caravan of pilgrims from Mecca, and, consequently, there was unusual stir in the city. That evening the trees of the Ezbekiyeh were hung with lamps, and the broader avenues were lined with tents and booths, in which the howling dervishes performed their worship. Of course, the park was alive with spectators of every age, colour, sex, and nation. In each tent a band of dervishes were conducting their noisy ceremony. Their dress was not uniform, though their action seemed to be the result of drilling. Their performances commence by reading in chorus the Koran, with an intonation reminding one of the priestly chanting in the Romanist churches of Europe, and they then rise, and, standing either in a row or circle, begin a succession of low and dignified bows, calling out in tones of singular hoarseness the name of "Allah," "Allah." Their bowing and enunciation become gradually faster, until an undefined sound, more like the bellowing of a bull than any other known noise, is all that is heard, while their bodies vibrate with the rapidity and apparently mechanical action of a steam-engine. This they continue sometimes for an hour, when, exhausted, they seat themselves, and find refreshment in pipes and coffee. Often they continue their wild worship till they fall, foaming in frenzy, to the ground. This was certainly a startling spectacle with which to begin our observations of the Moslem faith, but the scene that awaited us on the morrow far surpassed this, both in novelty and fanaticism. The Ezbekiyeh was fairly jammed with human beings, in all the gay-colored drapery of the East. The *Doseh* was about to take place. The birth of the Prophet was to be commemorated by a ceremony as remarkable as any in the annals of superstition. The immense crowd moved with impatience as the sun shone hotly upon them. After a long delay, there was a parting of the mass, and a hundred half-naked dervishes came rushing to a point near our station, where they cast themselves upon the ground, with the incessant cry of "Allah." A quasi police force arranged their prostrate figures in due order, packing them as closely as was possible, with their faces downward and their feet extended. This done, the Sheikh of the Saadiyeh dervishes, mounted on a strong horse, rode over the living pavement, an escort of footmen attending. Immediately after his passage, the devotees rose shrieking, whether in pain or religious frenzy we could not tell. We were told that two of those ridden over died that day, but Mussulmans declare that no injury ensues, owing to a miraculous restraining power possessed by the Sheikh. While waiting for the performance of this ceremony, naked wrestlers with oiled bodies had gone through their disgusting exercises before us, and after the ceremony, some of the dervishes tore living vipers with their teeth—a customary accompaniment to this day's programme.

The origin of this curious and revolting ceremony I know not, though the first human cause was, doubtless, the natural desire to expiate sin by one's own suffering —the great self-righteous principle, which, springing from pride and ignorance, has always resisted the plain but humbling truths of the Gospel, and appears in every phase of false religion. No doubt, a blind attachment to custom influences some of these dervishes in the Doseh, and a desire of praise may prove incentive to others, but I imagine that a sense of personal expiation for sin and a holiness thus purchased, is with many still the impelling motive to this absurd and debasing action.

Cairo and its Environs.

CAIRO—HELIOPOLIS—OLD CAIRO—PYRAMIDS.

OPHTHALMIA prevails in Egypt to a frightful extent, and, like the Goitre in Switzerland, it is attributed by different theorists to widely different causes. Some consider it the result of the exhalations after the overflow of the Nile—others, as proceeding from the dust that is raised by the slightest wind in a land where rain is so seldom known. A third theory finds its cause in checked perspiration. A fourth in the reflection of the sunlight by the sand. Of these hypotheses the first has the greatest probability.

A source of constant annoyance to a sensitive traveller is the abundance of vermin which is the inevitable portion that falls to his lot throughout the East. The third and fourth plagues of Egypt have left their traces, and no portion of the land can claim exemption, as of old. It is only to travellers, however, that the vermin prove vexatious, the natives apparently regarding as a luxury that which is to many the direst discomfort. It may be said of the Egyptian, equally with the Neapolitan lazzarone, that the banishment of vermin from his person and dress would cast him into unspeakable sorrow, as cutting off one of his principal sources of amusement and occupation. Were it not that with Mussulmans washing is a religious duty, the Egyptians would be intolerably filthy, as we may certainly know from their personal uncleanliness in spite of the prescribed lavations. The Egyptians deserve credit, however, for their good-heartedness, a strong set-off to their faults. We ever experienced kindness at their hands, and were witnesses of refined courtesies among them, that might have caused some of the most enlightened nations of the earth a blush for their own shortcomings. Their demands for " backsheesh" must not be adduced as objections to this character. How can a people, bowed to the dust by tyrannical oppression, and living abjectly on the crumbs that fall from their tyrants' tables, avoid seeking support from the strangers that pass among them, whose imagined wealth is to them the consolation of every wo? If they are a *begging* people, it is because they are an *oppressed* people; and God forbid that we should blame those for their importunity whom man has driven to the last necessity. It was on our first Sunday in Cairo, that we walked to the little chapel of Mr. Lieder, the worthy representative of the Church Missionary Society of England. A door-way, of the size and appearance of a front-door to a dwelling-house, leads from the Ezbekiyeh to the Coptic quarter, in which the chapel is situated. We then pass through streets about six feet in width, resembling dark entries in a large house, where the approach of a camel or donkey drives the pedestrian to the wall. After a little labyrinthine exercise, we entered the little court, through which we passed to the chapel, a pleasant room, neatly and comfortably fitted up with pulpit, desk, chancel, and pews. The unpainted window-sashes and little panes reminded of Switzerland. About thirty-five persons were present, chiefly travellers and English residents, to whom Mr. Lieder delivered an admirable practical discourse on the great themes of repentance and faith. During the services, the sweetest singing-birds were sporting about the windows and mingling their songs with the voice of God's ambassador. It was strangely appropriate; the Gospel was delivered in a land of Moslems; the birds were those of February.

That afternoon we saw old Mohammed Ali pass in his European carriage. His reason was well nigh gone, and little sensation was excited by his presence; the ass can kick the dead lion. He reclined in one corner of the vehicle, and paid no attention to things about him. His fine white beard and well-formed features comported well with the dignity of his robes and turban. We afterwards saw him often in his drives, in the same posture, and with the same indifferent expression. Abbas Pacha was then in Constantinople, receiving the ratification of his succession at the hands of the Sultan.

Cairo possesses no antiquities itself, except the fragments of ancient buildings which have been transferred to modern erections; but its neighbourhood is unparalleled for interest in the antiquary's eye. It was a bright morning (as every morning is in Egypt) that we drove to the site of Heliopolis in a European barouche. We rode for about two hours N. E. of the city, over the fertile plain, and past two or three villages of the same stamp as those before seen. A wheeled vehicle not being able to make further progress, by reason of ditches and dykes, we alighted, and, calling a shepherd to guide us, reached a slight sand-hill, whence we saw the lone obelisk rising behind some houses and trees, in a situation far different from what I had anticipated. I had imagined it rising solitary in the midst of a sandy

plain, but on the contrary it stands in a garden, and almost *within* the village of Matariyeh, though these localities, 'tis true, are not far removed from the actual desert, a distance of a stone's throw only intervening. Heliopolis, known in Scripture as On, Beth-Shemesh and Aven, is first heard of as the residence of the priest Potipherah, whose daughter was married to Joseph. According to Berosus, this was the city of Moses, and here he became learned in all the wisdom of the Egyptians. Herodotus also declares that the Heliopolites were reckoned the wisest of the Egyptians. Jeremiah denounces this city and prophesies its injury by Nebuchadnezzar, and Ezekiel foretells the destruction of its young warriors by the hand of the same conqueror. Sixty years after, Cambyses, the furious successor of Cyrus, made havoc with its edifices. About a century after this conquest, Herodotus, Plato, and Eudoxus, successively visited Heliopolis, and attended the instructions of the priests of the college established there. Strabo, however, relates that when he visited Heliopolis, a few years before Christ, it was a mass of splendid ruins, among which were shown the houses of Eudoxus and Plato. The rise of Alexandria had probably undermined the prosperity of Heliopolis, and gradually reduced it to the size of a village. Its original name was probably *On*; in hieroglyphics it is called Phré (the Sun), hence the Hebrew name Beth-Shemesh (house of the Sun), and the Greek Heliopolis, (city of the Sun), the city having been dedicated to the Sun, to which a magnificent temple had been erected.[*]
The name of Aven, in Ezekiel, is probably a play upon the name On, which words in Hebrew are very similar,

---

[*] It is said that a fountain, now called "Ain Shems" (fountain of the Sun) preserves the old name, and that the Greek title Heliopolis is still seen in a village called "Kelioub." But these I did not see.

the prophet taking advantage of the name of the city to give it the similar and appropriate title of Aven (iniquity). The Hebrew writing for On and Aven is אן and און, there being but the difference of one letter (wav) inserted.

To return to the obelisk, now the sole representative of the Egyptian Athens, unless we regard the mounds which extend for half-a-mile as remnants of the fallen city. This obelisk is at present 60 feet in height, being much covered at the base by the deposit of alluvium. It is a noble shaft of Syenite granite, and shows marks of a former metallic covering on its apex. Its hieroglyphics are large and comparatively few. They declare its erection by Osirtasen the 1st, whose reign is by some placed contemporary with Joseph, by others 300 years previous. It would be an interesting work to explore the alluvial deposit in the neighbourhood, and thereby expose other remnants of the splendid ruins that greeted Strabo's eyes. It is not my design to record the method by which the hieroglyphics of Egypt have yielded a chronicle of ancient history, which was a sealed book for ages, nor to explain the mystic writing in any way; but I take the interpretations of Champollion and his successors (as I would the translations of a Greek manuscript,) as incontrovertibly correct, though liable in a few cases to the mistakes that attach to all translations. At Heliopolis is shown a sycamore, under which Joseph and Mary reposed after the flight into Egypt. This and the house of the Virgin at Old Cairo may stand as fair samples of the value of monkish tradition.

The third day of our sojourn at Cairo was devoted to the Pyramids. A party of twenty, mounted on sprightly donkeys, and attended by a legion of donkey-boys, in full pursuit, we galloped through the narrow streets, putting the worthy inhabitants to the wall, turning abrupt corners innumerable, till, reaching the gate and emerging from the city, we found ourselves on a pretty shaded road. Four miles of riding brought us to Old Cairo, called by the Arabs Musr el Atikeh, or the Old Musr, to distinguish it from Musr el Kahira, or the victorious Musr, the Arabian title of Grand Cairo. This Old Cairo is a shabby place, of probably 3,000 souls, and was (after the conquest of Egypt by the Saracens, and previous to the foundation of the present capital) the chief city and seat of government of the Caliphs. It was built on the site of the Egyptian Babylon. Opposite Old Cairo is the long island of Roda, on which are the pretty villas of several grandees, and at the end of which is the famous Nilometer. Descending the steep mud banks, we embarked in one of the myriad of dirty boats that are constantly waiting for customers, while our donkeys found passage in another, the usual accompaniment of an Egyptian thoroughfare—ceaseless vociferations—being not wanting. On the western shore we landed at Ghizeh, a miserable village, that has the honour, however, of giving the common name to the neighbouring Pyramids. Leaving this as soon as possible, we hurried over the level plain that lay, green with the luxuriant growth of the Nile valley, between us and the objects of our excursion. Here and there we galloped through a squalid village, slightly raised above the plain to escape the inundation, and from which we were assailed by the familiar cry of "Backsheesh, backsheesh, ya hawagee" (Money, money, your honor). The mighty monuments of the Pharaohs grew more majestic as we approached. We arrived at the limit of Nile-giving fertility, passed the frontier-village, and entered the sandy district, the outskirts of the great Lybian desert. Just beyond this limit rises the rocky elevation on which the Pyramids are built, a height of probably fifty feet. Ascending this, we were at the foot of the Great Pyramid. The spirit cannot be human that can stand here for the first time and look up these huge sides and along that extended surface of immense hewn stones, and feel no astonishment and awe. The thought of its human origin enhances this sensation; we look upon a mountain, but the habit of associating such a work with the omnipotent hand of Deity has, the effect of dulling our sensibilities in its contemplation—but gaze at the Great Pyramid, the work of man, with which all else that he has wrought is dust and ashes, and we are overpowered; the idea of mystery at once connects itself with our thoughts. It is certainly more startling to the mind to witness a gigantic result from a diminutive cause, than to behold the harmonious proportion of cause and effect, of whatever mutual magnitude the latter may be in comparison.

The Pyramids, on a near approach, lose the smooth appearance which they possess when seen at a distance. It then becomes strikingly evident that generation after generation have quarried from them, as from mountains of stone, to erect the edifices of successive cities that have risen in this neighbourhood. In this manner the smooth surfaces of the Pyramids have become indented like giant stairways, and the epithet of "ruins" is clearly suitable to these venerable relics of the earlier ages of man. The Pyramids stand in an imposing situation, on the brow of the low Lybian hills that form the western border of the Nile valley. Just beyond the green vale, they rise solemnly above the dreary sand, for they that were laid within them had left the beauty and joy of life for that which had by them been regarded as the sad wilderness of the invisible world. That they were built for tombs there can be no question.

Their position in the grand cemetery of Memphis, their interior arrangement, and the voice of history, are sufficient testimony on this point. Herodotus, who visited Egypt probably about B. C. 455, thus writes regarding the Pyramids (his information having been obtained from the Egyptian priests): "Cheops, who succeeded Rhampsinitus, degenerated into the extremest profligacy of conduct. He barred the avenues to every temple, and forbade the Egyptians to offer sacrifices; he proceeded next to make them labour servilely for himself. Some he compelled to hew stones in the quarries of the Arabian mountains, and drag them to the banks of the Nile; others were appointed to receive them in vessels, and transport them to the so-called Lybian Mountain.* For this service a hundred thousand men were employed, who were relieved every three months. Ten years were consumed in the hard labour of forming the road through which these stones were to be drawn; a work, in my estimation, of no less fatigue and difficulty than the pyramid itself. This causeway is five stadia in length, forty cubits wide, and its extreme height thirty-two cubits; the whole is of polished marble, adorned with the figures of animals. Ten years, as I remarked, were exhausted in forming this causeway, not to mention the time employed in the vaults of the hill on which the Pyramids are erected. These he intended as a place of burial for himself, and were in an island which he formed by introducing the waters of the Nile. The pyramid itself was a work of twenty years; it is of a square form; every front is eight plethra long and as many in height. The stones are very skilfully cemented, and none of them of less dimensions than thirty feet. The ascent of the pyramid

---

* Wrongly translated by Beloe, "to *a* mountain of Lybia."

was regularly graduated by what some call steps and others altars. Having finished the first flight, they elevated the stones to the second by the aid of machines constructed of short pieces of wood; from the second, by a similar engine, they were raised to the third, and so on to the summit. Thus there were as many machines as there were regular divisions in the ascent of the pyramid, though, in fact, there might only be one, which, being easily manageable, might be removed from one range of buildings to another, as often as occasion made it necessary; both modes have been told me, and I know not which best deserves credit. The summit of the pyramid was first of all finished: descending thence, they regularly completed the whole. On the outside were inscribed, in Egyptian characters, the various sums of money expended in the progress of the work, for the radishes, onions, and garlic consumed by the artificers. This, I well remember, my interpreter informed me, amounted to no less a sum than 1,600 talents. If this be true, how much more must it have necessarily cost for iron-tools, food, and clothes for the workmen, particularly when we consider the length of time they were employed in the building itself, adding what was spent in the hewing and conveyance of the stones, and the construction of the subterraneous apartments. * * * According to the Egyptians, this Cheops reigned fifty years. His brother Cephren succeeded to the throne, and adopted a similar conduct. He also built a pyramid, but this was less than his brother's, for I measured them both; it has no subterranean chambers, nor any channel for the admission of the Nile, which in the other surrounds an island, where the body of Cheops is said to be deposited. This Cephren reigned fifty-six years; the pyramid he built stands on the same hill with that erected by his brother; the hill itself is near one hundred feet high. * * * Mycernuis, the son of Cheops, succeeded Cephren. * * * This prince also built a pyramid, but it was not by twenty feet so large as his father's. It was a regular square, on every side 300 feet, and, as far as the middle, of Ethiopian stone."

Such is the account of Herodotus, and from its minuteness, we must grant it a considerable degree of credibility. This portion of history certainly belonged to times long anterior to the Grecian writers, yet it is probable that something like a true account had been preserved by the priests, who were the literary caste. In the dimensions of the Pyramids, Herodotus widely errs in one instance, as the following will show:—*

| Former perpendicular height of Great Pyramid, as known by mathematical calculation, given by Col. Howard Vyse, 480.9 feet; length of base, 764. | The same, as given by Herodotus, 8 plethra, i. e., 800 feet; length of base, 800 feet. |

The proximate correctness of the second amount induces us to believe that the former is an insertion in the text. The words thus inserted would be the two small ones ὕψος ἴσον.

His other declaration, that the base of the third pyramid was 300 feet in length, is near enough as a rough estimate to the real base, which is 354 feet. Strabo, the geographer, who flourished at the time of our Saviour's birth, thus writes:—

"To one going forty stadia from Memphis, there is a certain brow of a hill, on which are many pyramids, royal sepulchres; three are remarkable, and two of them are reckoned among the seven wonders of the world. They are straight [or, a stadium] in their ele-

* Beloe wrongly translates "300 feet *high*."

vation; square in shape, having a height somewhat greater than each side, and the one is somewhat greater than the other. There is a stone, capable of removal, about midway between the top and base, on the sides, and when removed a tortuous passage leads to the tomb. These are near to one another, on the same level; but farther off, on a greater elevation of the hill, is the third, much smaller than the two, but of far more expensive workmanship; for, from the foundation almost to the centre, it is built of black stone, which they bring from the mountains of Ethiopia, and from which they make mortars. This stone being hard and difficult to work, rendered the building extremely expensive. * * * I must not omit one of the wonderful sights at the Pyramids. There are masses of stone lying before them, and among these are found fragments, both in shape and size like lentils. * * * These are said to be the petrified remnants of the workmen's provisions; nor is it improbable."

Diodorus Siculus, who lived at the same period as Strabo, thus speaks regarding the Pyramids:—" Chembis (or Chemmis) a Memphite, who reigned fifty years, built the largest of the three pyramids, which are reckoned among the seven wonders of the world. They stand on the Lybian side (of the Nile), distant from Memphis 120 stadia, and 45 from the river. They strike every beholder with wonder, both from their size and the skill of their workmanship; for every side of the largest, at the base, is seven plethra in length and more than six in height. Decreasing in size towards the summit, it there measures six cubits (nine feet.) The whole is of solid stone, made with prodigious labour, and in the most durable manner, having lasted to our time, a period not less than 1,000 years, or, as some say, upwards of 3,400, the stones still preserving their original position, and the whole structure being uninjured. * * * It is reported that 360,000 men were employed in this work, and the time occupied in finishing the whole was scarcely less than twenty years.

"On the death of this king, his brother Cephren succeeded to the throne, and reigned fifty-six years. * * Wishing to emulate his predecessor, he built the second pyramid, similar to the other in its style of building, but far inferior in size, each face being only one stade in length at its base. * * * *

"After them came Mycernius, or, as some call it, Mechernius, the son of the founder of the Great Pyramid. He built the third, but died previous to its completion. Each side was made three plethra long at the base, with (a casing of) black stone, similar to that called Thebarc, as far as the fifteenth tier, the rest being completed with stone of the same quality as the other pyramids."

From these authors, we gather that the three kings, Cheops or Chembis, Cephren, and Mycerinus, erected the three main pyramids of Ghireh, and that the period of their reigns was uncertain 1,800 years ago. The difference in recorded sizes of the pyramids clearly shows that these authors of ancient days are not to be trusted for *precision* in their accounts. Additional testimony of the most important nature is had in the hieroglyphics discovered by Col. Vyse within the Great Pyramid. These hieroglyphics contained the king's name —Cheops. Within the third pyramid, moreover, was found, by the same indefatigable discoverer, a sarcophagus, a wooden coffin, which bore the name of Mycernuis. As to the date of the reign of Cheops, Wilkinson makes it 2,123 B.C., while others prefer a still more ancient date, harmonizing their opinion with the

Bible accounts by refusing Archbishop Usher's calculations, and considering the numbers of the Septuagint to be more correct than the Hebrew, which is supposed to have been altered. It is probable, that in the course of future investigations, more light will be thrown on this interesting subject. From the remark of Diodorus, that the Pyramids were uninjured in his day, we are led to accuse the Caliphs as plunderers of these monuments. To Moslem power, we are led to attribute the conflagration of the Alexandrine library; to the same power the ruin of the Pyramids; and in Mohammed Ali the spirit of destruction has continued its abominations in the annihilation of many of the most important relics of antiquity.

To return to our visit. We had gathered followers to our party as we advanced, as a rolling ball accumulates the snow, so that, when we alighted from our donkeys at the foot of the Pyramid, a hundred Arabs were loudly recommending themselves to our consideration as guides to the summit or interior. Some had handfulls of *antiquities*, such as stone scarabaei, mummy relics, and brazen ornaments, to tempt purchasers; and others were satisfied with importunately beseeching us for "backsheesh." Leaving the ladies below with the servants, I mounted the huge sides under an escort of two stalworth Arabs, one of whom, however, proved a greater hindrance than help. The other, a good-natured black, who rejoiced in the high-sounding name of Abdallah, was serviceable enough; though it is sufficiently easy for an active man to mount without help. The steps (formed by the removal of the casing) are from two to four feet in height, and broad enough to be perfectly safe. About half-way to the summit is a cavity, whence stone has been removed; in this the assisting Arabs are wont to stop with the traveller and demand pay before proceeding further; but a determined look is enough to frighten these bravos into their duty. From the summit the view is full of satisfaction. The flat valley of the Nile extends North and South, gay with every variety of green, in the midst of which flows the mighty river. Immediately beneath us, and extending to the Westward, are the dreary elevations of the Lybian desert, in which is the Mystic Shrine of Jupiter Ammon;* to the South other pyramids lift their summits, from the giant neighbour tomb of Cephren to the distant monuments of Dashoor. Beyond the Nile valley are the Mukattem hills and the Arabian desert. There is instruction in standing upon the sepulchre of a king, and gazing thence upon the country of his former sway. It is not so suitable a spot as the summit of an exceeding high mountain,† whence to tempt the ambition of a man. The platform upon the Great Pyramid is about thirty feet square, much of its height having been removed by the spoiler. On descending, we lit our torches and entered the colossal tomb. Bending double, we passed along the various galleries, in one place winding through a forced passage, until, nearly suffocated and thoroughly dusted, we arrived at the centre chamber. This room is surprisingly small when we consider the immense size of the edifice. The dimensions of the chamber are—height 19½ feet, length 34 feet, and width 17½ feet. The walls and roof of the room are not of the stone of which the rest of the pyramid is built, but of reddish granite; and at one end is an empty sarcophagus of the same kind of granite, which, when struck, gives a clear, ringing sound. Beneath this chamber is an-

---

* See St. John's adventures in the Lybian desert, for an interesting account of the Oasis of Ammon.
† Matthew, iv. 8.

other, of smaller dimensions, with a pointed roof, to which access is gained by a branch passage; and above the main room are five other small apartments, only 3½ feet in height, one situated above the other, and the uppermost having a pointed roof. Four of these last were discovered by Col. Vyse. Besides these, there is a chamber 105 feet below the surface of the ground, to which leads a direct continuation of the first passage entered from the opening. In each of the second and third pyramids a single chamber was alone found. These interiors had all been opened by the Arab caliphs, and reclosed. Who reopened the Great Pyramid I am not aware, but to Belzoni and Col. Vyse are we indebted for our present access into the chambers of the second and third. It was a strange scene for us within that mass of stone: a dozen dark Bedawin and half as many pale-faced strangers waking the echoes of that dismal hall in the uncertain light of our torches. A few minutes of contemplation, and we retreated through the close passages, and heartily enjoyed the recovery of sunlight and fresh air. Our appetites were soon in good condition, and the servants busily prepared our meal at the shady side of the Pyramid. The Arabs, who are generally *close* friends, had no idea of deserting us now, and we sat down to eat, with a hundred hungry mouths and wistful eyes surrounding. By their help we were soon rid of any eatables that might have troubled us on our return to Cairo. After our luncheon, we walked to the Sphynx, about 1,000 feet S. E. of the Great Pyramid. Its proximity to its lofty neighbours injures its effect, as its height is not 70 feet. Still, notwithstanding this disadvantage, and the fact that it is greatly covered by the sand, the Sphynx is a solemn thing to see. Its human face gives it the commanding interest of life, as it seems to look with a resigned sorrow on the tremendous changes that are ever occurring before it. The figure is cut out of the solid rock, excepting a part of the back, which is cased with stone where the rock was defective, and the forelegs, which excavation has shown to be of hewn stone. In front of its paws is a pavement, on which they lie. Between the paws is an altar. Three tablets were also discovered there, and a crouched lion looking towards the Sphynx. But all these were concealed by the accumulated sand at the time of our visit. On one of the tablets was found the name of Thothmes IV., who probably reigned shortly after the Exodus of the Children of Israel. By him it is likely this monument was formed, and in it he has left an almost undying portrait of himself to posterity, for we may believe the face to be a likeness of the monarch. The Sphynx is not female, as is commonly supposed, and therefore its sex can be no objection to its character as a portrait of Thothmes. The face is much mutilated, the nose being entirely gone, but its power over the mind remains in spite of its many injuries. The whole region of the Pyramids is filled with pits, excavations, and small structures, all which have doubtless been places of sepulture or mortuary temples, where services connected with the dead were performed. One of the most interesting of these tombs is that which bears the name of Colonel Campbell. It is a large square pit cut in the rock to a depth of 53½ feet. A short distance from the mouth of this pit is a trench cut in the rock to a depth of 73 feet, and forming a square about the pit, at the bottom of which I saw a stone sarcophagus. Behind the second pyramid, a series of chambers are hewn out of the rock, which has been left as a wall by the removal of a large mass to allow space for the base of the pyramid. One of these chambers has its rocky roof cut in imitation of palm trunks—a curious fact, and one which throws light on the construction of houses in the days of the Pharaohs. The Egyptians use palm trunks in the same manner to this day.

There are twenty-five pyramids in the vicinity of the ancient Memphis, only six of which, however, are of immense size; though, were they away, the others would rank high among the greater buildings of the world. Besides these, there are eight others in Egypt, and one hundred and thirty-nine in Dongola and Sennaar. Thus, altogether, we have one hundred and seventy-two pyramids in the valley of the Nile. After a day's delightful employment at these hoary remains, we disentangled ourselves from our attached Bedawin friends, and rode back to Cairo over the fertile plain. There are no carriage roads, no fences, no hedges, no walls—so that our ride had the appearance of trespass among the standing grain of the Egyptians. On our homeward route, we met on the outskirts of the city, riding in his barouche, Suleiman Pacha, the formerly French Colonel Séve, but now the Moslem grandee. Had we not been taught in our nurseries the history of an old woman who kissed a cow, and the moral axiom founded thereon, we should wonder at the perverted taste of this Gallic colonel.

Cairo and its Environs.

STREETS—MOSQUES—CITADEL—PALACES—SHOOBRA—PETRIFIED FOREST—PREPARATIONS TO LEAVE.

THE streets and bazaars of Cairo are ceaseless sources of amusement to the traveller. The thoroughfares, narrow, crooked, and unpaved, keep one's curiosity constantly in exercise. From their dimensions and serpentine character, the view is ever limited, and the walker or rider is thus continually changing the scene, and consequently attracted by new objects of interest; and, from experience in Cairo, one is led to conclude that it is far less tiresome to walk in the narrow streets than in the broad avenues of a city, unless a large changing crowd obviate the objection, by furnishing new feasts to the eye. Though I cannot charge this motive to the Saracen Caliphs in forming the ways of Grand Cairo, I have no doubt the pleasure of enjoying this philosophical fact has been the property of their subjects without their knowledge. The straitness of the streets also renders them cool, by excluding the rays of the sun; but it is probable the air is rendered more impure, and disease is thereby generated or increased with greater facility. As you pass along these lanes, you are particularly struck with the odour of the camel manure, which is used as fuel throughout

Egypt, by reason of the scarcity and great value of wood. As the streets are unpaved, the foot falls almost noiselessly to the ground, which, in a populous city, has a remarkably strange effect. This is heightened by the absence of wheeled vehicles, which are only seen in a few comparatively large and modern streets. Over these curious silent lanes project the latticed balconies, from which the inhabitant of the harem can look over unnoticed on those who pass below, and here and there an archway, which one would imagine an entrance to a dwelling, reveals another twilight avenue, down which the eye looks in vain to discover an outlet.

The bazaars differ from the streets in little. Stretch awnings of palm-leaves or canvass over the way, from house-top to house-top, form little stalls or cells on either side, where venders may expose their goods, and you have a bazaar. The mellowed light falls upon the attractive wares and upon the sedate face of the Moslem salesman, who, reclined on his little divan, slowly emits clouds of smoke from his long shebook, exhibiting none of that anxiety to arrest the attention of customers, that so marks the money-making Anglo-Saxon. Such are the streets and bazaars of Cairo, and to say that there is not a wondrous fascination in them, is to give the lie to every Frank who ever made a sojourn in the Caliph's capital.

There are 400 mosques within the walls, and here, as everywhere in the East, they form the chief architectural ornaments. We visited four, the Aliwan, Hassan, Tooloon, and the great Mosque of Mohammed Ali. The Aliwan is one of the ordinary mosques of the city, and has no beauty to recommend it to the visitor. It is a barn-like building, with plenty of filagree work ornaments suitable for a barber's shop. The tomb of the Sultan Aliwan is an ugly chest in the centre. The mosque of the Sultan Hassan is one of the most prominent buildings in Cairo. It stands on the large square Roumeileh over against the citadel, and was built by the Memlook Sultan of Egypt, E' Naser Hassan, about A.D. 1355. The entrance is lofty and imposing. The interior is a square court, open to the sky, with a high recess on each side, the openings of which to the court are four lofty pointed arches. In the eastern recess is the sanctum, where the services are conducted, and in this are numerous lamps suspended either from the ceiling or from side brackets. Behind this recess is the tomb-room, in which, beneath a large dome, lies the body of the royal builder. In the centre of the paved court is a wooden canopy, surmounted by a turban-shaped dome, under which a fountain was furnishing the faithful with the means of ablution.

The Mosque of Tooloon, before mentioned, is the oldest building in Cairo. It is in the Southern portion of the city, not far from the gate of the same name. It was built by the usurper Caliph Ahmed ebn e' Tooloon, the first independent Saracen sovereign of Egypt, in the year 879. It is a large quadrangle, 400 feet square, its centre open to the sky, surrounded by arcades on one side five arches deep. The material is plastered brick. In the centre of the court is a tank for ablution beneath a domed building; and on the north-west side of the mosque is a lofty minaret, with stairs winding around its exterior. But what is of peculiar interest in this structure, the arches of the court are *pointed*, showing the use of the pointed arch among the Saracens more than three centuries before its introduction into England. The Mosque is in a decaying condition, exhibiting only some melancholy efforts at repair. Rubbish is heaped everywhere, and we wandered about as among the ruins of a deserted city. The Arabs say that Noah's ark rested on the site of this sanctuary!

But the prince of Mosques at Cairo is the grand building, still unfinished, that Mohammed Ali has erected on the summit of the citadel hill, overlooking city and cemetery, Boulac and Old Cairo, and the rich valley of the Nile. It rises like a pyramid of domes, and four central minarets of exquisite form and colour stand at the four corners of the superb edifice. It is built of the Egyptian alabaster, and has before it a domed arcade, like the court of the Kaaba at Mecca. Few buildings in the world possess the noble situation and commanding aspect of this Oriental St. Peters. The citadel of Cairo is an elevated rock at the south-eastern corner of the city, which was fortified by the celebrated Saladin, about the year 1172. The ascent is by a fine zig-zag. Within the extensive enclosure is the above-named mosque of Mohammed Ali, his palace, his harem-palace, the arsenal, the barracks, courts of justice, etc. The palace of the Pacha is of moderate merit, posessing many Oriental and European comforts, but few elegancies. The Beer Yoosef (or Joseph's Well) is a well in the citadel, which bears marks of antiquity, but which derives its title from Saladin (whose full name was Yoosef Saladin), who removed the sand by which it was filled and restored it to usefulness. It has two parts, one above the other, and a winding stairway leads to the bottom, a depth of about 250 feet. Mr. Joseph Pitts, whose remarks have been before quoted, thus discourses concerning this well:—" There is a Well in the City of *Cairo*, of a very considerable depth, and about 20 Foot square; there is a way to go down half-way, dry, round about it, to which Light is given from the top of the Well, through great Holes dug in the sides of it. If I mistake not, there are about three Hundred broad Steps down to the half-way, where there is a Stable in which Oxen are kept to draw the Water from the bottom; and there is a great Cistern, into which the Water is emptied, from whence it is drawn by other Oxen, after the same manner, to the top. The Way of drawing it up is thus, viz.: They have a Wheel somewhat like a Mill-wheel, on which are two Ropes, and between these are fastened little earthen Pots to both of the Ropes, about four Foot distance one from the other. As the Ox goes round, so the Wheel goes round, and brings the Pots up full, which empty themselves into the Cistern, and so go down empty with their mouths downward, to take in more Water. This Contrivance is for their *Baths* and watering of *Gardens,* &c. But it is not so much for the sake of this *Machine* that I mention this Well, as for another Reason, viz.: Because this is affirmed by them to be the Well in which *Joseph* was kept a Prisoner by *Potiphar.*"(!) The tradition which wise Mr. Pitts here mentions, doubtless arose from a misconception of the origin of the title, Beer Yoosef, or Joseph's Well, the Saracen warrior being confounded with his namesake, who lived nearly 3,000 years before him. In one of the buildings of the citadel, the bastinado is administered, and in the same room are wooden cages in which the culprits are placed previous to punishment. In the corner of this room (which is a stone hall) sits on his divan the governor and his scribes, to whom the public appear to have the most perfectly democratic access. It was in this citadel that occurred the slaughter of the Memlooks by Mohammed Ali, and the spot is shown whence Emin Bey escaped by leaping his horse over the low wall and reaching the ground in safety. A wooden aqueduct was built by Saladin, to bring the water of the Nile to the citadel, which, after the Turkish conquest, was replaced by one of stone; this now forms a conspicuous object on the road to Old Cairo, whence to the citadel its lofty arches stretch over the plain.

The palace of Ibrahim Pacha, on the bank of the river opposite the north end of Roda, is probably the fairest specimen of a Cairene palace that a stranger can explore. It is a large building at the end of a broad avenue, and, with its projecting roof and surrounding gardens, wears the air of a comfortable country home.

Its interior is a mingling of luxury and comfort, of elegance and vulgarity, that is often seen in the Oriental mansions. There were delightful divans, floors of polished marble, and cooling fountains, but by the side of these may be seen a common pine table or a clumsy fresco painting, esteemed as valuable from its *Europeanity*. And *no books*—the Orientals have no taste for the most civilizing of the arts. You may pass through all the houses of the East, and the only book you are likely to see is the manuscript Koran, unless some Pacha, who has been brought into contact with things European, may have introduced a few French school-books into some corner of his palace. Let writing, printing, and publishing be brought into the East, and its civilization will be, in fifty years, not a whit behind that of Europe. A part of the roof of Ibrahim's palace, as of most large houses in Cairo, lifts up like the lid of a figure-four trap, so that the breeze may enter and cool the apartments. An Abyssinian slave acted as our cicerone, whose appearance in Frank dress of coat and pantaloons resembled that of a child in his grandfather's castoffs.

There are many palaces of the same general appearance in and about Cairo, belonging to the grandees of the vice-royalty, in the neighbourhood of each of which is generally a twin palace, appropriated to the harem of the noble. Just outside of the Ezbekiyeh is the unfinished palace of Abbas Pacha, which has risen only a few feet above the surface of the ground. According to its design, it would cover as much ground as the Ezbekiyeh itself. It seems that the young Abbas was rather hasty in his plans, and suddenly received a notification from his grandfather that he had made quite sufficient progress in his new mansion, as he had other methods of spending money than in building fine houses. Whether the youth, now that he has obtained the Pachalik, will revive the work, is uncertain. He probably will agree with his grandfather, and find that he has sufficient outlets for his surplus capital in other directions.

The passage of the Indian travellers always causes considerable bustle in the Frank quarter. Omnibuses and donkeys are in great demand, and the hotels swarm with human beings. They eat, perhaps, one or two meals, dash off to the Pyramids, sleep one night, and are away in the morning, either for Suez or Alexandria, as the case may be, and again all is quiet and subject to the regular routine. However full of anxiety and hurry these transitory visits are to the visiters themselves, they are inexpressibly ludicrous to the more fortunate man, who sits quietly at his window or calmly paces the hall and court, and complacently blesses himself that *he* is not in a hurry. He is amused to see his fellow-beings striving to effect a just compromise between sight-seeing and sleeping, and wavering, as their curiosity or fatigue preponderates. And the results are as various as the circumstances and characters. One, with an oath, sends all Egypt to perdition, and rushes in search of a room that has less than six beds; another is off at a wink for the Pyramids; a third cares only for the mosques; a fourth prefers *his* dose of Egypt in the obelisk form, and gallops away to Heliopolis, while many a bloated epicure bawls out, "Something to eat, and hang the antiquities!" Servants are constantly running over one another; a hundred Mohammeds answer at the call of the name; Hassans and Achmets, by the score, are mistaking and being mistaken; baggage is carried to one hotel and its owner to another; while the sedate Mussulman gazes with a look of consternation, and ourselves feel a mischievous satisfaction in the disasters of the Transit. Several times, during our stay at Cairo, these apparitions came and went, like the shifting scenes of the drama, and the curtain falling never failed to find us convulsed with laughter.

A pleasant excursion was that to Shoobra. Donkeys, as usual, and their attendant spirits. Four or five miles' ride over a lovely road, where the meeting acacias form a cool berceau, brought us to this country residence of the old Pacha. The house is large, but plain, the glory of Shoobra being its charming garden. Pretty avenues innumerable, with here and there a neat summer-house or sparkling fountain, groves of fragrant orange, and flowers of every sort delighted the senses. In the midst of the garden is the grand bath—a large quadrangle, surrounded by marble porticoes, and containing in the centre a superb white marble fountain of great size, about which are seats for musicians. In each corner of the portico is a lounging room, one of which is exquisitely furnished with large mirrors, velvet divans, and polished floors of inlaid wood.

Another excursion comprised the petrified forest. Leaving Cairo by the famous Bab el Nusr, or Gate of Victory, at the north-east corner of the city, we immediately find ourselves in the desert, among the straggling tombs of a Moslem cemetery, where some say the lamented Burckhardt lies. Passing the tombs of the Memlook sultans, we rode along a sand valley, on each side of which is a low, brown, rocky line of hills, in which were quarries and workmen engaged in extracting the stone. In somewhat more than two hours we reached the curious forest. This name is, however, inapplicable. A series of sand-hills, spreading as far as the eye can reach, is covered with fragments of silicified wood, lying in every position, and varying in size from an inch to forty feet in length. The extent of this region of petrifactions is unknown, though as far as Jebel Aweibid, sixty miles east of Cairo on the way to Suez, I afterwards found specimens. The origin of this phenomenon is enveloped in mystery. Dr. Binst, of Bombay, thus writes regarding the matter :—" They (the fragments) are hard and sharp as flints; they ring like cast-iron, strike fire with steel, and scratch glass. The sap-vessels and medullary rays, the very bark and marks of worms and insects, and even the spiral rays, remain entire; the minutes fibres of the vegetable structure are discernible by the microscope. Here you have the carbon—the most indestructible matter known to us—entirely withdrawn, and substituted in its place a mass of silica—a matter insoluble by any ordinary agent, and at any common heat. Yet so tranquilly has the exchange been accomplished, that not one atom has been disturbed; the finest tissues remain entire, the most delicate arrangements uninterfered with. * * * No theory of their silicification, or their appearance where they are found, has ever been attempted. The late Dr. Malcolmson found fragments of the wood imbedded in the conglomerate which contains the Egyptian jaspers, and threw it out as possible that they and the gravel of the desert, consisting almost entirely of jaspers, might possibly be the result of abrasion or denudation. This threw the difficulty only one step farther back; besides this, that the appearance of the forest is at variance with the theory. No agates or gravel appeared around. The trees seemed to be petrified as they lay; they looked like a forest felled by mighty winds. A further mystery was this, they lay on the surface of bare drift sand and gravel, and reposing on limestone rocks of the most recent tertiary formation—the texture and colour of the imbedded oyster-shells were as fresh and pure as if brought not six weeks from the sea." Of the sorts of trees which are here petrified, Wilkinson enumerates "thorn-bearing trees, and palms, and jointed stems, resembling bamboos, one of which is about fifteen feet long, broken at each of the knots." He also states that the same kind of petrifactions are found inland on the other side of the Nile, on the borders of Wady Fargh. On the way back to the city, I noticed a lizard of immense size, its body being as large as a kitten's. These lizards abound in the desert, many species of which we observed on our future journey to Palestine.

For several days Boulac was regularly visited. We were in search of a good dahabiyeh or passenger-boat, with which to make the ascent of the Nile. All along the bank were ranged the various species of Nile craft, like cattle in the stalls, and we spent hours in exploring their cabins and examining their decks, making particular inquiry concerning rats and other vermin, whose partiality for life on the water is well known in Egypt. After much hesitation, we selected a boat of comfortable appearance, with a smooth-faced Nubian rais or captain, and an apparently stalworth crew. We had already engaged an excellent dragoman, Ibrahim, whose service under Col. Vyse had furnished him with the distinguishing and distinguished name of his former employer, so that *Ibrahim Vyse*, like Saul among the children of Israel, stood in importance head and shoulders above the innumerable Ibrahims of Cairo. Ibrahim had also accompanied Dr. Robinson on his tour, and had afterwards served as dragoman to Mr. Bonar and the Scotch mission in their expedition to the Jews. With Ibrahim's experienced assistance, we soon obtained the requisites for housekeeping on the Nile, and were surrounded with a formidable array of crockery, ironware, and provision, for which the bazaars and the little store of Mr. Carlo Pini, an Italian resident, were thoroughly ransacked. Procuring, moreover, the indispensable services of a cook, a ponderous, good-natured, and intelligent fellow named Hassanein, we left the hotel on the evening of February 13th, and made a formal transfer of ourselves and apparatus to our dahabiyeh at Boulac, which dahabiyeh we forthwith denominated the "California," the news of that El Dorado having lately arrived at Cairo, with such a powerful influence as to induce even thence a contribution to the increasing population of the Sacramento valley.

The Nile.

BOATS—COMMENCEMENT OF VOYAGE—SCENES ON THE RIVER—BENISOOEF—COPTIC CONVENT—MINYEH—WASHINGTON'S BIRTHDAY—DAYR EL KOSSAYR.

The principal description of passenger-boats upon the Nile, are the *Dahabiyeh* and the *Cangia*, differing from one another principally in size, the former being the larger and the more suitable for a party, as they can accommodate, tolerably, four passengers. The dahabiyeh varies probably from forty to eighty feet in length. It rises at the bow and stern, has but one deck, which, by being shut in towards the stern, forms one or two small cabins, and carries, generally, two masts. These masts have each one large latteen sail, which adds to the picturesque, and detracts from the useful. The crew sleep on the deck or crawl into the hold beneath, as the weather influences them, while the double cabin affords separate accommodation for the ladies and gentlemen of the travelling party. Our crew consisted of rais, pilot, and eight sailors, besides whom we had a cook for the crew, a pleasant-faced Nubian boy, who was taken sick on the trip and returned home to Nubia. There were five other boats about starting at the same time with us: one American, one French, one English, and two Scotch. Each carried its national flag, and our rencounters upon the river were full of interest. Though we embarked on the evening of the 13th, it was not till the morning of the 15th that we left Shagget Mekkee, an island opposite Old Cairo, a strong south wind having previously rendered our progress impossible. In the meantime we had arranged our new home by constituting pantries, bookcases, wardrobes, &c., and having found our Hassanein a most finished knight of the spit, we were contented. In *ascending* the Nile, rowing is impracticable on account of the current: so that in a head wind, the crew drag the boat in canal fashion along the shores, which form a natural tow-path. In *descending*, dragging is never practised, as the current would drive the boat ashore, but rowing is then brought into use. The voyage on the Nile I give in journal form, as easier to be followed, though more desultory.

Feb. 15th.—This morning we were under way at half-past seven, though the clumsy manœuvres of our crew made our actual departure a quarter of an hour later. The wind continued contrary, and we made slow progress along the western shore by tracking. Several times during the day the "Cleopatra," one of the Scotch boats, passed us and was passed by us in turn. At sundown we were struck by a squall, which brought out the clumsiness of our swarthy crew to advantage. Soon after, we made fast to the western shore for the night, near the village of Massandra.

Tracking is a tedious way of advancement. Six sailors shoulder the long rope of matting that is fastened between the masts and tug along the bank; while two remain on the boat to assist by poling against the muddy bottom. When the trackers arrive at a small cove, they hoist their loose garments on their shoulders, and wade across the little bay without materially damaging their costume by the water. At noon the crew halt a half hour for their dinner; a like half hour is spent in the morning for breakfast. But breakfast and dinner seem to be alike: a large wooden bowl is filled with boiled lentils or soaked bread, and around this are gathered the whole company, gracefully squatted; their fingers are thrust into the sop, and convey the portions to their mouths, and after the dish is emptied, their mouths are again used as finger-bowls and napkins. We passed a conspicuous red mosque on the eastern shore; it was Attar e' Nebbee, where is preserved for the edification of the faithful, the footstep of the prophet. Not far from this was the village of E'Dayr, a Coptic convent, plain, but conspicuous. The religions seem to be neighbourly, if not harmonious. The great object of interest to-day has been the Mukattem hills, porous with excavations, which extend along the Arabian shore about two miles from the river. Then is seen the mighty mount whence were born the pyramids. Those barren yellow heights of rock have been the source of a world's astonishment. Beneath these is the village of Toora, where is situated a large school and hospital of the Pacha, finely shaded and forming an attractive object from the river. The villages of the Nile, though generally built of mud or unbaked brick, are rendered picturesque by their palms, which ever hang gracefully over the abodes of the *fellahin* or peasantry. We have passed successively on the western shore, the pyramids of Ghizeh, Abooseer, Sakkarah and Dashoor, differing in size and form, but all telling the same story of power and decay. Before stopping for the night, we met a small steamer, looking strangely out of place, smoking impudently in the face of the pyramids. We felt a slight thrill of civilization as she paddled past, and could not but think it was an improvement on the vessels of bulrushes. It was Ibrahim Pacha's steamer, which had been lent to a German prince of unpronounceable title, one of the 1001 cousins of Prince Albert, wherewith to enjoy the Nile, by cunningly avoiding its beauties and antiquities in night travelling.

Feb. 16.—Day before yesterday we sent a droll member of our crew to purchase a drum—an approved toy of an Egyptian sailor—but he did not return that day; yesterday came and went without his appearing, but this morning the fellow stepped aboard, somewhat tired, having walked thirty miles in pursuit. My friend C—— and myself made a land excursion, strolling among dirty villages and labouring fellahin, and reaching the river again far ahead of our craft. Here we saw the other American boat, which we hailed, and with which we exchanged salutations.

We generally stop during the night, the wind failing and our Arabs needing rest; but when the breeze continues favourable, we make the best use of the night, while the crew alternate their rest by watches. We get off about half-past six in the morning, and stop at night about eight. Then the crew gather around a bivouac fire upon the bank, and look their best in the picturesque, while a solemn conversation goes on among them, now and then running over with a little Arabic or Nubian loud gutturality. At noon we came up with our American friends, but some specimens of awkward seamanship soon put us back. We passed the low pyramids of Lisht on our right, and near them a rocky elevation much resembling those curious structures. Our Scotch friends ran into a boat-load of Albanians. One of the valiant Grecians instantly boarded the Scotchman, and commenced a summary chastisement of the crew. He found himself rather unequal to the task, while, to his confusion, the "Cleopatra" made sail, and carried this doughty hero away from his companions. He was finally restored to their company, rather the worse for his chivalry. The Haram el Kedab, or False Pyramid, was seen on the western shore, of curious shape, and deriving its name from a former supposition that it was partly native rock.

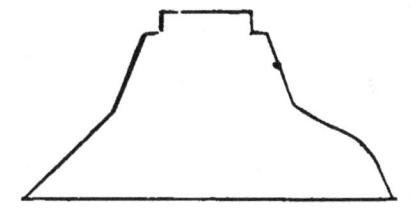

A lovely sunset completed the day, and we anchored near to the west bank, by the village of Rigga. As we advanced, we purchased fowls, eggs, milk, and the like, at the villages,—only such luxuries as oranges, sherbet, tobacco, etc., being brought from Cairo.* Following the usual and reasonable custom of travellers, we pushed on up the river, postponing visits to ruins until our descent, the current of the river being always a means of descending, while adverse winds might retard us greatly in the ascent. The immediate banks of the river preserve a uniform aspect. They are now (low Nile) about twenty feet high, of loose alluvion, and as level as a road, here and there intersected by tracts of sand. Numerous villages are constantly in sight, with their clustered palms,—camels, donkeys, and buffaloes, are seen everywhere, the last often up to their necks in water, to avoid the heat and insects. The peasant women, enveloped in their blue garments, look like

---

* For expenses and necessary outfit of a Nile voyage, see Appendix.

animated mummies, as they come in knots to the river side and fill their earthen jars, then poise them on their head, and return to their village. At short intervals we pass sakias and shadoofs, both instruments of irrigation. The former is a succession of jars strung upon a wheel, which, revolving by the means of buffaloes, lifts the water and empties it into reservoirs or gutters provided for the purpose. The latter is a long pole, poised near the centre, having a bucket of leather at one end and a heavy weight of stone or baked mud at the other. The stone, being the heaviest, draws up the bucket whenever a man stationed at the bucket end has filled it with water. This is emptied on the land, and the bucket let down for another load. The men at the shadoofs sometimes accompany their work with a melancholy air, which, mellowed by the distance, comes over the water and strikes the ear favourably. We have only seen one tool used in the fields, and that a short-handled hoe. No carts are used for transportation of produce, but donkeys are loaded with the grain or grass till the animal is concealed, and the load has the appearance of possessing a mysterious animation. Camels are also used in place of wagons and carts.

Feb. 17.—To-day I walked ahead of the boat, and having selected a pleasant spot, attempted to wash my feet in the holy river; but I cannot recommend his holiness as a foot-basin; there being no rocks for a seat or footing, and the brink of the river being muddy, as fast as one foot had received the benefit of a towel, it was ready for another ablution. After regaining the boat by being carried over the shallows on the shoulders of the Arabs, a pleasant breeze bore us on, and, like all who are in prosperous circumstances, we began building various large edifices of hope, but a sudden cessation of the treacherous wind ruined these airy structures, and Thebes, which had a moment before been within grasp, retired indefinitely before our mental vision. We ran alongside the eastern shore, and made fast to the bank, near Dayr Conigh. The calm, but current-marked Nile, the low shores fringed with the beautiful palm, the frequent latteen sail, the distant pyramid, and the golden hues of sunset bathing all, filled us with an indescribable delight. Going ashore, we found hills of very curious formation, scarcely to be distinguished from massive remains of ancient buildings. Long rows of huge steps ran regularly for a mile, forming terraces varying in size and shape, and on one of these seemed to rise the ruins of a Titanic temple. We wandered thoughtfully over these strange heights, as night gradually settled upon the scene, throwing its appropriate shadows over these mysterious wilds. Returning, we found our boat in its old companionship with the "Cleopatra," and the lights of our American friends were gleaming across the quiet river.

Feb. 18.—To-day a tolerably good wind has carried us about thirty miles on our course. The river's banks have been sandy and dreary. We were gratified by seeing a boat approach, carrying the American flag; it passed us with nearly the width of the river between us. My gun was fired, and the salute returned, but the vexatious distance precluded speaking, so that I was forced to put up with a disappointed curiosity and the loss of the pleasure of greeting personally some fellow-countrymen. But we had not proceeded far when we discovered a little boat coming towards us down the river; she hauled alongside, and we were soon chatting busily with Messrs. S. and P., New Yorkers, like ourselves, whose boat had passed us, but who had been on a visit to our American friends ahead, and now were kindly seeking us. After a pleasant interview, we bade them adieu, and, entering their rowboat, they pulled for their dahabìyeh.

At four P. M. we passed Benisooef, the first large town since leaving Cairo. Its palm trees and factories were an agreeable sight. Don't smile, reader, at the idea of a factory being an agreeable sight. An Egyptian factory is not a huge, ugly, staring mass of brick and windows, such as wear the name in Europe and America, but long, low, neat, country houses, with projecting eaves, and girt with the foliage of numerous trees. Passing on without stopping, we halted for the night about ten miles beyond Benisooef, in company with the other Americans.

Feb. 19.—For nearly two hours we were detained baling out our leaky boat, the rais having deceived us in regard to its tightness and good condition. We were also not a little troubled with the rats, that made night hideous in our contracted cabins, which, with the attacks of an unnumbered army of fleas and other small enemies, gave us a realizing insight into Eastern life.

After our boat was cleared of the water, we pushed on, and towards noon halted at the village of Feshn, where we obtained a quasi carpenter, who, conjointly with our worthy crew, patched up the opening timbers. Thus three hours of the day were lost. While we were hoping to recover this time by harder work, the wind became so violent from the westward, that we were forced to fasten to the west bank, on a sandy strip that there bordered the water. The wind blew a hurricane, filling the air with sand and causing us to retreat into our cabins. Four of the men laid down upon the shore under the lee of a sand-hill, and while there, a strong gust loosened us from the bank and bore us across the river, leaving our men sleeping, in utter ignorance of our departure. We thumped against the eastern bank for two or three hours, when the wind abating, allowed us to return for our men, who had been sufficiently dismayed on waking. On we went, till, the wind increasing to a gale, we scudded under bare poles. After a tedious day, we came to for the night about 10 P. M., off Jebel Sheikh em-Barak. The mountains of the Arabian side, level-topped yellow heights of rock, here border the river, while the Lybian range are correspondingly retired. The crew perform daily on the drum, which is a broad-based, thin-necked jar, whose bottom is removed and replaced by a sheepskin. With this there is a vocal accompaniment in the minor key, inexpressibly harsh.

Feb. 20.—Delays crowd upon us. About 11 this morning, after a succession of lesser mishaps, caused by the extreme verdancy of our men, we closed the ceremonies with a glorious plunge into the bank, carrying away half of our rudder. With a compulsory resignation, we drifted back to the nearest village— El-Meragha. While some dozen villagers were playing the carpenter about the fractured helm, whose fragments had been collected and laid out upon the bank, we sauntered into the village and explored its mud walls and palm grove. Sitting under the rude portico of a mud-built café, we indulged the curiosity of the settlement by taking the mocha in their midst. Just below the village, a short distance from the western bank is the Hagar e' Salam—or "Stone of Welfare," which in the eyes of the Nile boatmen has some connection with the good luck of their voyages. It is a dull rock, lifting itself a few feet out of the water. After two or three hours' visit to the hospitable inhabitants of El Meragha, we found our unfortunate "California" in condition to proceed. With a fair wind, we passed the village of Sharona, supposed by Wilkinson to be the ancient Shenero. A little beyond was a large red mound, called "Kom Ahmar" where are the remains of brick and masonry; why is not *this* Shenero, whose name (as is often the case with a ruined town) is removed to the neighbouring village? Aboo-Girgeh, about two miles from the bank, showed extensive mounds, the remains, doubtless, of a Pharaonic city. We discover that Hassanein is an unrivalled cook. To-day, a most complicated castellated structure of candy and fruit, the result of his skill in kitchen architecture, made its appearance on our table. We almost suspected him a disguised Frenchman.

We are forcibly struck with the horizontal summit of the low mountains which bound the Nile valley; not a peak is to be observed. This flat appearance of the summits, with the sides slightly departing from a perpendicular, is very ingeniously supposed by some to be the origin of the Egyptian style of buildings as seen in the ruined temples. The Nile preserves the average width of half-a-mile, and, contrary to my expectations, has a very tortuous course. On this account, like the Mississippi, it has cut off repeatedly large tongues of land by forming a new and more direct channel—and in one case nearly destroyed the town of Manfaloot by the operation.

We were forced this morning to exercise our austerity for the first time in punishing two of our crew. They had delayed us by running off without permission into the country, and, as the only means of drilling order and obedience into a Nile boatman, we had recourse to the whip, the rais acting as executor of the penalty. Much as the whip is to be avoided, yet in a land where it is not considered an indignity, and where it is the usual method of punishment, there can be no impropriety in its limited exercise. At 11 o'clock, we halted at the village of Galosanee.

Feb. 21.—To-day we have had a good run. Leaving our night-quarters at Galosanee at 6½ in the morning, we have reached Beni Hassan this evening. We passed the town of Samaloot about noon. It is away from the river westward, and is famous for its minaret, which tradition says was considered so fine by the Caliph at the time of its erection, that he had the hand of the artist amputated lest he should build another like it. I mounted the bank to look at it, but was disappointed. It is lofty, but of ordinary appearance, and manifestly crooked. At 3 P. M. we passed Minyeh, a Moslem town of large size and pleasant aspect. The Pacha's house and the factories are very neat in appearance, and a shaded sheikh's tomb is a conspicuous object. Nearly opposite is Souadee, where is a rum distillery of the Pacha. This is one of the civilizing influences that Moslem principles of abstinence have not been able to withstand. Rum has an insinuating power everywhere.

Before reaching Minyeh, the eastern mountains touched the water, their high yellow cliffs giving an air of wildness to the river. On their summit is the Coptic convent of Sitteh Mariam el Adra (Lady Mary the Virgin). On approaching this point we had heard, faint, in the distance, the hallooing voices of men upon the rocks, and on arriving opposite the cliffs we saw the figures tumbling from rock to rock, until, on reaching the river, they swam off to our boat, crying incessantly " Ana Christian, ya hawagee " (I'm a Christian, sir). They made no hesitation in mounting the deck, with no other costume than nature furnished, and enforcing their Christian character upon the attention of the ladies, as a claim to their charitable consideration. We hurried them off as expeditiously as possible, with powerful exhortations to modify their Christianity by assuming a decent apparel. A few piastres and some empty bottles were to them rich prizes for the treasury of their unique convent.

On this side of Minyeh, and on the opposite shore, is Zowyeb, a remarkable place, as being the cemetery of Minyeh, to which the dead are ferried over; the same custom being retained as was prevalent in ancient Egypt,—a custom which gave rise to the Grecian myth of the Styx. Near this is another Kom Ahmar, or "Red Mound," supposed to be the site of the ancient Alabastron; it is a mass of red brick and pottery.

One never wearies of the Nile. The strongly-marked yellow hills, the graceful palms, the busy sakias, and shadoofs, the clear atmosphere, the delicious temperature, and the pleasure of travelling in one's own house, is enough to satisfy the most fastidious of voyagers.

Feb. 22.—The Eastern Mountains have to-day appeared, honey-combed with natural and artificial excavations; the same softness of rock which yielded to the elements having offered inducements to the Egyptians there to carve their sepulchres. Thus the curious grottoes of Beni Hassan and Tel el Amarna, so important in elucidation of Egyptian antiquity, are seen in the neighbourhood of many water-hewn caverns.

Fine echoes answer the boatman's song along these imposing cliffs, and the various water fowl scream wildly from their dwellings in the jagged rock. We met another steamer, towing a dahabiyeh which carried Nuzleh Hanem, Mohammed Ali's daughter, and widow of the infamous Defterdar. An infinity of rope intervened between the tug and its honoured follower, a distance formed to keep the fair occupants of the dahabiyeh unseen by the rougher sex on board the steamer. The tall chimney of the Rauda sugar factory rose prominently on the shore, and the puffing steamer paddled past,—the Egyptian Phthah is become the Grecian Hephaestus on the banks of the Nile.

A very interesting relic of the past greets the traveller on the river, in the remnants, here and there seen, of a wall running parallel with the stream, called "Gisr el Agoos" or "Dyke of the Old Woman," supposed to have extended from Nubia to the sea, and built as a defence against incursions from the Arabian desert. It is strange that no ancient author refers to this structure. Only small portions are now seen running across the mouths of ravines at different points on the river. Mounds of ruined towns are seen daily —the undistinguishable remnants of communities Pharaonic, Persian, Ptolemaic or Roman. They are the most melancholy of all ruins, as baffling all attempts at theoretic restoration, and impressing the sole idea of destruction. Often modern villages are built on these mounds, the people finding them fitted by their elevation to escape the inundation.

Washington's birth-day was duly remembered, and our patriotism oozed out in many musical tributes to the honor of the "everlasting Yankees." Not the least of our performances was the ascent of a palm tree, as a rostrum, whence to discourse sweet music to the bewildered natives. At sunset we fired four guns (or rather, pistols) in memory of the founder of American freedom, and drank to his remembrance with sincere feeling, though my friend C. *did* announce the toast, "To the *health* of George Washington."

Quantities of birds are seen on the banks of the river, or flying across its surface, or sailing gracefully therein. Wild duck and wild geese, of many varieties, snipe, hoopoos, quail and kingfishers, swallows and sparrows, hawks and crows, the ibis and pelican, and the curious little crocodile-bird, besides many other birds peculiar to the Nile. The crocodile-bird is small and snipe-like, of mingled black and white, its body being black, its neck white, and its wings gray. It stretches out its neck at each chirp most ludicrously. It is this bird that is said to awaken the sleeping crocodile on approach of danger, and with its sharp hook at the point of its wing to extract the flies from its throat. Doves also abound, and frequently visit our deck in innocent security. Tame pigeons swarm at every village and form clouds in their flight, the houses of the villagers having often structures on their roofs as pigeon-cotes, which furnish a castellated appearance, frequently very deceptive.

We are in the sugar-cane district. On all sides the plant is cultivated, and factories, native and European, are seen at intervals, for the manufacture of the sugar.

Moored at 10 P. M., at the west bank, a mile north of Daroot e' Shereef, having made about thirty miles in the day.

Feb. 23.—Another delay. About 1 o'clock, our skilful sailors brought us in contact with a dilapidated sakia on the bank, tearing our sail from yard to deck. Three hours were devoted to its repair, all the crew officiating as seamstresses or sailmakers. C—— and I employed the time by running up the mountain a half mile off, and exploring a fine artificial cavern, that showed well from the river. It is on the west face of the cliffs, and perhaps 150 feet in depth. Three rude square columns support its front, but its seven interior columns of similar form have been knocked away, and their fragments remain like huge stalactites and stalagmites from the roof and floor. We fired a pistol with grand effect. From the summit of the range we had a glorious view of the green valley. On the west rose an endless succession of such hills as those on which we stood, and in their sides are numberless caverns. The mountains are far from the river on the western shore. We noticed the first specimens of the Dôm or Theban palm near our place of halt. It differs in many respects from the common palm, but principally in its being ramiferous, each branch separating into two. The Governor of Dayr el Kossayr (or Sheikh el Belled, as he is called) gave us several specimens of the unripe fruit.

With a westerly wind we passed Manfaloot, and still continue under sail, this being our first progress at so late an hour of the night (midnight).

The Nile.

SIOUT—ARAB CUSTOMS AND PRICES—THE GEBELS—SONGS—
ARRIVAL AT THEBES.

Feb. 24.—We continued moving last night until three o'clock, when we anchored about ten miles south of Manfaloot. At sunrise this morning we were again loose—and with the usual alternatives of sailing, tracking, and poling, came into El Hamra, the port of Siout, at noon.

Just before reaching this, we passed two dahabiyehs carrying the English flag. We had met another yesterday. Still another English boat was lying at Siout. Its occupant visited us, and informed us of a fever on board one of the English boats we had met, stating that the same fever had attacked another Englishman farther up the river. This was not welcome news, as we knew we were too late on the river, and had some scruples regarding the propriety of making farther advance. Still it was a more unpleasant thought to return, and we decided, in unison with our inclinations, to persevere steadfastly until Thebes was seen. Syout, Siout, or Osiout (as it is variously written) is a large town, and the capital of Upper Egypt. It is distant a mile from the river, and has no beauty except in its minarets and shady entrance from the East. It is surrounded by a beautifully green country, which Miss Martineau compares to an Illinois prairie. El Hamra, the port, is a mean mud village. Having to remain 24 hours here for our crew to bake their bread, a custom always pursued by the boatmen of dahabiyehs, we mounted a selection of the many-offered donkeys, and made our way along the tree-lined causeway to the town. The entrance to Siout was really very pretty; the gate admitted us into a beautiful shady court, near or on which were the gubernatorial residence and palace of Mohammed Ali. Around this pleasant spot, groups of Orientals were lounging and smoking. They gazed placidly upon us as we rode through and entered the meaner portions of the town. The streets are dirty and the bazaars shabby. Galloping away from them out of the western side of the town, we hurried to the mountain side that rises behind Siout, up whose steep face we climbed to see some cave-workmanship of Abraham's time! The cliffs are limestone, and completely perforated by human labour.

The principal caverns lie in ranges, one above the other, to the summit. The first we entered was the largest, and called "Stabl Antar," or "Stable of the Architect." It has an arched entrance or vestibule, from which a door-way leads to the principal chamber, at the extremity of which are many hieroglyphics, much defaced. We entered several others, and found painted hieroglyphics in some. The rooms are all of irregular shape, and contain pits for mummies. The uppermost range are smaller than the rest, and communicate with one another, but whether originally or by the operations of modern research, I know not. We serpentined through a number, examined the hieroglyphics, read many modern names upon the walls (among others those of Irby and Mangles), enjoyed the uncommonly fine view from the cliff-top, and then, with our donkeys and donkey-boys, retraced our way to Siout, where we rejoined one of our ladies, who reported herself to have been followed by crowds, staring in wonder at the unveiled Christian, for it is not often that the worthy citizens of Siout are treated with the sight of a Christian female. After avoiding with difficulty a herd of buffaloes that were driven through the narrow bazaar without any regard to unfortunate wayfarers, we again passed along the lovely road down to our boat.

Here the donkey-boys were clamorous for more "backsheesh," and raised an unearthly uproar at the side of our craft. Wishing to improve the sport, I threw an orange among them, which caused an incredible amount of scuffle, and which was at last devoured, amid terrific persecution, by a sore-eyed urchin. C—— wishing to add his quota to the fun, threw a lemon, which, taken for an orange, was treated in the same manner, and one youngster sunk his teeth into the tempting bait. As he discovered his mistake by wry faces and choked expectorations, a universal roar of laughter from his brethren saluted him—under which we made a regular charge upon them with eggs and other handy missiles, which drove them in confusion from the bank, and left us to the peaceful enjoyment of our mirth.

Feb. 25.—Our crew wear the Mohammedan religion with great ease and indifference, and had the prophet no more ardent followers than they, the crescent would soon set for ever. Not one of them, (nor our servants either) have made a prayer since we left Cairo, for a Moslem prayer is so girt with ceremony that it defies concealment, and a believer of easy conscience is readily discovered.

In spite of their impiety, we found the people exceedingly amiable and obliging, and easily persuaded. Why is not Egypt more cultivated as a missionary field? I fully believe it is white for the harvest, and laborers only are needed to convert this moral desert to a garden. I trust our American Board of Commissioners will not be long without a representative in this deeply interesting land.

We often meet large rafts formed of stone jars bound together by matting, and guided by a few of the fellahin. These come from Ballas, near Thebes, where is an extensive manufactory of these useful utensils, which supplies all Egypt; from the place of their origin they are termed *Ballas*. The largest jars cost originally only one piastre, or five cents each. The next size, which are used by the women as water jars, cost but a half piastre or two cents each—while the smallest size, the *goolahs*, which serve as pitchers, bring four paras each, or half a cent.

While speaking of these low prices, it is well to note that all the necessaries of life are found in Egypt at the lowest rates. Eggs are often purchased at sixty or eighty for a piastre, that is, twelve or sixteen for a cent; lentils can be bought at twenty-five cents a bushel; a palm tree is worth from one dollar to five; and a neat comfortable woollen rug, capable of seating four, is valued at thirty cents! Indeed, it is said that for five cents a day, an Egyptian can board, lodge, and clothe himself, and have a surplus of pocket money. Each of our sailors receives as wages but two dollars and a half per month, and the pilot about a dollar and a quarter besides. A good sheep can be bought for a dollar, and a lamb for sixty cents; and Egyptian segars (deliver me from their smoke) are sold at three for a cent. Travelling is correspondingly cheap. We pay for the use of our dahabiyeh for a voyage of six weeks only one hundred and twenty dollars, or thirty dollars for each person.*

We spent last night at the port of Siout, and on waking this morning found the "Cleopatra," the French boat, (which had received the name of "Le Pirat,") and the English boat, by our side. Visits were exchanged, afterwhich, at 10 A. M., we left with a good breeze, the Scotch and English vessels remaining for their crews to bake bread, while "Le Pirat" kept us company. After a delightful run of twenty-seven miles, we came to our night's halt.

Feb. 26.—We were moving as early as two o'clock, and about sunrise met with a provoking delay on a sand-bank. This is one of the almost unavoidable accidents in ascending the Nile at this season, the river being very low and the sand-banks innumerable and ever changing their position. With a fine breeze we passed the precipitous cliffs of Gebel Sheikh Hereedee, another abutment of the Arabian mountains. We supposed their height to be about 800 feet.

These various mountains that bear different names are only portions of the same long chain which extends from Cairo to Nubia. They present the same character of yellow precipitous cliffs, hanging over the river. Such are the Gebel El Hereedee here noticed, the Gebel Aboofoda, near Manfaloot, the Gebel Sheikh Said, near Melawee, the Gebel e'Tayr, near Minyeh, and the Gebel Sheikh Em-Barak, half way between Minyeh and Benisooef. All these are the points of the chain that touch the river, and all are found on the East bank, the mountains nowhere approaching the river on the West side, between Thebes and Cairo,

---

* For other particulars, see Appendix.

except at Siout, and there they are more than a mile distant.

The name of some Sheikh (or Moslem Saint) is given to these mountains, from their tombs being situated upon them—little white-domed monuments, that never failed to remind us of our Saviour's allusion to "whited sepulchres."

We have observed the men of the country spinning and the women at work in the fields. In the British Museum is a manuscript of the thirteenth century, a large folio of one hundred and twenty-two parchment leaves, containing many drawings illustrative of Scripture history, both written and traditional. Among these is one representing a scene in those ancient days

"When Adam delv'd and Eve span,"

where the first pair are depicted at these pursuits. So it seems by this most erudite authority, that the civilized nations of the earth have preserved the original distribution of employments, while the inhabitants of Upper Egypt have strangely reversed the proper works of the sexes. It may be, however, that this is a step in the greatly-extolled modern improvement, which is known to make men hair-dressers and women the heads of families.

The women of the country wear a spot of paint upon their chin and another upon their forehead, giving their ugly faces a still more revolting aspect. The nose-rings, worn through the outer partition of the nostril, add to their unseemly appearance, though I cannot see greater impropriety in the use of these ornaments than in the ear-rings of our own ladies. Some great female reformer is needed among us, who shall sweep away the disfiguring and hurtful fashions that now hold the females of enlightened Europe and America in the worst of bondage. In such reform, ear-rings will find the same fate with the senseless rib-compressing article of dress, at mention of which before gentlemen, ladies forthwith faint, or find refuge in hysterics, but which they nevertheless most undisguisedly thrust before every gentleman's eyes, in their wasp-like deformities of figure.

The utility of the palm tree is a beautiful instance of the provident manner in which Nature supplies human wants. Its trunk forms floor-timber and fuel; its stems are used for boxes, chairs, and whips; the ribbon-like strings beneath its leaves supply cord and rope; the leaves themselves are employed in baskets and fly-brushes, and the fruit is either eaten or compressed to form a liquor used among the Arabs.

The boat-songs of the Nile are amusing, but by no means musical. Some travellers find in them Iliads and Æneids, Horatian lyrics and Petrarchian amatory odes, but I tried in vain to extract a grain of merit from them all. A few of the principal songs given by our sailors, I here record, that the reader may judge of the beauties of the Nile muse :—

"El yôm ya Saidée—"
(It is your day, Saidée.)

This is one which they repeat by the hour. It calls for the protection of a Moslem santon, Saidée.

Another is (I write it from ear),

"Law b'gau, ya nebbee"
(Help us, O prophet.)

A third signifies,

"Best horses come from Arabia."

A fourth is,

"Iskandrian woman is coming from the bath,
I'll go home with her, when her husband is away."

This is the general style of their songs—the burden being exceedingly brief, but often repeated.

What is amusing in these performances, is the tone of voice in which they are uttered, and the expression of countenance that the men sometimes assume, as they throw themselves in the most grotesque attitudes. When pushing the boat by poles, they generally use the words

"Hay, hayly sah,"

the signification of which I am not Arabian enough to comprehend; and, when tracking, some of their notes are inexpressibly ludicrous, more like the heavings of a donkey than aught else. But their most remarkable use of the lungs is when the boat strikes a sand-bank, and they leap naked into the water and apply their shoulders to the bows in order to push her again into deep water. Then comes rolling to the cabin such a mixture of pathetic and ridiculous, such an unearthly groaning as would drive the most *Nil admirari* philosopher off from his centre of gravity. That sound I despair utterly of describing, and must leave to the reader's very fertile imagination.

The songs of more polished Arabs on shore, such as the story of Antar, of course, are far different things, in composition, sense, and music. We stopped to-day at the large town of Girgeh, where we met another English dahabiyeh on its way down to Cairo. The Englishman, poor fellow, was returning from an unfinished trip, sickness having forbidden his farther progress upwards. After leaving Girgeh (which had no attractions), we again grounded and went through the usual tedious method of getting off during a high wind. The wind subsiding, we left the sand-bank and saw "Le Pirat" coming up with its bright lights. We have moored together by the shore, and while we have made merriment in our little cabin with our united forces, our two crews have joined in music and dance on our deck. This Nile life grows in interest, and is the most fascinating travelling imaginable.

Feb. 27.—A calm day forced us to the slow system of tracking, and this evening we had to rest content with about fifteen miles of progress as the sum of our day's work. The village near which we halt bears the euphonious name of Gezeert Abou Neknag. The day was closed by an entertainment on board "Le Pirat," where our French friends furnished us with the luxuries of the Parisian *cuisine*. Our amusements have been augmented since passing Beni Hassan, by the presence of crocodiles, and our ineffectual attempts to carry one off as a prize. These animals are seldom seen on the river below the twenty-eighth parallel. They lie upon the sand-banks on the very edge of the river, like long black logs, and, at the approach of a boat or the report of a gun, flounder clumsily into the water. Our French friends hailed us from the shore, at one time, as we were passing on, proclaiming their success at having killed one of these monsters. We had heard the successive reports of their pieces, and now saw the creature lying dead upon the beach. But, unfortunately, the poor beast had long since died a natural death, and every passer lately had put a ball in his body, supposing himself the successful sportsman, until a closer examination told both eyes and nose of the sad mistake. The company of "Le Pirat," consequently, say as little as possible on the subject of crocodile-shooting.

Among the superstitions of a Mussulman, is the appropriation of Thursday as washing-day, Monday wherein to cut their nails, and Friday as the time for shaving. We cannot ridicule this folly, while we have thousands at home who will not commence any undertaking on a Friday, and who carefully take their first sight at the new moon over the right shoulder. Half the follies of the Pagan and Mohammedan world might be discovered in our own conduct, with a slight microscopic observation.

The agriculture of Egypt seems in a lamentably backward state. As before said, the little hoe appears to be the only implement of husbandry, and watermelons are planted along the mud-banks of the river with no other tool but the hands to scoop out a resting-place for the seed. The same produce is derived from the Nile valley as in the time of Israel's bondage. We see constantly the leeks, onions, and garlic, the melons and the cucumbers, for which Egypt has ever been famous. Besides these, are cultivated the sugar-cane, peas, lupins, barley, wheat, clover, and tobacco. The varied colours of these crops, as viewed from either range of mountains, give the flat valley the appearance of a variegated carpet of richest material. Of trees, Egypt has a scanty assortment. We do not see the oaks, beeches, hemlocks, and myriad other forest-trees that border our own magnificent rivers; Egypt's glory is other than this. The sycamore is, however, a dweller by the Nile, and the acacia is seen in beautiful groups, at intervals, upon the banks. The orange only grows in palace-gardens, preserved, like the harems, from the vulgar gaze. But *the* tree of Egypt is the palm, which flourishes luxuriantly in every part of the land, and in a hundred varieties. From Thebes to the sea, the palms cluster gracefully along the banks, and seem as much identified with the country as the Nile itself.

Feb. 28.—Another delay in order to bale out our still leaky boat. This and the want of wind has given us another day of small advancement, and we now lie moored at Kasr e' Syad, opposite which are the mounds of old Chênoboscion, which was an asylum for Egyptian geese, who were there fed at the public expense.

The towns on the Nile are either called Bender or Belled—the former being the larger, and having the government of a Hakim Effendi—the latter being analagous to our "Village," and under the authority of a Sheikh el Belled, or Village Chief. There are also "Governors of the Nile" stationed at various points on the river, whose province it is to settle disputes connected with the navigation. The term "Sheikh," probably finds the nearest English synonyme in "Chief." It is applied both to civil and religious characters, as the sheikh of a village, the sheikh of a college of dervishes; and a Sheikh (*par excellence*) is the title of a Moslem Saint. It is often used besides, as a courteous title of address to any one—thus, "Sabál Khayr, ya Sheikh," is "Good morning, Sir."

The tobacco of the Nile is of the vilest sort, and when prepared for use could scarcely be recognized as the article it professes to be. It resembles a mixture of stubble and bark. One cent's worth lasts an Egyptian for two days, but I verily believe would last an American a lifetime. For this stuff they pay the government 10 per cent. of the sale. Its bad quality is more than half attributable to the neglect of its proper cultivation, bad government and natural laziness rendering the people utterly careless of improvement in any branch of employment.

The Orientals are well known to be very punctilious in their salutations. When one presents you with a pipe, he touches his lips and forehead, to which you respond by a like movement. Sometimes the heart is also touched. When a pacha passes, the people bend nearly double, and with their right hand perform an imaginary scooping up of water from the ground; then standing erect, they touch the lips and forehead, while the pacha merely lays his hand upon his heart.

March 1.—To-day we passed Dendera, but could not distinguish the temple. The banks of the river are here of a lovely green, and rich in palms. On the eastern side we noticed a few jagged peaks upon the mountains. These and one or two near Benisooef are the only exceptions to the horizontal summits that we have observed.

Discipline is a thing unknown in our boat equipage. We hear the men and rais often involved in the disentanglement of some knotty questions, in which hard epithets fly thickly from both sides, but either party seems to have peculiar aversion to blows, being satisfied with piling upon one another overwhelming loads of Arabic anathemas. The rais receives the title of "Dog" from his unruly crew, as if it was his undoubted cognomen, and shortly after is smoking peaceably in their midst. We are moored to-night at Ballas, the great jar-factory of Egypt, "Le Pirat" lying behind.

March 2.—Almost in sight of Thebes the whole day, and yet prevented arriving there by the total lack of wind. We passed *Koos*, now an insignificant place, but the emporium of Upper Egypt 500 years ago. We are in night-quarters, four miles from Thebes, enjoying one of the most serene evenings I ever beheld. Not a sound disturbs the air; the Nile is as placid as a sheltered lake, and with the structures of the distant

Past around us, we feel as if Time itself was slumbering.

March 3.—Thebes at last! It is eighteen days since we left Boulac, and the distance only 450 miles! So 25 miles has been our daily average. By urging the crew and avoiding stoppages, the other American boat had outstripped us by three days. It has been an oppressively hot day, but we lost no time, on arriving, to commence our visits to the ruins. We moored our boat at Gournou or Gournah, one of the villages now occupying the site of Thebes.

Thebes.

THE RUINS—TOMBS—LUXOR—KARNAC—A DINNER PARTY.

To describe Thebes, I leave my diary, to resume it again on the descent of the river.

We spent four days among Theban antiquities, and were forced to great diligence to explore its principal wonders in that time, for to see thoroughly *all* the relics of this great city would consume a month at the least, and I doubt not years might be profitably and delightfully spent among its ruins.

The name of Thebes is the Greek Θηβαι, and stated by Wilkinson to be a corruption of the Coptic Tápé, which was pronounced in the Memphitic dialect Thaba. The hieroglyphic name is Ap or Apé, which, with the article, is Tápé, and signifies "the head," and refers to its rank as capital of the country. Its date of foundation is involved in mystery, but we have every reason to believe it existed nearly 2000 years before Christ. It is supposed to have reached the acme of its glory about 1000 B. C. It suffered probably at the invasion of the Ethiopians, about the year 778 B. C.; and to this Nahum the Jewish prophet refers when, in predicting the destruction of Nineveh, he uses this language: "Art thou better than populous No (or as in the Hebrew *No-ammon**) that was situate among the rivers, that had the waters round about it, whose rampart was the sea, and her wall was from the sea? (The Nile is still termed by the natives "The Sea.") Ethiopia and Egypt were her strength, and it was infinite; Put and Lubim were thy helpers. Yet was she carried away; her young children also were dashed in pieces at the top of all the streets; and they cast lots for her honourable men, and all her great men were bound in chains." It doubtless suffered again in the incursion of Nebuchadnezzar, about 600 B. C. And we know that the mad Persian Cambyses laid it waste with fire and sword, in 525 B. C., and the marks of his savage hand are, without doubt, seen in many of the ruined walls that now mourn over the desolate site. Its final destruction, however, was by Ptolemy Lathyrus, 81 B. C., who plundered it after a three years' siege. About eighty years thereafter, Strabo writes: "Now traces of the magnitude of Thebes are seen for a space of eighty stadia in length (that is, ten miles), including many temples, whose splendour Cambyses has greatly defaced—but now a few villages occupy the site!" From that period to this, the plundering hordes of Roman, Saracen, Turk, and Frank, have assisted in its demolition, and the driven sands have covered many of its mighty monuments.

The temple of Gournah, lying nearest our boat, was first visited. It is really a temple and a palace conjoined, dedicated to Ammon or Jupiter, by Osirei, and completed by his son Ramses II., the supposed Sesostris. The beginning of the reign of Osirei is placed by Wilkinson at 1385 B. C., shortly after the death of

---

* That by this is meant Thebes, the title of Ammon or Jupiter, to whom Thebes was dedicated, the Septuagint Translation of Diospolis (the known Greek name of Thebes) and the context all prove.

Joshua. I leave descriptions of pyla and propyla, and the technical architecture of Egyptian temples, to those who have made it their study, and with brevity mention the leading features of the remains. The columns of the portico of this temple of Gournah are made to represent a bundle of stalks of water-plants, and are as beautiful as they are unique. A dromos of Sphinxes, which was the splendid approach to the sanctuary, can be traced by the mutilated fragments. A dozen different apartments are seen in greater or less ruin, all exhibiting the distinguishing characteristics of Egyptian architecture. The temple portion is small, being only fifty-seven feet in length, though this hall is but a trifling part of the whole edifice. In the neighbourhood of this ruin are seen two prostrate statues of Ramses II., and a relief of Ramses III., who reigned about fifty years after. Other confused masses of ruins lie about, and mounds testify to the existence of hidden remnants of the ancient city. The appearance of one of these Egyptian temples in their day of glory must have been vastly imposing. Imagine a noble structure of huge stones, covered with the skilfully-carved hieroglyphics, rising majestically over the plain. A massive portico fronts the edifice, and before this again is raised a pylon, or gateway, on each side of which rise the lofty towers of the propylaca. To this gateway leads a broad avenue, bordered on either side by a row of stone Sphinxes, the sacred guardians of the way, and along this unrivalled path march, in all the pomp of heathen ritual, the bands of priests and people, the most enchanting music accompanying their progress, and gold and silver sparkling in their garments and waving banners. The heart sinks in sadness as the imagination of such glorious scenes is exchanged for the view of the weed-grown fragments that remain from all that splendour.

A mile to the southwest of Gournah is the celebrated Memnonium, now more properly called by the antiquaries the Ramsesium, as having been built by the same monarch who completed the temple of Gournah. This temple is 500 feet in length, and varies in breadth from 180 to 130 feet. Its propyla remain in massive majesty, and opposite these, in the first grand area, is the broken Colossus of Ramses II., the largest stone statue in the world. It contains, according to calculations, nearly three times the solid contents of the great obelisk at Karnac, and weighs 887 tons! It is a mystery even to account for the manner in which Cambyses (for it was doubtless his work) overthrew this mass of stone; much more to conceive the method of its transportation hither. The upper part of the statue lies gloomily in the sand, and from the humbled monarch the miserable Arabs have cut their millstones. Another and another hall disclose their grandeur to the visiter, the weighty columns still in many cases at their post, waiting for time to give the signal for their departure. Some of these pillars are 21 feet in circumference. All notion of grandeur is by comparison, for here, among these huge structures, that seem upreared by Titans, if we cast our thoughts to that great day when an assembled universe shall hear in awful silence the final awards of a righteous God, and ten thousand worlds shall sound the praises of Jehovah, the temples of Thebes and their mighty builders will become less than the smallest dust of the balance, and utterly lost in their insignificance.

A mile farther south is the temple and palace of Medeenet Abou, so called from the decayed village that obstructs the ruins. The oldest part of this group was built by Amun-neit Gori, supposed to be one of the Pharaohs who oppressed the children of Israel. His two successors made additions, and Ramses III., some two or three centuries thereafter, built the palace. The buildings are so confounded by the ruins and modern obstructions, that it is very difficult to obtain a correct idea of their arrangement. On mounting to the second story of the palace, which is supposed to have been the private portion of the king's residence, a very curious sculpture is seen among many admirable efforts. It is the king and one of his favourites engaged in playing chess, the chess-men being all alike, and resembling our pawns. Wilkinson states that a similar sculpture is seen in one of the grottoes of Beni Hassan, which dates 500 years earlier, in the time of Joseph. Another striking peculiarity in this group of ruins is seen in a large open hall, which has on one side *eight circular* columns, and on the other *seven Osiride* pillars, the Osiride pillars being square, with a colossus relief of Osiris on one face. This want of symmetry is often seen in ancient Egyptian architecture. The walls, like those of all the temples of Thebes, are covered with sculptures, the principal subject being the battles and triumphs of the various monarchs. The eastern portion of this temple is the work of several Cæsars, whose names are found inscribed upon the pylon.

Still farther south is a neat little temple of the time of the Ptolemies.

Dayr el Medeeneh is a small Ptolemaic temple beyond the Memnonium, chiefly interesting from the sycamore cramps, which bind the stones together, still remaining in this dry climate.

Dayr el Bahree is a name given to a ruined temple, lying west of Gournah, whose outline can be traced by its faint remains. It must have been the main temple on this side the river. Its plainly defined dromos was 1600 feet long. This dromos corresponds in line to that of Karnac opposite, with which it was probably connected by a bridge, thus forming the most majestic avenue in the world.

Out in the open fields, between these ruins and the Nile, are the two colossi of the plain, discovered by Champollion to be the work of Amunoph III., whose reign is placed by Wilkinson 1430 before Christ, that is, about the time of Joshua.

These immense seated statues, though much mutilated, wear an awe inspiring dignity, and for 3000 years have called forth the wonder and respect, nay, sometimes the worship of the successive generations who have come and gone before them. There they still sit, calmly and in grandeur, with faces turned towards the holy river, and there they shall sit, doubtless, until the trump whose voice shall startle a universe shall call them to the common fate of all things earthly. One of these figures (the most northern) was the Memnon of the Roman writers, whose mysterious chaunt saluted the rising sun. This miraculous song is well supposed to have been the striking of the stone in the lap of the figure. I sent a boy up into the lap by a fissure in the back, and the sounds he caused by striking the stone, while he was entirely hidden from those below, were decidedly musical. This was an Egyptian device of furnishing " sermons from stones;" at least a charitable mind will erect this hypothesis.

The mountains behind Thebes are rich in tombs, which have proved to the world the richest contributions to the elucidation of ancient Egyptian history. Beneath these rocky cliffs, and in various retired valleys, are these excavated homes of the dead. In one section are gathered the priests—in another the ancient queens of the valley of the Nile; but in greater splendour than all the others are buried the embalmed remains of the Pharaohs themselves. The mountain over these last rises to a natural pyramidal summit, a noble monument to surmount these royal sepulchres. The doorways of the tombs are on a level with the valley, and usually, a descent by inclined plane or staircase leads to the subterranean chambers. Wilkinson has painted numbers on the outside of each tomb, in order to render reference more easy. The main tomb (No. 17) bears the name of Belzoni, having been opened by that enterprising discoverer. A sinking of the ground above betrayed its existence to some fellahin, and they communicated their suspicions to Belzoni. He forced an entrance, and passing down a double stairway and along a narrow passage, found himself in a chamber twelve feet by fourteen. At the end of this chamber was a deep pit, evidently intended for the corpse, and marking the limit of the tomb. The privilege of unlocking mystery forms one of the keenest enjoyments of the mind. If we analyze this enjoyment we find in it a benevolent and selfish principle; benevolent, in exposing to our fellows new feasts of pleasure, and selfish, in obtaining ourselves the first fresh taste of these. These principles are, of course, by no means of equal weight in every one, but in proportion as either one predominates, so is the individual of enlarged or contracted mind. But however this may be, in all cases there is a vehement enjoyment derived from discovery, and we may imagine that a discovery in such an interesting field as Egyptian antiquities, would have a peculiar flavour of delight, and this was Belzoni's reward. He had here disclosed the important secrets of a treasure-house that for thousands of years had never been whispered to the ear of man. He followed pathways where even the footsteps of Time had left no impress, and he entered the chamber where Death had held its lonely habitation for long, long centuries, where the noise of the wheels of Life had not penetrated, and whence Light, Life's emblem, had been banished. How his heart must have swelled with emotion as those grim old carvings looked down upon him from their silent ranks, and the sullen echo that answered to his tread must have fallen on his ear as the voice of the forgotten Past!

But his astonished soul was yet to find new sources of surprise. This pit was not the limit of the mysterious tomb. No! that farther wall returns a hollow sound —that narrow crevice bretrays some novel wonder— and the discoverer forgets the prize just won, in his eager pursuit of the new wealth that is now offered for his grasp. A palm tree is brought to act against the barrier, which proves a vain guardian to the inner vault, for the prostrate wall soon reveals the dazzling splendour that has stood so long concealed within, but which now shines in its pristine lustre, upon the daring intruder.

Four large pillars, adorned with sculptures glowing in richest colours, support the roof of rock—and around this brilliant hall are vivid representations of regal life and mystic symbols, of the fairest design and colouring. Beyond this rich apartment is another, in which are seen the figures left by the draughtsmen upon the walls, but which the sculptor had not yet touched with his chisel; for the death of the king, or the outbreak of civil disturbance, had closed the portal ere this subterranean palace had attained its completion. Still more chambers lie beyond, among which is a grand hall of six pillars, at the extremity of which stood an alabaster sarcophagus. Yet farther passages led to apartments more remote, but the fallen roof has excluded their investigation. Who can visit these suites of excavations in the bowels of the earth, or read a description of their wonders, without having brought vividly to mind the words of Ezekiel; " When I looked, behold a hole in the wall. Then said he unto me, ' Son of man, dig now in the wall:' and when I had digged in the wall, behold a door. And he said unto me, ' Go in and behold the wicked abominations that they do here.' So I went in and saw: and behold, every form of creeping things and abominable beasts, and all the idols of the house of Israel portrayed upon the wall round about." The idolatry of Israel here described was undoubtedly derived from the practices of Egypt, and the " chambers of imagery" that called forth divine censure were the copies of these Theban excavations.

It was with great surprise and pleasure that, in the midst of our meditations in this curious spot, we read inscribed upon the wall of an unfinished apartment, the familiar names of three New York friends, who, thirteen years before, had like us been here as admiring visitants. Our thoughts immediately turned to Broadway, and, in spite of the attractive works of ancient Egypt's painters, sculptors, and architects, our bodies alone were in those gorgeous vaults, for our spirits had flown to the abodes of the Manhattoes.

Bruce's tomb, (No. 11), also called from one of its paintings the Harper's Tomb, is of great interest, from the accurate pictures of the manners and customs of the old Egyptians, that occupy its walls. Here are seen in bright colours the various processes of butchery and baking, navigation and the art of war. Moreover, the finest furniture, household utensils of every description, musical instruments, fruits, birds, and the different agricultural employments, are all vividly depicted, throwing an intense light upon Egyptian history, and showing a high state of civilization in the Nile Valley, 1200 years before the birth of Christ. This tomb bears the name of Ramses III., and Belzoni's that of Osirei, the father of Sesostris.

We entered many others of inferior merit, but a description of one is amply sufficient to any one who desires a *general* knowlege of things Egyptian; and as my readers, I trust, are of this sort, I will at the same time please them, and avoid a large amount of statistical trouble, by dealing in *generalities*.

These tombs, or many of them, have probably been rifled at various epochs, from their construction to the days of the Cæsars. By the account of Diodorus, who states that only seventeen remained in the time of Ptolemy Lagus out of an original number of forty-seven, we may suppose that the rest were covered and concealed previous to the days of the Ptolemies, and have so continued until modern discoverers have again made public their remarkable interiors. It is only by the hypothesis of their plunder, that we may account for the absence of valuable relics, and even of the body itself, in many of the tombs.

These sepulchres (at least those known at the time) are called by the Greeks and Romans συριγγες, or tunnels, and that they were visited by the travelling gentry of those days is known by the many scribblings on the walls. One Roman thus records his visit, scratching the record among the hieroglyphics. " Janvarius P. P. Vidi et miravi locum." A Greek, who seems to have had but little antiquarian taste, writes his sentiments as follows : " Επιφανιος ιστορησα ουδεν δε εθαυμασα η μη τον λιθον," (I Epiphanius saw nothing wonderful but the stone), meaning, probably, the large sarcophagus near which he has written his contemptuous opinion.

It was a day of intense heat in which we visited these tombs. Their interiors were cool and pleasant, but on passing from them to the close sandy valley, surrounded by rocks that seemed to blister in the sun, we almost fainted with the reflected heat, in spite of our constant recourse to the goolahs of water that a small army of Arab boys carried after us. As we wound along the curves of this oven-like ravine, we met our American friends, Dr. W. and Mr. M., arrayed in costume that would have convulsed an occidental community, riding through the scorching heat to take a final look at the tombs, previous to leaving for Cairo in the evening. They gave us an invitation to dine on their boat after the toils of the day were over, and that evening there was as comfortable a dinner-party off Thebes as New York ever had represented on the Nile. That night our friends gave us their farewell salutes, a dozen guns disturbing the quiet of the evening air; and as their boat disappeared in the darkness, and the sound of their oars became lost in the distance, we felt our loneliness and strove to entertain the hope that a future day might bring us to a meeting in our own and distant land.

For deep interest, it is probable, the tombs of Thebes exceed its other relics; but for *grandeur* we must cross the Nile and bow before the majesty of Karnac. Karnac and Luxor are the two points on the eastern shore where the power of ancient Egypt has left its most remarkable tokens. At Luxor rise the lofty walls and pillars of a temple built by Amunoph III., the Memnon of the vocal statue, and embellished by the great Sesostris, whose magic hand seems to have been felt in every part of the vast extent of Thebes. The great colonnade of this temple is one of the finest sights of Egypt, the lotus capitals exhibiting a perpetual bloom, symbolical of the eternal youth of art. A miserable Arab village clings to the temple's sides, and fills its areas, disfiguring its beauty, though these habitations have the effect of assisting the grandeur of the edifice by comparison. On either side of the pylon is a colossal statue of Ramses seated, but the effigies of the old king are like his history—almost concealed from view. The sand has accumulated around these giant statues, so that the king has really four feet in the grave. Indeed one of these colossi only shows the head above ground. Seeing an Arab matron and her babes gathered about this surviving portion, who will chide me for pitying the unhappy monarch, who, notwithstanding his calamitous condition, has the weight of a family on his shoulders?

Before these statues is the widowed obelisk, its mate having been removed by the French to Paris, where it forms one of the greatest ornaments of that capital. A dromos formerly connected the temples of Luxor and Karnac, which are a mile and a half apart. The Sphinxes that lined this dromos are still seen in fragments near the latter temple—many of them the criosphinxes or ram-head sphinxes. Of Karnac it is impossible to convey a correct idea. It is a stupendous pile of buildings, some two miles in circuit, and of every date from the time of Osirtasen (supposed to be the Pharaoh of Joseph's day) to that of Ptolemy Physcon, B. C. 145—a period of 1650 years. The grand hall was the work of Osirei, the father of Sesostris, and for grandeur, casts in the shade every other room ever constructed on earth. This apartment is 329 feet long and 170 feet wide, and is supported by

134 columns, 12 of which are 66 feet high and 12 feet in diameter, and the rest 42 feet high and 9 feet in diameter! The mention of these numbers will give a faint conception of the prodigious size and massive appearance of this hall. On column and wall and roof are innumerable paintings of the Egyptian school, giving a tone of life to the desolate temple. Among these entangled ruins two obelisks still remain upright, one of which is of the surprising height of 92 feet. Colossi are sprinkled about with a lavishness befitting the statuettes of a plaster-cast merchant; pylæ or propyla, pillars and obelisks, walls and roofs, sphinxes and relievos, paintings and hieroglyphics, are everywhere in indescribable confusion.

From the summit of the lofty propyla, we saw the sun go down behind the western hills, bathing the ruins in a mellow light, which seemed the rays escaped from heaven's portal, so full of sweet joy and peace, so softly brilliant, were those brief gleams of setting day. The darkness of night soon enveloped Karnac in its folds, rendering the ruins a shapeless mass, and drove us to our boat, where we were shortly busy with dreams of Thebes and Sesostris in all their glory.

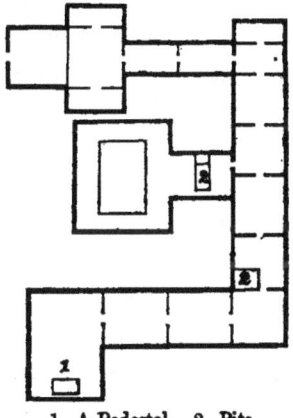

1. A Pedestal.   2. Pits.

There is a tomb upon the western shore I cannot omit to mention. It is that of the priest Petamunap, who is supposed to have flourished not long before the inroad of Cambyses. It is the largest tomb in Thebes, and shows remarkable peculiarity of arrangement.

The foregoing is an *approximate* sketch of its interior, taken merely from a passing view of its apartments.

Besides the floor here given, are two lower.

The direct length of apartments is 862 feet, not including the lateral chambers or the other floors. This Petamunap was, doubtless, the Wolsey of his day, and had no idea of the church being considered inferior to the state, and while the Pharaohs were erecting their noble palaces in the face of heaven, the cunning priest was mouse-like gnawing out the interior of the earth and forming a palace for his corpse, that should remain sound in every item when the lofty domes of the monarchs were crumbled into dust.

We have thus enumerated the principal relics of ancient Thebes, marks of the earlier civilization of our world. Here in this beautiful valley were flourishing the arts and sciences, when Europe was a wilderness of savages, or even an uninhabited wild. From these temples and palaces flowed the civilizing stream through Greece and Rome to the kingdoms of modern Europe and the extended shores of a New World; and while these climes are well watered by this vivifying stream, its sources among the sands of Egypt are nearly dry. However much we may admire the great advance of ancient Egypt in the arts, it is folly to attribute to those early times a farther progress than is enjoyed by us. Some antiquaries, surprised at the wonderful delineations of the successful practice of many arts depicted on the ruins of Egypt, have, like the bent bow, sprung from incredulity into the most fanatical ideas regarding the ancient civilization of the Nile valley, and its vast superiority to that of the present day; and they declare, in accordance with these notions, that man was created not a savage, but a civilized being, and that therefore, in the earlier stages of the world's history we must expect to find the golden age of civilization. This reasoning is based on two false assumptions—that man deteriorates as the world grows older, and that man's original civilization, received directly from his Creator, comprehended an enlightened knowledge of the arts. As regards the first assumption, the history of particular nations may be summoned to testify to man's faculties of improvement. Are not nations daily advancing in every branch of civilization before our eyes? Is European refinement of the nineteenth century inferior to that of the fourteenth? And is the march of improvement in the Sandwich Islands retrograde? Or, if the opponent says that these improvements in particular quarters are nevertheless accompanied by a deterioration in the whole mass of the world's inhabitants, we would merely ask him to compare the world's civilization now and that of the middle ages. Take the whole globe, and in full view we have its rapid advance in civilization within the last four centuries.

We therefore see no argument for the ancient superiority of Egyptian civilization in the natural deterioration of the human race; nor do we find support for the theory of the wonderful advancement of that land in the arts, in the fact that man was created a civilized being; for though his mental faculties may have been the keenest in perceiving the relations of cause and effect, and his manners may have exhibited the most perfect refinement, yet he could not have been acquainted with the myriad mechanical arts, as they were both unnecessary for his wants and too numerous for his attention. Indeed, Scripture also tells us of the discovery of the useful arts long after the creation of man, for Tubal Cain was not indebted to Adam for his smith-work.

We are therefore unbelievers in the imagined superiority of Egyptian civilization over our own; and with the printing-press, the steam-engine, the majestic telegraph, and the preached Gospel, we defy comparison.

Yet Egypt undoubtedly was a wise and polished nation. The comforts and luxuries of life were there enjoyed, and wholesome laws encouraged the labours of the artisan. This we could learn from the monuments, were history silent; but history is *not* silent, and from Grecian and Roman authors we have full testimony to the enlightened condition of the Egyptian nation.

While lying at Luxor, we ventured on giving a dinner-party. Our Scotch friends were to be our guests. Dragoman and cook were carefully admonished to keep up the dignity of our dahabiyeh, which, however, was an imaginary quality, but nevertheless a fulcrum by which to raise the energies of our Fridays in preparing a good feast. From the village was levied the due quantity of live stock for slaughter, and a dozen officious Arabs acted as butchers and scullions, content to receive payment in a chance handful of fragments. Our fire smoked as if our boat had been transformed into a steamer, and the pompous Hassanein assumed the bearing of a general on the eve of battle. Ibrahim, however, struck terror into our hearts in the midst of our arrangements. He had made an inventory of our table furniture, and found it rather limited, unless we should take dinner in rotation. This would be well enough for our principal guest, who of course would have the first morsels; but as it would be horrid cruelty to those succeeding, who would thus from guests become *waiters*, and whose hunger would rival in extent and manner of treatment the thirst of Tantalus, we discarded the idea, a little pride and selfishness mingling in our decision. But what were we to do? It was impossible to make seven plates out of four, or seven chairs out of two. To be sure, cups and saucers might be used as plates, and boxes as chairs, but then there are still the knives, forks, and spoons wanting. At Ibrahim's suggestion (to whose knowledge of Egyptian etiquette we bowed implicitly), we adopted a happy expedient. We added a Nota Bene to our note of invitation, which then ran somewhat as follows:

Luxor, *March* 6, 1849.

Mr. and Mrs —— request the pleasure of Mrs. and Messrs. G——'s company to dinner this evening at 6 o'clock.

N. B.—Please bring with you six plates, ten knives and forks, twelve spoons, a coffee-pot, a table, and four chairs. Also, several tumblers and wine-glasses.

Thus were our forebodings set at rest by the rare device of our worthy Ibrahim, our hospitality being enlarged to the invitation of guests both animate and inanimate. It is a well-known fact in the daily or nightly history of city fashion at home, that the display of silver and crockery upon the supper-table is borrowed splendour. What more reasonable than that such loans should be made by the partakers of the banquet? This, to us, was a rational theory on the Nile, and its practice succeeded to a charm.

The distribution of the company was the next thought, and we began to calculate the square inches necessary for a human being to have to himself in order to preserve life. When our guests arrived, we shrewdly remarked that it was so much more delightful in the open air than under a roof; this stopped the gentlemen on the deck, where fortunately was verge enough. The oriental use of divans was of saving importance to us, for we immediately passed off our beds for the most approved divans, and the want of space for our borrowed chairs was most gracefully concealed by the adoption of an Egyptian style. Many other curious peculiarities, that found a parent in invention's mother, were naively attributed to a refined taste. A lantern received high encomiums as avoiding the flare that would have inevitably attended a candelabra,—a pitcher with a broken handle was reckoned an imitation of Etruscan form,—and some shocking brandy was straightway supposed to be a novel species of foreign wine. Hassanein and Ibrahim were ecstatic with the delight of successful practicians, and our swarthy crew looked towards the cabin as to an elysium graciously brought within range of their mortal vision. In spite of our perplexities, we made a good dinner, and separated with those peculiar feelings that are the portion of those who dine heartily beneath the ruins of Luxor. Next morning our Scotch friends passed on, in their way up to Edfou; but the desert was before us, and we had reached the limits of our Nile voyage, for the increasing heat would soon render desert-travelling dangerous.

The Nile.

DENDERA—A TURKISH BATH—AN ADVENTURE—ABYDUS—NIGHT ADVENTURE.

On the evening of the 7th March, we dropped quietly down the stream, bearing away from Thebes an enlarged stock of knowledge, pleasant memories, and a miniature museum of antiquities. In this last department several mummies testified to our zeal. I had become possessed of a lady's hand—a hand which had probably had a hundred suitors 3000 years ago, but was left for a stranger from the land of the setting sun, thirty centuries after the fair owner had made her debut; Egyptian old maids had no reason to fear increasing age. The ring upon my acquired hand had been placed there by some hopeful gallant, a subject of the Osirtasens and Amunophs—but in vain; a rival he had not suspected was to carry both ring and hand away, and bear them to an unknown shore. A cat, moreover, (that had mewed and purred by some Theban fireside, when the household was discussing a new victory of Sesostris, and counting him a promising fellow,) was another ornament to our cabin; all swaddled, as if to avert the chill of death, she was soon detected by our domestic rats, and these feline enemies immediately commenced a revengeful attack upon her fair form, as though in her was the source of all the ills that rat-life is heir to, and pussy would have fallen a victim to these avenging spirits, had not her lifeless claws and stiffened jaws been removed to a safer position.

C—— had brought away a veritable human head—skin, features, and hair, complete—who knows, but the visage of a Pharaoh? It was duly suspended in our cabin, and formed a peaceable addition to our travelling party; like the modern Egyptians, he travelled without a trunk.

To resume the diary.

March 8.—A strong head wind has kept us all day lying quietly between Kopt and Koos, only twelve miles from Thebes. The scenery being tame, we have had recourse to our library for pastime; and we have watched the women, as they come for water to the river, wondering at the weight they bear upon their heads, and the steadiness with which they manage their loads. Though the wind blew violently, these women would bear their large filled jars upon their heads perfectly upright, scarcely ever using their hands as support. This use of head for hands, so manifestly inappropriate for the rounded skull, Nature never designed, unless for the Flat-head Indians; but the women of Egypt (though no blue-stockings) invariably prefer head work to hand work, and have as little regard for nature as the most civilized being could exhibit.

In descending the Nile, the main-mast of a dahabiyeh is raised from its socket and laid lengthwise along the boat, resting on the cabin roof, and bound at the other end to the surviving mast. This gives room for the crew to perform their inimitable feats in rowing, in which their aim seems to consist in making the most violent movements with the oars, and obtain the least benefit in progress. The end of the oar in the water is entirely forgotten in their amusement with the end they have in their hands, so that a traveller who expects any other agency in descending the Nile than wind and current, will be wofully mistaken. There is an immense amount of the ludicrous in his crew's manœuvres; so he must enjoy the fun and pocket the disappointment.

It is near our present position that the trade of Upper Egypt for ages flowed—the costly goods of Indian fabric reaching Kopt (or Coptos) from the port of Berenice on the Red Sea, and hence being taken by the Nile to the nations of the Mediterranean. Even now there is a caravan route from Kossayr upon the Red Sea to Kopt, but Suez and Cairo have proved more advantageous positions for the course of modern trade, and Upper Egypt is robbed of all her glories.

March 9.—Ibrahim roused me from bed about 7 o'clock, chiding my lateness, and telling me that we were nearly at Kenneh; I hurriedly dressed, and found our boat about stopping among a motley company of Nile craft, by the mud bank of the town. As our object was to see Dendera, (which lies opposite,) and not to give the crew an opportunity of desertion at Kenneh, I ordered the rais instantly to cross the river, and land at the opposite side, where was no tempting village to entice our worthies ashore. To this the Nubian had decided objections. It wasn't customary, and the water opposite was too shallow for the boat, and Kenneh was worth seeing, and I don't know how many more reasons for remaining where we were, arose in the mind of the rais, and were successively poured out in our ears. But his devices were fruitless.

I gave him, in turn, my reason for crossing, viz., that I wished to go; and he reluctantly found it his better policy to give up all the anticipated delights of a ramble in Kenneh. We thereupon crossed, and found the river not so shallow but that we could reach a point about twenty feet from the shore, and, by means of planks, this was got over by us dry-shod.

We had ordered donkeys over from Kenneh, and a tub-like scow had brought them. Mounting these sorry specimens, we rode for a mile over the plain, grown with " halfeh," a coarse grass, before we reached the sandy mounds of Tentyris (Dendera). From the banks of the river the top of the front portico of the great temple had been visible over the intervening mounds, but the remainder of the ruins were concealed from view until we had reached the site. The main temple, erected to Athor, the Egyptian Venus, by one of the late Ptolemies, and completed by the Cæsars, remains almost in a perfect state. It has been thoroughly excavated, so that you may enter every apartment from ground to roof, as in the days of its youth. The temple is 220 feet long by 100 broad, and is approached by a dromos of 260 feet, before which is a pylon bearing the names of Domitian and Trajan. This building exhibits a striking instance of the importance of Champollion's discovery. Former antiquarians had used this ruin as a proof against Bible chronology —boldly declaring that it boasted of an antiquity far antecedent to the biblical epoch of creation; but Champollion blew their cobwebs to the wind when he read " the writing on the wall," and fixed its date at the beginning of the Christian era. Such a signal defeat should make us exceedingly wary in receiving the dogmas of infidel philosophers, whose enmity to religion renders them capable of urging the most extra-

THE TEMPLE.   99

vagant doctrines with a boldness that gives plausibility and begets belief.

The grand portico of the temple is supported by twenty-four pillars, surmounted by heads of Athor as capitals, and bears the name of Tiberius in Greek, plainly visible from below, on its front. The carvings are most skilful, and in prodigious quantity. Within the farthest room is an enclosed chamber, or sanctum, like the structure within the church of the Holy Sepulchre at Jerusalem. This inner spot was the heart of the temple, and the abode of the goddess. Upon the external surface of the back wall is a carved portrait of the famous Cleopatra, which, if a correct likeness, proves rumour a flattering herald, or shows a wonderful difference between ancient and modern

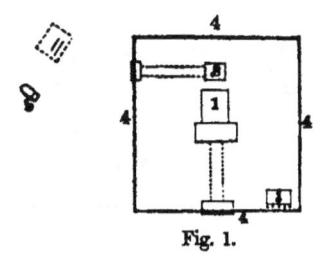

Fig. 1.

Fig. 2.

Fig. 1. The entire field of ruins.
Fig. 2. The main temple (on a larger scale).

1. Temple of Athor, dromos and pylon.
2. Temple of Isis, dromos and pylon.
3. A building probably belonging to No. 1.
4. Remnants of brick wall.
5. Pylon and temple, very ruined.

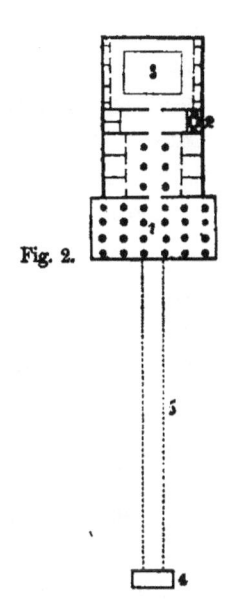

1. Grand portico.
2. Stairway.
3. Sanctum.
4. Pylon.
5. Dromos.

standards of beauty. A winding stairway, with square corners, leads to the roof, where are the remnants of small chapel-like rooms. Besides this main building, there are other remains of Roman date, but of inferior interest, still existing on the site, not yet completely covered by the invading sand. The foregoing rude sketches will show their position, and give a general idea of the ground plan of the principal temple.

On the ceiling of the portico of the great temple is the famous zodiac, which, before Champollion's investigations, formed a bone of contention among the savans of Europe. Dendera or Tentyris, (supposed by Wilkinson to be derived from *Tei-n-Athor*, the abode of Athor) though probably a town of Pharaonic antiquity, yet must have reached its highest prosperity about the first century of the Christian era, when the massive temple was erected that now calls out the admiration of the traveller. The Tentyrites were great enemies of the crocodile, while the people of Kom Ombos paid it divine honours—hence arose endless feuds between these two parties. The more the Tentyrites persecuted the crocodiles, the more the Kom-Ombites prayed to their scaly gods, and their zeal of opposition waxed so hot, that Tentyris became a slaughter-house, and the good people of Kom Ombos almost wore their knees out in their worship. Then they took to blows upon each other—first the crocodile-party would gain the day, and then the temples of Kom Ombos were filled with devout worshippers—then came success to the anti-crocodilers, and the Tentyrites would treat their captives on crocodile-steak. As in all religious controversies, neither side was converted, and the crocodiles had to stay up the river and keep a sharp look-out towards Dendera. Strabo relates that the Tentyrites were so fearless of their amphibious enemy, that they would boldly swim amongst them, and adds, that the enterprising managers of the Zoological Gardens at Rome had imported some Tentyrites, with their crocodiles, in order to make out a more attractive bill. Land and water accommodation was afforded the Egyptian leviathans, in the shape of a duck-pond, and a wooden staging on the side; and the Tentyrite performance consisted in pulling these monsters from one element to the other, with an ease perfectly astonishing to the Roman snobs. Poor Dendera! how changed! One crocodile could now dwell as undisturbed master of its temples and palaces—and I doubt not that many a grim old crocodile, well-informed in traditionary lore, thrusts his huge jaws out of water as he passes this desolate site, and shakes his stony features at its fallen glory, with all the sneering triumph of a satisfied revenge.

On returning over the plain of "halfeh" to our boat, we met the Governor of the district, mounted, like the judges of Israel, on an ass, and possessed of a most benevolent and patriarchal countenance. The old Turk saluted us with a gracious "Sabal khayr" which we translated to him in a genuine Saxon "Good morning."

After reaching the dahabiyeh, we paddled over to Kenneh in a small boat. This town is a mile away from the river, on a canal. It is the ancient Kainopolis (New-town) and its present name is probably a corruption of that word. It has the same character with all Egyptian towns—quaint, dirty, and crowded. I here essayed the Turkish bath for the first time, and feel it due to my friends, as a survivor of the operation, to narrate my perilous experience. I entered a dull vault-like building, into which the light struggled through small windows in the roof, and throughout

8

which floated an atmosphere of steam. In the first chamber I unrobed, upon an elevated divan, of doubtful purity, and thence proceeded, with one towel around my loins, another over my head and shoulders, and a pair of wooden pattens on my feet, through a passage of undisguised filth (so placed probably to enhance the luxury of purification), and passed the Tepidarium or "cooling-room" to the Caldarium, or "hot-house." The heat here was choking, and I felt my substance gradually melting away. The Arab guide laughed at my uneasiness, as I thought of the suffocation of the English princes, sundry deaths from the fumes of charcoal, and other kindred subjects. But comforting myself with the knowledge that a man cannot die but once, I allowed myself to be seated on a very warm stone, and submitted heroically to the manipulations of a lank Arab. First, he used his long black fingers, and rubbed me into a fearful state of nervousness. He then procured a hair-glove as an instrument of torture, and practised on me with the zeal of a groom with his curry-comb. This was nothing to the next step in the cleansing process. I was coolly (no, not coolly, but deliberately,) pitched into a stone trough of water, almost boiling, while a spout above poured forth the liquid still hotter, if possible, upon every portion of my persecuted frame that dared attempt an escape. This was too much. I vowed I would keep out of hot-water forever after, if once clear of this Tophet, and I felt the sincerest sympathy for Latimer and Ridley. I remembered, too, the injunctions of my childhood, not to get *over-heated*, but the penalty following such childish imprudence seemed nectar to me, and I fondly wished I might take *cold* as soon as possible. Released from my burning coffin, I was deluged with soap-suds till I looked a man of snow, but it was only appearance, I assure you, for to my glowing body, the few sun-beams that had forced their way through the vaporous atmosphere seemed to possess a coolness, so sadly were my perceptions askew. Then came bucket after bucket of the smothering water upon my head—then I was plunged anew into the scorching trough, and then, O bliss! I was transported (yea, it *was* transport) into the cooling-room, where, wrapped in sheets and towels, I was suffered to rest, but not before a huge Arab had pressed me from head to foot with his giant arms, and made every bone in my body crack with the pressure. A cup of coffee and a shebook were indubitable blessings, and I began to feel somewhat kind-hearted in spite of my late afflictions. A barber pared my nails, and trimmed my beard, and at length I dressed and quitted the establishment, meditating on cleanliness and its inconveniences, and concluding that if a Turkish bath was the only method of its attainment, mankind would be fully justified in its neglect, and uncleanness would have become a virtue. I even looked with favour on the squalid beggar-boys, and wished to warn them against all hot-house methods of forcing a clean skin, for I felt keenly for them when I thought of the furnace of affliction that inevitably awaited their advancing years.

While in Kenneh, I witnessed some dances of the Almeh women, and can only contradict the romantic accounts of some sentimental travellers by stamping the women as beastly specimens of female depravity, and their dances as graceless and disgusting.

Leaving the town, we passed under the welcome shade of some fine trees that ornamented the road before the factory, and thence along the dyke and over the sandy beach to the river. We had just started in the dahabiyeh, when we found some Kenneh salesman had given Ibrahim some molasses for honey—and so off goes Ibrahim again to cudgel the merchant and make him give "sweets for the sweet." Another two or three hours is added to our delay, and we leave Dendera at length at 7 P. M., instead of 11 in the morning, as intended.

March 10.—To-day we've been contending with a violent head wind. We've crossed and recrossed the river, rowed to larboard and rowed to starboard, tried to pull and tried to tow, and spun around like a top, but all to no purpose. The Minaret of Hoo has provokingly laughed at us all day, and I fancy the muezzin relaxed his solemn countenance, as every time he reached his post on the turret he saw us laboring, as fruitlessly as the leopard, to change our spots. At sunset we fastened to the bank by the Farshoot factories. We visited a factory on the bank, where a French superintendent very politely showed us through the different rooms, and explained the sugar-refining process as practised in Egypt. There are three factories here, one being as yet unfinished; in the others they both make and refine the sugar. The Frenchman was a regular gossip; he talked indiscriminately of Europe and his garden, General Washington and sugar, and concluded his agreeability by offering us some absinth and tomatoes, a refreshment as variegated as his conversation. From the boat we saw a crowd collected around a defunct crocodile, which they were stuffing for preservation. Knots of Arabs were gathered for their evening's smoking and chaf, and a few tarbouched and slippered Frenchmen looked exceedingly comfortable under a leafy portico.

March 11.—On rising, I found the boat gliding rapidly along the green sloping banks of Lower Farshoot, and we continued prosperously to Belliany, where we have halted for the night, in order to visit Abydus in the morning, this being the nearest point to that ruined city. A lovely palm grove ornaments the bank at our side. Taking the ladies, I made an excursion through the village. In the centre of the place we saw the governor and his assembled councillors smoking profusely on an open divan. The usual amount of dogs and naked children adorned the dirty lanes. On our return to the boat, we stopped to look at a native sugar-factory, a rude shanty within a crude brick enclosure. Buffaloes turned a mill that resembled a cider-press, from which flowed the juice. Soon satisfied with a view of the advance of mechanical arts in Egypt, we turned to retire, when I observed a Nubian shut and lock the gate of the yard. I remarked the fact to Ibrahim, who accompanied me, but he thought me mistaken. However, on reaching the door, my surmise was found correct. The Nubian refused to open the door unless "backsheesh" was forthcoming—and twenty rascals supported his demand. I had nothing but a club in my hands, and on threatening the black with a visit from it, he flung the key into some ashes, in order more effectually to prohibit our departure. It was growing night, and the ladies became greatly alarmed. Without suffering the scamps to obtain the first advantage, I pushed the Nubian after his key, and hauled him to the door. A general row ensued, when the gate was opened and we made a sortie. I took the ladies to the boat, procured my gun, and calling Ibrahim with me, marched off straightway to the governor's. He referred me to the agent of Kamil Pacha, who owned the factory, as possessing the sole jurisdiction within its limits. I met this worthy in the street, a full-conditioned Turk, with a goodly quantity of liquor aboard. He hiccoughed all sorts of apologies for the insult I had received, and vowed he'd have me revenged. I told him that revenge was not my motive in addressing him, but a desire to make the people of the country shy in injuring travellers, by filling them with respect for their power. He swore it was all the same in results, and took up as straight a line of march for the factory as his soaked system was capable of prosecuting. He burst on the astonished Nubian and his compeers like a thunder-clap, and in a twinkling the black rascal was roaring under the blows of the bastinado. The governor was determined to give him 300, but a compromise was effected for 30. After the punishment had so rapidly succeeded the offence, (for the bastinado follows on the *heel* of crime,) I harangued the trembling offender on the extreme inconvenience attending upon the bad treatment of strangers, and then urged the rest to digest their comrade's case thoroughly before they followed his example. I left the factory, after thanking the gubernatorial agent and inviting him to our boat, fully believing that the artisans of that establishment were under unspeakable obligations to me for delivering them from future bastinadoes by my warning lecture, accompanied by illustrations.

Now, a Turkish officer never was guilty of doing his duty gratis; and consequently, we had invited our red-faced friend to the boat to receive our thanks more formally by a substantial token. In about an hour, a slave came down the bank bearing a huge jar of sugar-juice as avant-courier of his excellency; then another and another made their appearance, with stalks of sugar-cane as offerings of his most sincere friendship, which consisted of a strong desire for a transfer of property of some sort in his favour. At length came the Effendi himself, with a dignity entirely incommensurate with the contracted size of our dahabiyeh. We offered him a chair, and he tried to sit, but fidgeted himself down on the divan, where his bent-up limbs found more congenial repose. He magnificently handled an offered pipe, and hurried through his coffee as if he had an eye on some ulterior blessing. We took the hint, and asked his Mohammedan excellency if he would have anything stronger as a beverage. He winked most pleasantly, and his looks spoke volumes against his belief in the abstinence of the Koran. Unfortunately we had nothing but rum on board, and so informed him. His eyes were brilliant as he told us confidingly that rum was just the thing. We offered him the article with some water, but he preferred "rum au naturel," and to our astonishment drained our entire stock. Discovering he had found the bottom of our hospitality, he most benignly received some powder as a mark of our high esteem, and bade us an affecting adieu, not, however, before promising us Arabian steeds of noblest breed and gloriously caparisoned for our morrow's ride to Abydus. Our official friend had by his visit postponed our supper until our appetites had become unruly. His departure was the signal for immediate action, and the table was instantly furnished. But our haste was our hindrance, for the table gave way beneath our impetuosity, and we were fully convinced of the truth of the instruction we had received as children, that *china* lay directly beneath our feet. Our cabin was a true Canaan, flowing with milk and honey, and we precipitately made Pisgahs of our divans. We did not retire, however, before the wreck was removed, and we had acquired the contentment that follows an appeased appetite.

March 12.—A Turk's promise is pure theory, and any attempt to reduce it to practice will only plunge the experimenter into a labyrinth of disasters equal to his, who endeavors to square the circle. Of course, therefore, our Arabian steeds were as phantom-like as a night-mare, and we were content to hire donkeys of ignoble breed, without even the ornamental utilities of stirrups, saddle, or bridle, whereby to visit the ruins of Abydus. I found some rope accoutrements of questionable merit, and we performed our seven miles' trip to the foot of the Libyan Mountains in three hours, our long-eared chargers evidently having as little to do with *fast*-days as their irreligious masters. The plain was lovely with the verdant growth of peas, beans, wheat, barely, lentils, and clover. Here and there we passed the usual village scenes of hideous females, naked children, and barking dogs, when we reached Arabat el Matfoon (the buried Arabat), the village that now unworthily represents the fallen Abydus. About a quarter of a mile behind the village, and just within the bounds of the desert, are the principal remains of this great city, now nearly concealed by the accumulated sand. Abydus is said by Strabo to have been second to Thebes for size, though in his day it was a small village. He also mentions, as its principal glory, the Memnonium, which was a stone building resembling in interior the described arrangement of the labyrinth. He reports this to have been called in his day the work of Memnon, whom he thinks to be the same with Ismandes, who also erected some splendid edifices at Thebes. He also mentions a temple of Osiris, in which no music was allowed.

The two grand edifices now partially seen at Abydus, are of exceeding interest. Their roofs are on a level with the surrounding sand. It is discovered that they are the works of Osirei and Ramses the Great, and are probably the Memnonium and Temple of Osiris mentioned by Strabo. In that case, the Roman Memnon would be the Egyptian Ramses—though it is probable that the Romans gave the name of Memnon to several Egyptian kings whose reigns were little known. We crawled into the great temple, and looked at the fresh colours on the walls and the interesting carvings. The ceiling of a portion is formed of single stones, laid across and hollowed on the under side, to imitate an arch. It was in one of the chambers of the smaller temple that Mr. Bankes discovered, in 1818, the tablet containing a list of Egyptian monarchs who preceded Ramses the Great. Abydus is by some supposed to be the still more ancient This. It is finely situated in an alcove of the Libyan cliffs, the points of which are some four miles apart. It is well placed for defence, and that was probably a reason for its site, as well as to avoid taking up any of the tillable land, which was so valuable to a large population. West of the ruins runs the road to the Great Oasis over the Libyan hills—a steep, climbing path. Miss Martineau calls it an opening in the hills: it is as much an opening as a cat's track over a fence. We had to rest satisfied with looking at the merest fragments of Abydus, and trust to our imaginations for an idea of its old reality. It was very hot, and we were glad to exchange the burning sand for the coolness of a sweet green palm grove, where we sat ourselves comfortably to a primitive luncheon. By one o'clock we were back at our boat, and soon pushed off into the stream. In four hours and a half we reached Girgeh, its minarets and palms showing well from its high position. We here stopped two hours, and shopped in the bazaars. We are now off again for Achmim.

March 13.—Visited Achmim, the ancient Chemmis or Panopolis, which Strabo speaks of as a town of workers in linen and stone. What connexion there was between the trades I can't conceive. The modern town is of the usual Egyptian type. The ancient remains are found behind the town. Those of the supposed Temple of Perseus lie in a palmy hollow, and consist of huge stones in confused groups. I saw two with a carved work of united stars upon them, as if they had been portions of a roof. Another fragment had two hieroglyphical ovals. West of these I saw the large stone mentioned by Wilkinson. With a crowd of Arabs brimful of curiosity gathered about me, I took down the inscription of Trajan. It marks the date of the edifice to which it belonged to be the twelfth year of the reign of Trajan. It would be as easy to build a seventy-four from a gooseberry-bush as to arrange any theory of these structures from the slender remains that lie scattered behind Achmim. We must here, as in many other places, be contented with the wildest guesses. To-night our rais has begged me to be ready against attack, as he knows this part of the river to be well stocked with robbers. Whether he be a coward or a cheat I know not, but I have no question the Nile is as devoid of danger as the Hudson, unless it holds true here that "*delays* are dangerous." If so, a Nile voyage is a risky affair. To be sure, if I had a tendency to encourage romantic ideas of robbery and murder, this would be a good place. The grim cliffs of Gebel Sheikh Hereedee frown down gloomily in the twilight. Two suspicious looking craft are a short distance ahead of us, and the place is wretchedly lonely. But I could scare up the same ghosts on the Hudson.

March 15.—The river at one point, yesterday (between Gow and Abooteg), was so narrow that I could nearly cast a stone across. Of course the stream was very rapid at this point. Near Motmar our eyes were regaled by the loveliest groves of acacia, almost too tempting to allow our passing them unvisited. The days are hot and the nights cool, and the changes of temperature I have noticed as great as in New York. The thermometer, one day at 96°, has fallen the next to 70°, and the wind has proved as changeable as the weather, utterly laughing at the story of the steady character of Æolus in Egypt. The fellahin are now harvesting their barley, but the wheat has not changed colour. This reminds us of the plague of hail, by which the barley was smitten, for it was in the ear; but the wheat was not smitten, for it was not grown up (Exodus ix., 31, 32), the relative advancement of the two crops being the same now as in the time of Moses.

At Thebes one of our Nubian sailors had thrown up his commission in our service, without the usual etiquette considered necessary on such occasions; and on our downward voyage another oarsman had pursued the same independent system, or rather lack of system, thus leaving us unexpectedly in the condition of the famous Master Nellis of the Museums, viz., minus *two hands*. We had ordered our rais to supply the vacancies, according to contract, but that smooth-faced commander manifestly saw better policy in saving the wages of two sailors than in conforming to the terms of a contract. Our plausible friend was not rude, however, in his obstinacy. By no means. He exhibited the graces of a Chesterfield, and clothed his total dissent from our conclusions with all the flattering drapery of full agreement. He assured us of results, to prevent which was his decided aim, and he issued promises with all the benevolent zeal of a broken bank. But promises, good in their place, are of little value as a propelling power in things purely material, and we grew impatient. Village after village, each the expected source of our recuperated energy, was passed, and still the two oars dragged neglected by the vessel's side. The interest was fast accumulating on the promissory notes of the rais, and at length I threatened the oily-tongued worthy with an application of the usual Egyptian method of arranging such debts. I summoned him to the *poop*, and there held a very *stern* manner of speech. I reminded him that one Lattif Bey, the Governor of Upper Egypt, dwelt at Siout, which place lay not far distant. I further assured him that the said Lattif added to his other Oriental accomplishments a singular proficiency in managing the bastinado. I lastly introduced, as a relevant subject, the necessity of procuring our complement of crew, at Siout, and then dismissed him to study at his leisure the inter-relations of the various parts of my discourse.

Well, we arrived at Siout yesterday at 5 P. M. I rode up to the town and took a last look at its bazaars, and then regained the boat in so weary a frame, that I soon dropped asleep in the cabin. On waking, I discovered we had left Siout and were floating down the river. Hastening to the deck, I found we were some five miles below the town, and the easy rais was about mooring the boat for the night at the petty village of Welladiyeh. The men had rested six hours during the day, and now a drift current was assisting our progress. Of course, I forbade all thoughts of so early a stoppage, it being only 9 o'clock. But another look altered my determination. The vacancies were still unfilled. I permitted the halt and we were soon fastened to the bank. "Now, rais," cried I, "put on your walking gear, and I'll join you in a promenade." The fellow was thrown off his equilibrium. The night was dark, and what could I mean. "Where would you go, Hawagee?" "To Siout—be quick," was my reply. A good hoax, thought the Nubian, and he smilingly donned his outer robe. Ibrahim and Hassanein each procured a lantern. I threw my double-barrel over my shoulder, and, joined by the rais, we gained the bank. As aforesaid, it was a night of literal Egyptian darkness, and Siout was five miles distant. We followed the river-side, stumbling, in spite of lanterns, into ditches and over stumps innumerable. The rais suddenly struck an idea: it was no hoax, and he was actually on the way to see Lattif Bey. His countenance fell. A paleness even gleamed through his swarthy skin, and he trembled like an autumn leaf. Placing him between Ibrahim and Hassanein, I led on more rapidly, passed the quiet hamlet of Hamra, the port of Siout, and then struck westward from the river to reach the town.

In a little more than an hour from the boat, we were before the gate. What an odd scene! The capital city of Upper Egypt was as silent as a farm-house at midnight—as motionless and apparently as lifeless as ruined Thebes.

Our flickering lamps just served to lighten the old gate, and make the gloom of night oppressive. We hammered stoutly at the portal, but our own breathing, or a rustle among the trees, was the only experience of our tympana. Another rap, and a hoarse growl from a roused dog gave answer. Still another, and the growl became a bark, which found its echo everywhere, till all the canine voices of Siout were lifted in chorus. This concert stirred the slumbering porter, and a voice half gruff and half terrified was heard from within. "Who, in the name of Allah and the blessed Mohammed, creates such infernal din?" "Eftah (open)—eftah," we impatiently cried in a commanding tone. At this sesame the bars were taken down, the bolts drawn back, and the astounded Moslem opened the gate sufficiently to squint at his visiters. We interrupted his reconnoitre, and, dashing him back, stalked into the town. Turning to the amazed Cerberus, I ordered him to conduct us straightway to the Palace of Lattif Bey. No sooner had he heard the Governor's name, than he girded up his loins and led us hastily through the winding lanes. We stepped over snoring Arabs, lying like bales of goods in the narrow ways, and here and there encountered a foxy dog, bolder in bark than bite. Still the city slumbered as if in death. As we passed on, the trembling rais reached the side of our new-found guide, and my suspicions were excited. I ordered him to fall back, and we continued our midnight tramp. We turned a hundred corners, roused the porters of the door-like gates that shut in the different quarters of the city, ascended and descended until my feet sank beneath me. I smelt a trick. "Where is Lattif Bey?" I thundered, when down we went after our ragged leader into a forlorn cellar of insufferable stench, as dark and dirty as a harpy's cavern. "What's all this?" I cried in exasperation. "The palace of Lattif Bey," coolly replied the villain. The bribe of the rais had operated. I leaped forward, and grasping the miscreant porter by the throat, flung him into a corner and placed the muzzle of my gun at his head. I knew not how many confederates he might have in the vicinity, but I *did* know that now was high time for decisive measures. With my gun at his head, the rascal squealed apologies, and again I set him on the track. My two barrels had converted him effectually, and, leaving the filthy cellar, we soon reached the court of the Governor's residence. But a new difficulty arose. Slaves on tiptoe came down to us and whispered that the mighty satrap of Upper Egypt was busy in dreams, that he was a dreadful personage, and that the man's head was doomed who should dare awake him.

I entreated, urged, commanded—but in vain. At length, Ibrahim offered to make the hazardous experiment; but he was my right-hand man and I dared not risk him in the peril. I made a virtue of necessity, and turning to the rais, who was almost lifeless with fear, dispensed to him my full forgiveness of his faults, on condition that the next morning should witness our restored complement of boat-equipage. Should this condition be neglected, I assured him, I should *then* persevere in cementing an intimacy between himself and Lattif Bey. The rejoicing captain fell at my feet, kissed my hands convulsively, and blessed the prophet. Meantime our guide had attempted to make off, fearing the effects of my indignation; but I had ordered Hassanein to stand guard over the reprobate, and we now issued from the gubernatorial hall, requesting him to show us the nearest route to Welladiyeh, where our boat was moored. He objected, and I urged him with the same argument I had used in the cellar. I planted the muzzle between his shoulder-blades, and told him the moment he stopped I would shoot. He hobbled on in trepidation, ever and anon casting his eyes over his shoulder, to judge of my hostile intentions, and his chances of escape. The poor fellow felt the muzzle of the gun, and pushed on, consenting to his doom, only asking in subdued tone that his "backsheesh" might be remembered. He drew comfort from the assurance that we should faithfully render him his deserts, and clenched his fingers around the imaginary piastres.

We returned by a different route to the village, more direct but less evident, over fields of grain and under groves of dark acacias. At length we reached the bank, and leaped aboard the dahabiyeh. Abdallah, the guide, who had stood aside to let me enter the boat, was at my heels. It was now my turn. "What, in the name of Mohammed, do you want?" "Backsheesh, ya Hawagee." "Backsheesh!" roared I in mock dramatic. "Off! imshee! away with your villany!"

But the Egyptian moved not. The craving after the piastres was a more powerful influence than my stentorian ejaculations in broken Arabic. He remained rooted to the spot, whining out his redundant theme, till I feared an experience similar to that of Sinbad with the old man was waiting me. But I remembered the cellar, and raised my gun—the charm was broken, and Abdallah was over the side of the boat in a twinkling. Here our intimacy ceased. I retired to the cabin, and slept soundly after the long march.

This morning we have a full crew.

The rais now beholds me in a different light. I am looked upon with marked respect as able to enforce my orders, and my least command is obeyed with an alacrity as pleasing as it is novel. This decided action is the only means of managing an Egyptian. Persuasion is valueless, unless it has a silver lining, and then it is a hurtful method of success. Let your lenity be tempered with decision, so that it wear not the aspect of impotency, and a Nile sailor is your humble servant to command.

We halted at Manfaloot, to-day, for an hour. Like some enthusiastic travellers, it has almost been *carried away* by the Nile. It is a forlorn town, just ready to drop away into the river. I went with Ibrahim to supply our kitchen from the bazaars. He was an original at a purchase. He would take up an article and fling down what he considered an equivalent, and march off, leaving the huckster using unavailing shouts of protestation, but afraid to abandon his remaining wares in pursuit of his unsatisfactory customer.

Passing the high wall-like cliffs of Gebel Aboofoda, that abound in caverns, and show plainly the mark of the height of the river in the inundation, we have stopped opposite Tel el Amarna.

The Nile.

ANTINOE—BENI-HASSAN—DASHOOR—MEMPHIS—LAST GLANCES AT CAIRO.

MARCH 16.—An interesting day. Our first halt was at Dayr es Nakhl. Leaving the boat, we had a scorching hot tramp of two and a half miles, over field and desert, to the foot of the hills behind the village and convent. Climbing the north side of a deep ravine, we found numerous excavated tombs—among them the one for which we were searching. It is near the summit of the hill, and has the remains of an entrance adorned with fine hieroglyphics. Entering, we found a room about twenty feet square, with a niche in the farther wall, where probably the corpse was placed. Much of the south wall had been destroyed by the Turks, and the entrance was in like condition. The ceiling had a fearful rent from corner to corner. This ceiling was finely ornamented with gold-coloured stars, with a string of hieroglyphics dividing it into two parts. The great attraction of the tomb is an excellent painting of a Colossus upon a sledge, being drawn to the place of its permanent location. The picture of the Colossus is about three feet high. It is a seated statue, and represented as bound to the sledge by several stout ropes, which are tightened by an inserted stick, as in the handle of a wooden saw. Four rows of men, numbering in all 172, are pulling by four ropes connected with the sledge, the head man of each row carrying the rope upon his shoulder, but the rest bearing it by their side. One man in front is offering incense to the statue—another, standing on its knees, is clapping his hands in time, to enable the men to pull simultaneously,—and a third, stationed in the front of the sledge, is pouring grease upon the track to ease the labour. Below are seen servants bearing water for the refreshment of the workmen. All the men appeared black, except the incense offerer. The date of this painting is placed by Wilkinson (from an interpretation of the hieroglyphics) in the reign of Osirtasen II., about 1650 B. C., during Joseph's abode in Egypt. The name of the occupant of the tomb is recorded— *Thoth-otp.* This painting is a clear testimony of the manner in which the wonderful Colossi of Egypt were moved, and sets at rest all speculation on the subject. It is a whole volume in itself, and one of the most interesting and instructive remains of ancient Egypt. No traveller on the Nile should leave this tomb unseen, and yet I believe that very few ever take the trouble to make the tedious walk necessary to reach the spot. The height of the painted Colossus being about four times the height of the men, would make the real image nearly twenty-four feet in stature. The colours have the freshness of a work of yesterday—so gentle are the hands of Time in this delicious climate. The view from the entrance of the tomb was grand. Beyond the Nile were the towns of Mellawee and Reramoon; farther down was Rauda and its sugar-factories. On this side were Dayr es Nakhl, and other villages, below the hills,—the beautiful valley stretched north and south, and at our side a dreary ravine of rock, honey-combed with caverns, ran among the hills, resembling (as Ibrahim says) the grim defiles of Petra. Our second halt was at the village of Sheikh Abadeh. Here are the ruins of Adrian's city of "Antinoe." From Dion Cassius (himself a Bithynian) we learn that Adrian was greatly attached to a Bithynian youth named Antinous, who accompanied him in his Egyptian tour. Adrian, having consulted the celebrated oracle of Besa, was informed that a great danger threatened him, and could only be averted by the death of one much beloved. At this, Antinous flung himself into the Nile as the desired offering, and Adrian caused to be erected opposite the place of his death the city that bore the name of the youth. Its theatre, its hippodrome, and its quadrivium, are still seen, the first two without and the last within the modern village of Sheikh Abadeh. The columns stand oddly in the centre of a dirty Arab village. They do not show any great beauty, yet testify to the importance of the ancient town. It is probable that the ancient streets were porticoed to shield the pedestrian from the sun's rays,—the remnants of columns would lead to this belief. An immense sycamore, that one might imagine coeval with the ancient city, stands upon the river's bank. We gladly sought its shade, and felt an agreeable coolness in this shelter, though even here the mercury (Fahr.) was at 96 deg.

Our third halt was at Beni Hassan. Here thirty or forty tombs are cut in the side of the cliffs that face the river; the ascent is by the inclined planes that their ancient framers caused to be made as roads to their lofty sepulchres. I visited nearly all these highly interesting remains. Their antiquity is indisputable. The eyes of Joseph were doubtless often turned in admiration at this majestically-situated cemetery,—

and perhaps he himself had attended the long procession that followed some noble to his last earthly habitation in this hollowed cliff. Some of the richest illustrations of ancient Egyptian life have been found here, and unknown authors have, by their speaking delineations on these solemn walls, formed an enduring history of their times. The most northern two of the tombs are of greatest interest. All sorts of trades and amusements are pictured; scenes in agriculture and the chase, and the solemn rites of religion; a hundred wrestlers in different postures; harpers; nets; fruits, and all the objects of every-day life.

In the second tomb is the famous painting supposed by some to represent Joseph and his brethren. But every internal evidence is against this. Above all, the person supposed to be Joseph, to whom the offerings are made by his so-called brethren, is evidently the proprietor of the tomb; and Joseph, we know, had his sepulchre in Canaan. Still, the painting is of intense interest, and has undoubted reference to some tribes east of Egypt. Several of the tombs have beautiful columns, representing, I suppose, the lotus in bud.

Others have three aisles, separated by two rows of

columns which we call Doric, but which were here erected hundreds of years before Doris had its name, unless we believe these columns to have been originally square, and altered to their present shape by the Greeks. Each tomb has a pit for the body, and several have a niche and statues. In many tombs are Greek scribblings, written by the gossiping travelling gentry of twenty centuries ago. The view from the ledge of rock before the tombs is magnificent, comprising the old scenery,—the silver Nile winding through its green valley. The minarets of Minyeh could be seen on the extreme right. Soon after reaching our boat, another dahabiyeh passed, and, in its rapid course, gave us a fleeting vision of the American flag. It was an American on his way to Thebes, but his name we were unable to learn.

March 17.—Stopped at Minyeh two hours. We lounged in a few cafés having fronts gayly daubed with representations of nondescript animals and unearthly plants, bargained with some Greek renegades for provision, and were off. After leaving Minyeh, a violent north wind arose, and we were forced to lie near the village of Gebel e' Tayr, where I have been practising medicine, and have created already a fame that would make a country doctor's eyes glisten. Ophthalmia has been the chief subject of my medicinal management, and a whole village has turned out to be doctored. Having plenty of water with which to refill my emptied bottles, I gave lavish doses, and performed as wonderful cures as ever are heralded in huge capitals on the pages of a puffing journal. Another American hailed us to-day, in passing upward; we began to feel that Egypt was entirely too common a road for travellers, and to turn our thoughts to the desert as more becoming. We must go to Mount Sinai before a railroad is built. We are now in the neighbourhood of the convent whose Christian inhabitants gave us so kind a visit on our way to Thebes. Curzon gives an amusing account of his excursion to this monastery. After toiling up the cliffs by means of a fissure, he found the building of square shape, about two hundred feet being the length of each side, and the walls having a height of twenty feet. It had been originally built of small square stones, but having fallen into decay, had been repaired with mud and sunburnt bricks. He entered by a low doorway, and found himself in a sort of barnyard—men, women, hens, and a large dog were all vociferous at sight of the stranger; the abbot, who had hitherto been strangely deficient in clothing, now leading the way to the church. A crowd followed them, who told Mr. Curzon that the monastery was founded by a rich lady named Halané, who was the daughter of a certain Kostandi, king of Roum. They by this, of course, referred to the convent-crazy St. Helena, mother (not daughter) of Constantine. The church is partly subterranean, and is covered by a flat roof of palm-trunks. The height of the interior is about twenty-five feet. Mr. Curzon also mentions the general arrangement of the church to be that of a Latin basilica—and this form, we know, was originally adopted from the Roman halls of court— often those very buildings having been converted into churches. This convent is a good sample of the many Coptic institutions of the same sort in Egypt. They have become more like villages than monastic edifices, being littered up with all sexes, ages, and domestic animals.

March 18.—To-day the convent sent its usual embassy, having profited nothing by our good counsel when ascending the river.

March 22.—A violent head wind has for four days baffled us, and we have only made Benisooef to-day, eighty-two miles from Minyeh. We have passed the time in short excursions, shooting Nile fowl, watching the peculiar habits of the fellahin, and planning for our future journey. Before arriving at Benisooef, C—— and I, with Ibrahim, left the boat in order to reach the town earlier and have our purchases ready, to avoid delay. Benisooef's minarets were ahead, and we made for them in direct line, as in a steeple-chase. We had not gone far, when an arm of the river, some thirty feet wide, stopped our progress. Ibrahim proposed carrying us over the shallow, but the mud appearing very soft, and Ibrahim being but slightly built, I preferred taking off shoes and stockings and wading over. After repeated efforts, wherein I fully tested the yielding properties of mud and the moistening qualities of water, I at last reached the other side, shook myself off like a water-dog after his swim, and sat myself coolly down to watch C—— and Ibrahim. C—— mounted Ibrahim's shoulders, thus avoiding the trouble of removing any of his apparel. Foot-deep, ankle-deep, knee-deep, came poor floundering Ibrahim, and C—— drew himself higher on his bearer's shoulders as the water made nearer approximation. A moment of hesitation, and back they puffed to the shore. Here they spent five minutes in anxious contemplation. I was fearful of disappointment, for I was already laughing internally at an imaginary catastrophe, and therefore hallooed in encouragement. Again was C—— mounted, and with resolute courage Ibrahim again essayed the task. Foot-deep, ankle-deep, knee-deep again; but what of that? on they come—when Ibrahim appears to totter; C—— is fairly on his carrier's head—a fearful lurch and over they go on all fours. A succession of plunges to recover their pristine condition is fruitless, and they splash manfully for the shore; C—— comes out on my side, but Ibrahim has regained the point whence he set out. I comfort my dripping friend by showing him my dry clothes, and comment kindly on the advantages of getting over difficulties on another's shoulders. Poor Ibrahim had now become perfectly desperate, and rushed wildly into the slough, dashed spitefully through stream and mire, and wrung himself out by our side. At length we reached Benisooef, and to our surprise a steamer was at the bank. We discovered it was carrying a relative on a trip to Thebes—so odd are some of the incidents of travel.

March 24.—Two more sorry days, in which we have made about fifteen miles progress. However, we have taken the opportunity to ramble over the bister-coloured Arabian hills, and collect curious specimens of their geological structure. We have chased jackals, and roused hawks and eagles from their eyries. Seeing a white, aristocratic-looking building in the distance, we walked to it and found it the residence of one Mahmoud Effendi, an agent of Hassan Bey, the great land proprietor hereabouts. There was a fine garden in front, stocked with mulberry trees and grape vines, à l'Italienne, as if the possessor had seen things European in his day. We were politely shown everything by an attaché of the establishment. Figs and oranges grew luxuriantly in the ornamented garden, which was well watered by noble sakias. The stables particularly attracted our attention: they stood around a huge hypæthral quadrangle 200 feet square.

March 26.—We have reached Masgoon, a sweet palm grove, from which we to-morrow make the excursion to the pyramids of Dashoor and Saccara. In the grove are tethered camels, horses, donkeys, and buffaloes, brought from the upper country, and on their way for sale at the great fair of Tanta in the Delta. At Tanta is buried a great Moslem saint, Said Ahmet el Bedowee, and at his tomb are held two celebrated fêtes every year, to which all Egypt flocks as to a domestic Mecca. From the inland side of the palm grove, we looked over the sand upon thirteen pyramids, the most prominent being the two great stone pyramids of Dashoor.

March 27.—At 8 A. M. we set off on bridleless, stirrupless donkeys, with the mercury at 90 degrees in the shade. After reaching the limit of cultivated land and passing the paltry village of Dashoor, we had two miles of hot sand-hills and sand-plains to the most southern pyramid. This structure is of peculiar form, the angle of inclination of its sides receiving a great diminution about half-way to the apex. Its height is probably three hundred and forty feet, and its base about seven hundred.

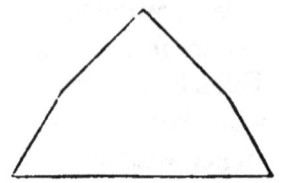

It strikes the beholder with almost as much awe as the great pyramid of Ghizeh. Wilkinson supposes the want of uniformity in the planes of the sides is owing to a desire to complete the fabric sooner. Probably the funds gave out, and they made a virtue of necessity by giving the structure an original form. By its south side is a small stone pyramid about one hundred feet high. The other large stone pyramid is of the regular form, and of about the same dimensions as the one described.

We rode over the plain a mile to the eastward, to examine one of the two brick pyramids. At a distance, it appears to be a fantastically-shaped mass of dark rich soil rising above the plain, but as you approach, you perceive it to be the misshapen ruins of a pyramid of unburnt brick. Only one hundred and fifty feet of height remain, though we have reason to suppose the original structure was one hundred feet higher. It must have been a sorry affair even in its glory, when compared with its stone neighbours. The time of erection of this pyramid is involved in obscurity. I venture a rude sketch of its ruder appearance, when the reader will see how little claim it *now* has to the name of *pyramid*.

The other brick pyramid has similar characteristics but is considerably less in its present remains. The heat was almost intolerable as we left the desert for the green plain again, and took our way over fields sparkling with beautiful flowers to and through the village of Saccara. Then through a palm-grove, where we met some strolling Bedawin, to the desert again—and up the low sand ridge to the large pyramid of Saccara. This is built in terraces and is surrounded by a sacred enclosure, 1750 by 950 feet.

Whether these terraces were so originally formed,

or whether they were produced by the removal of stones in later ages, is uncertain. I thought I could trace remnants of smaller terraces intervening between the larger; if so, I should suppose the original edifice had this peculiarity. The regularity of the terraces is also against the probability of its having suffered change.

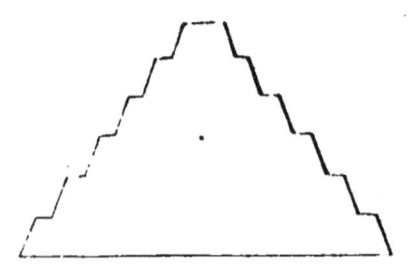

I found the platform on top oblong, being twice as long E. and W. as N. and S. The entrance to the interior is now entirely blocked up with sand. From the summit I counted twenty-five pyramids; four at Dashoor—four at Saccara—five between these groups—three at Abooseer, and nine at Ghizeh. A great object of interest at Saccara is the mummy settlement. Vast catacombs have been here discovered full of mummied oxen, sheep, snakes, ibises, and men. The ibis pits are in a hot sandy basin or wady, a quarter of an hour north of the great Saccara pyramid. We were obliged to crawl in on hands and knees, and in some places drag ourselves snake-like along the dark passages, our hands clutching fragments of mummies, jars, and rags at every grasp. We so came to an apartment piled high with earthen pots. We broke open many, and found the preserved ibises rather the worse for damp, being reduced mostly to a black powder. Crawling out of this highly fragrant region, we passed over a plain of mummied remains of all descriptions to the edge of the hills, where we entered a finely painted and sculptured tomb of the time of Psammaticus II., 600 years B. C. The roof is an *arch*.

The whole region from Dashoor to Ghizeh, a distance of fourteen miles, was the great cemetery of Memphis, and the pyramids are merely tomb-stones over sundry graves in this grave-yard. Memphis lay between this necropolis and the river. To the remains of Memphis we now directed our steps. These remains are but a few mounds about the village of Mitrahenny, and a huge Colossus of Ramses II. prostrate, with its fine face kissing the earth. Add a few fragments of breccia, and you have Memphis in 1849. These remnants are situated among smiling green fields and graceful palm-groves.

We met our boat at Bedreshayn, after a very fatiguing trip of eight hours. The minarets of Cairo are in sight, and we feel towards it as towards a home.

On March 28 we reached Cairo, having consumed forty-two and a half days in our Nile expedition.

The ensuing twelve days which we spent in Cairo were much employed in preparing for our desert-journey. Ibrahim had brought to me old Besharah, the Bedawee Sheikh of the Towarah, whose name is known to Americans as the Sheikh of Dr. Robinson's party. Besharah embraced me with the apparent affection of a long-tried friend, kissing me vehemently on both cheeks. Notwithstanding his eye to the profit of an acquaintance, I have no doubt the wily Sheikh had some good feeling in his breast. After a thorough experience of Besharah's Sheikhship, and a full examination of his character, I must award him some good traits of disposition. He is kind-hearted and docile, and a real friend to the Frank traveller—yet justice requires me to say, that he is an arrant beggar, and an old granny.

Several Bedawin sheikhs had applied to carry us over the desert, but we had preferred Besharah, from his knowledge of the wants of Franks, and his conceded experience. The season was late for a desert trip, and it was with great anxiety I thought of the expedition. I especially feared for the ladies, having an unformed notion of the perils and difficulties of the route for females to undertake. In our designed tour to Sinai, Akabah, and Petra, we would be at least a month among Bedawin, and exposed to the extreme heat of the desert. Many friends in Cairo called our project folly, and even experienced travellers told us we could form no conception of the heat we were to encounter. This was all bitters to my palate. I had left America chiefly to see the desert and the Promised Land, and now should I abandon the design when I was upon the threshold of its enjoyment? The ladies were perfectly willing to go, and I decided accordingly. Ibrahim procured a new cook (for Hassanein had left us) and a third servant to assist. I set all three immediately to work in procuring stores for the journey, and all the tent and travelling apparatus necessary. Besharah was to have his camels all in readiness on the 7th of April, and then we should taste desert-life for the first time. Meantime we saw more and more of Cairo, made valuable acquaintances of fellow-travellers, and became more intimate with Oriental life.

We visited the Nilometer on the Island of Roda. It is a square well, in the centre of which is a stone pillar, graduated to mark the height of the river, which has access to this pit. It was built (it is said) long before the foundation of Cairo, by Mamoon, son of the celebrated Haroun e' Rasheed. The alluvion deposited by the river has covered the bottom of the well to a considerable depth, and the whole affair presents the decaying, melancholy appearance of everything Oriental.

The gardens of Roda are pleasant promenades, kept in order by a *Scotch* gardener, who finds a great enemy in the Nile, which overflows all his parterres every year, and puts him in the condition of Penelope in the morning, with all the labour to be again wrought. However, the rich deposit of the unruly river compensates for its destructive propensities, and flowers and fruits wear a luxuriant aspect in the gardens of Roda. Ibrahim Pacha was the proprietor of these amphibious acres, though they probably now belong to his nephew Abbas, the reigning Pacha. The said Abbas had returned from Constantinople, rich in the invested dignity of the viceroyalty, and we frequently saw him riding out in a beautiful English chariot, accompanied by the high personages of his court. His looks are not at all prepossessing, and report says badly of his character. Everybody speaks of Ibrahim Pacha's death as caused by poison administered at Constantinople, and Abbas Pacha is said to be under like treatment. If so, the reason may be to destroy the whole family of Mohammed Ali, to whom the viceregal crown of Egypt is entailed, and make the throne free again to the chosen deputy of the Sultan. But as the old Mohammed has a goodly host of descendants, the work of their destruction will prove rather tedious and difficult even for a Turkish sultan. But before anything of this kind can occur, England will probably be quietly resting her paws on the Nile valley, and Sultan and Pacha be alike worthy subjects of European sovereignty. Then steamboats will be crowding the astonished Nile from the cataracts to the sea—railways will conduct the traveller to the Oases and Abyssinia—and where the children of Israel crossed the Red Sea dry-shod, *we'll* do the same—on a bridge. The Moslem power is rapidly waning; its destiny is accomplished; it will find its grave in the energetic spirit of the age; or rather, assimilated to the genius of modern improvement, it will give additional impetus to the onward course of an enlightened civilization,—a civilization before which all the boasted attainments of antiquity pale to disappearing.

The tombs of the Circassian Memlooks, though in a condition of decay, are among the principal objects of interest about Cairo. These tombs have the dimensions and appearance of mosques. They form a fine cluster of buildings just out of the city, to the northeast. Like most Egyptian places of burial, both ancient and modern, they are appropriately situated on the sands of the desert, where all is desolate, and lonely, and noiseless. The Circassian Memlooks were the last kings of Egypt previous to the Turkish conquest. The dynasty continued in power from 1382 to 1517. The tombs are of stone, and striped horizontally black and white, or red and white, like many Italian churches. The most noble edifice of this group is the tomb of Kaitbay, a famous sovereign of the dynasty, who was more than a match for the Turks, and who, by his valour, delayed materially their conquest of Egypt. The interiors of these mosque-tombs show the remains of former splendour in fine paved courts, walls ornamented with mother-of-pearl and polished stones, and the richness of Saracenic architecture,—but dust and decay are in close embrace with these beautiful works, which seem to be now mere homes for a few ragged families. In one of the tombs we were shown the impress of the prophet's feet and hand, which our attendants most devoutly kissed. These precious relics had been brought from Mecca by the monarch who was there buried. According to the mark of the prophet's hand, Mohammed must have been a Titan. From these tombs we passed behind the city and the citadel, along the edge of the desert, and through innumerable straggling cemeteries, whose tombstones rose up above the surface of the hot sand like buoys in the water, to the tomb-edifice of Mohammed Ali's family, at the south of the city. It is a three-domed structure, of no great beauty, and with an interior positively ugly and gaudy with gilt and paint. A magnificent camel's hair shawl covered the tomb of Ibrahim Pacha; the tomb itself was not completed. The tombs are arranged in two apartments, and somewhat resemble a collection of dog-houses. Besides Ibrahim's are those of Toosoom and Ismail, Mohammed Ali's other sons,—of the Defterdar, and a host of other minor members of the family.

The Deserts of Suez and Shur.

PREPARATIONS FOR DESERT-TRAVEL—ROUTE FROM CAIRO TO SUEZ—AYUN MOUSA—MARAH—ELIM.

THE 7th of April had been appointed as our day of departure from Cairo for Mount Sinai, but a recurrence of an old fever and ague kept me in bed on that day, and it was not until Monday morning the 9th, that we left the hotel on donkeys to join the camels which were waiting without the city. My delight at entering upon the novel scenes of the desert was sadly tempered by my sense of the difficulties before me. We were much too late in the season—it was now the period of the Khamseen, the hot desert wind with which so many fearful stories are connected. We could expect no water for the first ten days, except the supply we carried from the Nile—and the tribes of the desert were said to be growing unmanageable, owing to the imbecility of Mohammed Ali, whose name formerly held them in check. Moreover, I had the care of two ladies, who had never previously known the fatigues that lay before them, and all our Cairo friends had urged us to abandon the design. Per contra, I had left home *principally* to see the Desert and Palestine. We were all in good health and spirits—I knew that if the present opportunity were passed, my hopes of visiting Sinai and Petra would become indefinitely small, and we had mustered a party of eight, with seven servants. These latter considerations proved the weightier, and we consequently persevered in our intention. We had, moreover, lately received a note by Besharah, from a kind English friend, who had been conducted by Besharah to Akaba. This note advised our journey, and informed us of some excellent arrangements our friend had made with the celebrated Sheikh Hossein of Akaba, regarding Frank travellers.

Our party consisted of our three selves, our friend C——, of Boston, Mr. L—— and Capt. P——, of Scotland, Mr. F——, of England, and Mr. M——, of Wales. On riding out to the caravan, we found C—— full of his experience of desert life, for he had spent the night in his tent. He conducted us about as a veritable Bedawee, and looked upon us as neophytes by his side. He confessed, however, that it was not so agreeable in reality to sleep in a tent as in fancy, for he had commenced an acquaintance with several new entomological attachés, and he had listened all night to the growls of the camels. My heart sank within me, as I thought of the ensuing month and its imagined trials; but I committed my ways to a kind Providence, and took courage. We now had left the Hotel d'Orient and its comforts, Musr el Kahirah and its beauties, and civilization with its luxuries, to endure fatigue, heat, and privations, such as we had never before known. The scene that morning was spirited. The Bedawin were loudly calling to each other, our thirty-six camels were groaning pitifully while submitting to their loads, and our servants were busy at everything. Then there were the striking of tents, the Turkish costume of the gentlemen and the grotesque attire of the ladies, the intermingled donkeys and donkey boys, and a thousand other curious sights for our first taste of the desert. At 8½ A. M., we started in straggling order, with faces towards the grim desert on whose skirts we were already treading. The ladies at first felt ill at ease, but at length grew merry in their elevated position. An endless waste of sand hills and plains of a sombre yellow lay before us and on either hand, excepting on a portion of our left, where we caught glimpses of the green valley of the Nile as it spreads into the fertile Delta.

We proceed at the slow funereal gait of the camel (about two and a half miles per hour), and continued for seven hours without a halt—the caravan keeping no regular line of march, but each one going where he would. At 3½ P. M. we turned off the track into a scarcely perceptible wady (the Wady Suffra) and dismounted. The next half-hour was employed in unloading the camels and in pitching the tents, and then we were left to our meditations in the solemn silence of the desert. All along our day's course were seen the carcases of camels that had perished in their passage. Here and there they would rise before us like incarnations of the spirit of desolation, and cause a shudder as we gazed. The ways over the desert from Cairo to Suez are various. The Great Pilgrim or Haj route makes a northerly curve. The Derb el Hamra is more direct and is the road which the Transit has improved by clearing away the loose sand to the sides of the road. Along this road they have erected station houses, where horses are kept to supply the transit vans. These stations are small white building, partly of wood and partly of stucco, and are placed at intervals of five miles. They serve greatly to relieve the monotony of the route. The shortest route to Suez is the Derb el Ankibiyeh, reckoned by Dr. Robinson, who travelled it, to be about seventy-five miles in length. Farther south, beyond the Mukattem hills, is another route, the Derb el Besatin. We took the Derb el Hamra, its good condition from the Transit Company's care and the stations on its side being sufficient inducements. In most cases, these roads are merely beaten camel tracks (wide, from many camels travelling abreast) through a limitless field of sand. The wadys of this Suez desert are slightly depressed and broad channels, where the winter rains find a course, and where a few short herbs give token of a former moisture. At the time of our crossing, they were perfectly dry. It was interesting to see our good Ibrahim take his last look at Cairo. The minarets were just disappearing behind a sand hill, when he wheeled his dromedary and halted, with his eyes fixed on the distant city. "Farewell, my beloved Musr, may Allah restore me to your beauty," cried the enthusiastic Cairene, and bending gracefully on his saddle, he again turned his dromedary and rode amidst the caravan. The scene was touching, and irresistibly recalled to our minds the distance that intervened between us and *our* Musr on the Hudson. Our first day in the desert was marked with a mirage, and by the time of our arrival at Hebron, we had become familiar with this tantalizing phenomenon. The Derb el Hamra is quite hard to the foot, and our ideas of the quality of the desert sand suffered material alteration. Instead of the loose dust-like sand which we had expected, and which we had seen on the borders of the Nile valley, the road was formed of a well packed gravel, and presented excellent footing for the pedestrian. Mounted on a small sand hill, I complacently viewed our first desert encampment. Nine tents of various sizes and colours presented a formidable aspect. Around these were the camels, some browsing on the scanty herbage of the wady and some tied kneeling, the upper and lower portions of one fore-leg being so bound as to prevent rising. The Bedawin (who never carry tents in these passages through the desert) were gathered in squads about the piled baggage, chatting in an under tone, and the servants were busy preparing the meals for the different tents. Beyond and around was the awful desert, dreary and solemn. By placing the hill between myself and the camp, my silent feelings were wondrously strange. I had never seen anything so impressive. I had never been so completely removed from the world. In such a situation, with all creation a blank about him, a man turns his thoughts on himself and is almost painfully aware of his own existence. In the every-day life of a man, he has no time for such thoughts. Even though he be an idler, yet his eyes are attracted by objects of interest about him, and he unavoidably employs his thoughts upon these objects. But alone in the desert, man *must* look at himself, and is startled at the sight, unless he has been a self-meditative character. But that character is rare. The philosopher shuts his eyes and makes a virtual desert for his vision, but his thoughts rest on his theories and schemes, *not* on himself. The idler never shuts his eyes except when overcome by sleep. In the desert, the philosopher and idler are alike kept from theorizing and sleeping by the strange novelty of the scene, and the facts before them absorb each. It is the staring picture of *Himself*, with the sameness of the desert as a ground for the portrait. I was not sorry to return to the camp and relieve my social nature by again mingling among my kind.

The insects of Egypt were plentiful in the Suez desert, and greatly assisted in making us early risers. Every morning we rose at 4½ or 5, and were off about 6. Our day's journey was fixed at nine hours of consecutive travel. About 3 P. M., we encamped, dined at 4 or 5, and retired at 8. We were regular in these hours until our arrival in Palestine. The motion of the camels we never could fully enjoy. At the close of the day our backs would feel convinced of bad usage, and rest in our tents was unspeakably refreshing. We often relieved our weariness by dismounting and walking. I frequently would walk every third hour, and found in that a very desirable refreshment. The Bedawin walk almost altogether when conducting a caravan, only now and then making use of a loaded camel. The Sheikhs are exceptions, each Sheikh being provided with a riding camel.

We left Cairo on Monday morning at 8½ A. M., and arrived at Suez on Thursday at 12¼. Our travelling time was thirty-one hours, and the distance passed over is reckoned as eighty-two miles. This would make our rate of travel about two and two-third miles per hour. I should be rather inclined to think the distance about seventy-eight miles, and our rate of travel two and a half miles per hour.

Petrified wood I observed from time to time even as far east as Wady Seil Abu Zeid, fifty miles from Cairo. Half-way between Cairo and Suez, we saw, looming conspicuously before us, the lone acacia tree, called Dar el Hámra (the red House) or Om e' Sharameet (the mother of rags). It stands on a broad elevated plain called El Mukrih, and is hung with rags placed by the pilgrims. This is their first station on the way to Mecca. The sight of it set our whole caravan in convulsions. We had seen sand till we were tired, and a real green tree was too great a bait for our dignity to withstand. Pell mell, we galloped our dromedaries over the plain, shouting like madmen, and leaped off under the spreading branches of this out-of-place acacia. Blue and white rags were much more abundant than leaves, and formed an admirable substitute. Why these curious pendants are affixed to the branches is to me a mystery, unless it be as tokens of thanks for the pilgrims' safe return. If so, doubtless the pilgrims, like Diogenes, boast of their rags.

A few miles beyond this lovely tree is a little tomb erected to an Ethiopian pilgrim. It has a pyramidal dome. Its interior is about six feet square and ten feet high, and on its whitewashed walls are Arabic inscriptions rudely painted. Across the dome hung a cord, from which depended balls, apparently of mud.

This solitary building was, no doubt, erected by warm hearts, and its humble offerings placed there by a priceless affection. The tomb is called Kobbet e' Takrouree, and marks a stranger's grave. Still farther on, we passed a large mound, thrown up from an unsuccessful well, dug some eighty years since. A cockney would say that in attempting to make a *well* they made a *'ill*.

About ten miles farther on, we came among small stone-heaps called Rejum esh Shawaghiriyeh, the place of sepulture of a number who were there murdered while endeavouring to conduct a caravan from Suez to Cairo. Such little matters are full of interest in the loneliness of the desert, where is so little incident to attract attention. Passing the dark brown Jebel Aweibid upon our left, and having the loftier Jebel Attakeh (the famous mount of deliverance) upon our right, we entered the pass of Muntula. Low sand-hills on either side form the pass, which opens again into a basin a mile or two broad, and then re-closes. This pass is supposed by some to be the Scripture Migdol, and by such supposers is styled Muktula, but the Arabs did not know any other name for the spot but Muntula.

We saw several acacias between the Om E'Sharameet and Muntula, but they were mostly very small. The mirage deceived us regarding the Red Sea before entering the pass, exactly as it did with Dr. Robinson.

Sir Chas. Napier, on his way to India, overtook our caravan. He was travelling in Abbas Pacha's carriage, his suite following in vans. His luggage preceded him, borne on a long line of camels. We hauled our fleet on one side, and as the brave general passed, displayed the four flags of the party and gave him a salute of three hearty cheers. He awaited us at the next station, and held a few minutes' conversation. This was decidedly an incident, and relieved the tedium of the day. We encamped our third night in the pass of Muntula, and from the range of low hills at the South, I obtained my first view of the Red Sea, about fifteen miles off.

To the left was discernible the castle of Ajrud, the first of a series of fortified stations on the Pilgrims' route. The next morning, on issuing from the pass, we had a full view of the castle, lying north of our road, the Haj route running in that direction in order to pass around the head of the sea. The castle is a plain square wall, with round towers at the corners and at the centre of each side, excepting the south, where is the entrance between two square towers. Not far from it westward is a mosque, somewhat resembling a small fort in structure. Between the castle and mosque is a Santon's white tomb. We were now upon the plain of Suez, and far before us was the black-looking town. About three miles from the town, we came to the Well of Suez. This is an irregular castle-like enclosure of stone wall, with a gate. On the west side are troughs for camels, a spout, and a reservoir. The water was very brackish. At noon we entered Suez, having passed, without the walls, the mound of Kolzum or Clysma, the ancient port. An ugly dilapidated wall partially surrounds the wretched town, within which about twelve hundred human beings vegetate.

Nothing can be more desolate than the situation of Suez. A waste of yellow sands and an expanse of greenish water are all its environs. Not a green leaf is to be seen, nor any sign of Nature's power to be agreeable. Within the walls are miserable huts, filthy lanes, and a squalid population. The water of the sea (by reason of its sandy bottom) was of a light transparent green, unlike any I had ever before seen. Quantities of vessels were in the harbour and on the sands, all resembling old decayed frigate hulks with new peaked bows, completely devoid of masts or rigging. To our surprise, we found a fine large hotel, kept by an enterprising Scotchman, and by its side was the residence of Captain Linguist, which would have done credit to Cairo. This was finding pearls on a dunghill, and we gave ourselves up to the full enjoyment of the luxury.

I strolled out to the beach of the memorable sea, rendered famous to the end of time by one of the most startling exhibitions of Divine power. It was in this very neighbourhood that the children of Israel had crossed the restrained waters, and the Egyptian army had found its destruction in its presumptuous pursuit. The land of Goshen was, doubtless, along the Pelusiac arm of the Nile, and the departure of the Israelites was taken from Belbays or its vicinity.

The Israelites, without doubt, first directed their way towards Sinai, intending to pass north of the sea. They had reached Etham in this determination, Etham being probably a little north of the end of the gulf. Then (Exodus xiv. 1, 2) God commands them to *turn from* their intended course, and put the sea between them and their desired goal, that thereby the Egyptian king might be tempted on to his destruction. If it was not so, why was a divine command necessary at all? Moses knew well the way to Sinai, for he had lived there forty years, and he had been ordered by God to bring the people thither. He was on his route, and needed no new command, unless it was to *turn from* his direct course. In this way, the host of Israel was brought near the modern Suez, with the dark mountain of Attakeh precluding all farther progress southward, the sea before them, and the Egyptian army penning them in upon the west and north. Then came the murmur and the miracle.

We had now reached the track of the Israelites, and were to follow their wanderings to the borders of Canaan. The journey received a new aspect, and became of deeper interest. Our guide-book was 3000 years old, but was all we needed, for in those changeless wilds, a thousand years are as a day.

I turned from the sea and its strange memories. A few boats were receiving repairs along the beach, five lazy-looking cannon were gaping toward the water, (cannon that would have expired at the first exertion), some blacksmiths, not satisfied with the fierce heat of the day, were manufacturing a domestic supply in their rude booths, and a few Arabs were bathing and washing their garments in the green water.

Returning to the hotel, we enjoyed a dinner *in a house*, for which we paid the Suez price of two dollars apiece. To our great surprise, our French friends of the Nile walked in. They had left Cairo on Wednesday morning at 9 o'clock, and reached Suez at 3½ P. M. Thursday. They had performed the journey on donkeys, taking scarcely any rest, and giving their poor beasts no water. Yet they entered Suez on a gallop. This journey of eighty-two miles on donkeys, in 30½ hours, or nearly 2⅔ miles per hour inclusive of stoppages, and that for the most part beneath a burning sun, was a feat of no small difficulty. One of the French gentlemen was on his way to Abyssinia, and the others were about to return to Paris.

Through Captain Linguist's kindness, we were allowed the use of his boat to cross the sea to Ayun Mousa. Captain P., one of our party, was compelled, by sickness, to abandon us; and, thus weakened in numbers, we left Suez, our camels having gone around the head of the gulf.

The sea opposite Suez is only a mile or two in width, but Ayun Mousa is some distance down the Arabian coast, and is twelve miles distant from Suez. Our boat was well-cushioned and a pleasant sailer, and the variety in our method of progress was positively charming. The channel was tortuous, and we grounded repeatedly, so that we did not arrive opposite Ayun Mousa until 10 P. M., four hours after leaving Suez. Now came the brunt. The shallows did not permit a nearer approximation to the shore than a quarter of a mile's distance. It was a dark night, and we were wearied with the day's excitement. How were we to reach the beach? Our crew leaped into the water and offered us seats upon their shoulders. I ventured first to try the expedient. At the beginning my carrier performed well, but gradually his limbs trembled, and his knees knocked, his back bent more and more, and his plunges became fearful, till I found myself settled on my own pedestals, still far from the shore. The other members of the party, not sufficiently patient to await the result of my trial, had meantime mounted their several Arabs, and, with one or two exceptions, obtained a similar experience. There we were, not able to see one another, floundering in the water and taking every direction to reach the shore. Some were moving directly sea-ward, till our halloos restored them to a right course. Persevering and shouting encouragement to one another, we at length reached the land, where our considerate carriers were instantly clamorous for "backsheesh." It was too good a joke, and we rewarded them for our bath. We had to wait a half-hour in our dripping condition until the luggage could be brought ashore, and another half-hour was consumed in reaching Ayun Mousa, which lies back from the beach. The moon had now risen, and shone upon a dark object before us. As we advanced, we recognised a garden—an Eden in the midst of dreary sands. We passed through this fairy land as in a dream; flowers and fruit-trees were growing luxuriantly about our path, the air was filled with delicious perfumes, and we saw the gleam of water in the moonlight. Beyond were our tents, where Besharah was anxiously expecting us. It was half-past one in the morning before I lay down to rest. The next day I rose early, notwithstanding our late hour of retiring, and visited the gardens. The little Oasis of Ayun Mousa or Fountains of Moses consists of four fine gardens, well stocked with trees and vegetables, and supported in fertility by several wells. In each garden is a small house of tolerable comfort, and beyond the enclosures are two palm-trees, one being a curious assemblage of five stems from one root. The gardens belong to some gentlemen at Suez, who are connected with the Transit (Capt. Linguist among the number), and are worked by Arab servants. It was here, probably, that the Israelitish host halted after the overthrow of their enemies, and here sang Moses and Miriam, "I will sing unto the Lord, for he hath triumphed gloriously; the horse and his rider hath he cast into the sea."

The Turfa or Tamarisk was the principal kind of tree in these gardens. I saw one peach-tree laden with young peaches and some blossoms. Dr. Robinson describes Ayun Mousa as showing scarcely any vegetation; gardens are, therefore, of very late date, though there is every reason to suppose that gardens have previously occupied the site, the wells presenting a strong inducement to cultivation.

From the gardens we walked down to the sea, about a mile and a half distant. We had to enter a very great distance before we could find the water more than knee deep. The water abounded with the soft jelly-like "sting-galls" of enormous size, and blue colour,—small crabs ran in all directions,—and coral and shells of beautiful shape and colour were plenty upon the beach. Returning to the camp, we dined, and at 2 P. M. started, intending to stop for the night at Wady Sudr, about eighteen miles farther. By a misunderstanding on the part of the Arabs, we got no farther than Wady el Hattit (Dr. Robinson's el-Ahtha) where we formed our second Asiatic encampment. Our route now lay along the plain extending from the mountains of Et-Tih to the shore. This plain is intersected by broad and shallow water-courses that descend to the sea. These wadys are marked by a growth of herbs of various sorts, on which the camels feed eagerly. This part of the desert was excessively tedious, from the constant sameness of scenery. The mountains of Et-Tih rose some ten miles to our left, —the great sand waste extended thence to the sea, and apparently endless in front and rear,—and the grim mountains of Attakeh and Deraj, beyond the sea, bounded the western view. The heat was almost intolerable, and the water, both in casks and skins, was fairly putrid in taste and odour. We suffered greatly, but knowing that the faster we advanced the sooner our troubles would be over, we pushed on resolutely, and performed our regular day's journey of nine hours, with very few exceptions. On our third day from Suez, we reached Ain Howara, a fountain situated on a small hill to the left of the track, and which is thought (with much reasonableness) to be the Marah of Scripture. The fountain is merely a basin of a few feet in diameter, filled with brackish water, of which the camels drank freely, but the taste was to us much worse than that of our own high-flavoured store. The wady near this fountain bears the name of *Amarah.* This fact, and the situation of the spot, just three days' easy journey (thirty-eight miles) from Ayun Mousa, are strong arguments in favour of the identity of this fountain with the Scripture Marah. Dr. Robinson speaks frequently of the Ghurkud plant, and Burckhardt suggests that the juice of its berry may have sweetened the waters of Marah for the Israelites. Dr. R. brings forward a good objection to this suggestion, in the fact that the berries could not have been sufficiently mature at the early period of the year in which the Israelites passed,—and then he states that the Bedawin could not give him any information of methods to sweeten bad water. I made like inquiries of Besharah and his men, and, though they told me they had never heard of a plant called "Ghurkud," they all agreed that there was a shrub called "El Kedad," the berry of which they frequently put in brackish water, in order to sweeten it. They said it was abundant at Sinai and Wady Mousa, as well as in Wady Amarah and that neighbourhood.

But the words of Moses seem to rebut the idea of his having used *berries* in sweetening the waters of Marah. He says, "The Lord showed him *a tree*, which, when he had cast into the waters, the waters were made sweet." The Hebrew word translated "tree" is עץ, and is used to denote *the wood* which Abraham carried, whereon to sacrifice Isaac. From the immediate succession of the Lord's showing and Moses' casting, I should render the word here "A stick of wood." A branch of a tree happening to lie by the fountain, Moses is ordered to take that (as a near object) and cast it into the water. His faith was exercised in so doing, and the people saw, by the miracle, that God was with them. This is certainly a more *natural* interpretation than to attempt to explain away the miracle.

A half-hour beyond Ain Howarah we passed through a small basin-like tract called Nukeia el Fûl, and which the Arabs pronounce Gayelful. After the rains, beans and barley are grown here, but now there was not the slightest trace of vegetation. An hour more brought us to Wady Ghurundel, a deep dry water-course, filled with green bushes and shrubs. We gladly encamped near some palm-bushes. I had expected to find water here, and was disappointed to hear it was still a half-hour distant down the wady. Hot as it was (the thermometer indicating a heat of 101 deg. Fahr. in the coolest spot we could find), I ran eagerly down the wady, and in a half hour reached the desired water. Several shallow streamlets, about two feet in width, rise from the sandy bed and run slowly westward, seeming to disappear again in the sands. I drank recklessly, and thought the water nectar, yet the next day, when my thirst was not so urgent, I could scarce bear a drop of the nauseous stuff in my mouth. The ground around the springs was encrusted with salt. The wady was very verdant, a coarse sort of grass, of lily appearance, growing very plentifully. I got back to the camp in time to see our tents all take flight like a frightened flock of geese, and leave their inmates to write their journals in the open air,—a duty, however, on which they were certainly not *in-tent*. We all made chase after our runaway houses, and having caught them, bound them over to avoid future desertion. Tent-life has its advantages and disadvantages. There is a pleasing independence connected with it, utterly inconceivable to a worthy citizen. A man in the desert, however much he may be tied to his house, is not bound to one spot; as with the snail, his obsequious abode always waits on him like a drilled footman; then there is no running up and down stairs, and you need not be particular in cleaning your boots before you enter the house; more than all, you have no taxes to pay; yet, on the other hand, you find your house neither wind-proof nor eye-proof, and old Æolus or a prying Bedawee may call forth your anathemas, and while you are lying on your bed gazing thoughtfully at your canvass roof, it is very provoking to have this roof metamorphosed into a star-lit sky by the sudden flight of your domicile.

The Bedawee costume exhibits as easy a style of dress as a man could desire. If that unhappy Frenchman had adopted it, he would not have committed suicide on account of " this confounded buttoning and unbuttoning." A tunic of coarse dirty-white material is bound around the waist by a broad red leather belt, over which is thrown a sleeved cloak or toga of the same (or else of thick woollen striped brown and white). Sometimes they wear sandals of camel's hide. The Towarah (or Bedawin of the Sinai peninsula) wear the white turban, but the other tribes use the kefiyeh, or head-kerchief, tied about the forehead with a band of camel's hair or wool. They seem never to change their garments, and give every indication of retaining them faithfully until they fall to rags. The Bedawin are, consequently, not the cleanest people in the world. Indeed, the whole character of these Ishmaelites had been sadly misconceived by us. We had looked for the Bedawee of the French novelists, a white-bearded patriarch, full of honour and dignity, of noble stature and bearing, and the personification of justice and generosity. But such an Arab exists only in the imagination. It will not do in modern days, when almost every part of the globe is becoming as well known as a London street, to talk romantically about the perfection of any human character. Poor human nature is pretty much the same everywhere, and Utopia must be sought beyond our earth's atmosphere. We found the noble Bedawee a dirty being, of short stature and unprepossessing appearance, with just as much honour in his composition as in a highwayman. His ideas of justice were strangely askew—his own benefit seeming to be its unfailing standard. In short, the Bedawee's moral character is exactly that of every semi-barbarous people, where the weeds of man's natural disposition grow up with little restraint, and where, we confess, some pretty wild flowers are also seen. By intercourse with travellers, the border Bedawin have received a few of the virtues and many of the vices of civilization, and the love of money has induced them to resign some of their independency, and yield some subjection to the Pacha of Egypt. This is an admirable arrangement for travellers, but detracts from the small stock of Bedawee glory.

It has become fashionable to say that Abraham was a Bedawee, but such is not the case. Job was, no doubt, and so was Jethro; but Abraham, living in the fertile vales of Palestine, bore no more resemblance to a Bedawee than the modern Syrian of Nablous does to the rangers of the Arabian desert.

The Deserts of Sin and Sinai.

ELIM—ENCAMPMENT BY THE SEA—BUDERAH—WRITTEN VALLEY—
FEIRAN—NUKB HAWY—ARRIVAL AT SINAI.

We left Wady Ghurundel about half-past 5 in the morning (April 16), and commenced a sort of hilly travel southward, winding through a labyrinth of wadys and sand-hills. This was a luxury after three days of monotonous plain. We soon caught sight of Serbal, the highest peak of the peninsula mountains, nearly fifty miles south-east in a direct line.

Wady Ghurundel is generally supposed to be the Elim of Scripture; and the fact of its exhibiting more natural verdure than any point between Egypt and Mount Sinai (Wady Feiran excepted), is the main support of the hypothesis. But if Ain Hawara is Marah, the distance to Ghurundel, only five miles, is too *small* for a day's journey of the Israelitish host. Besides, the distance from Wady Ghurundel to "the encampment by the sea" (which next ensues, and which can be very clearly ascertained), is seventeen miles,—too *large* for one stage of the Israelitish progress. We should, therefore, place Elim at Wady Useit, which is nearly half-way between Ain Hawara and the "sea encampment." Wady Useit, it is true, exhibits scarcely any verdure, except immediately around the water, while Ghurundel is full of herbage and bush-growth for a mile's extent; but we are allowed to suppose sufficient change in this respect from natural causes during a period of three thousand years.

About an hour from Wady Ghurundel we passed two piles of loose stones, termed Husan Aboo Zenneh, or "The horse of Aboo Zenneh," so called as marking the grave of that animal unknown to fame. My camel leader gave one of the heaps a kick as he passed, uttering some Arabic formula, which is customary at this point. Besharah set off to find some rain-water on Jebel Hummâm, a mountain between us and the sea, but returned, after a long tramp, unsuccessful. We kept on among limestone hills and cliffs. In Wady Aboo Suweileh we passed a lonely acacia, and at 7 A. M. we entered a basin a half mile square, called el Medjas, surrounded by fort-like cliffs of gravel. Then came Wady Useit with its wee oasis, possessing brackish water in small sand hollows, and a dozen palm trees, some of sizeable respectability. Here we would place the Scriptural *Elim*, as before remarked. It was a hilly country we were now traversing, and the formations were very peculiar. One cliff resembled exactly a huge table, another was a thatched cottage, and a number bore striking similarity to a series of fortifications. The long, dark brown Jebel Hummâm was a wall upon our right, beyond which we were to turn down to the sea. Grasshoppers of extraordinary size and of the colour of the sand were frequent, and the curious angular-shaped lizards of the desert were constantly escaping from the path of the camels. Another rude heap of stones, ornamented with a dozen miniature flags, composed of rough sticks and dirty rags, bore the title of "Oreis Themmân, or "Bride of Themmân," such a character being there interred. What a dull home for a bride! Death had been her dowry and the sands her companions. At 11 A.M. we reached Wady Taiyibeh, and leaving Dr. Robinson's route, turned down to the sea. Here was a new species of scenery—the valley becoming narrow and the cliffs high on either side. The valley winds greatly on its course to the sea, about half-way to which is a pretty copse of turfa trees, where we made a temporary halt. About a half mile further flowed a tiny stream from under a ledge that rose in the centre of the wady, and continued toward the sea. In two hours from the entrance of the wady, we reached the sea, and found the sea-breeze peculiarly grateful. A small cave was hollowed in the cliff upon our left, and there to our surprise was an Italian botanist, arranging specimens of desert herbs he had collected. A few Bedawin and their camels were his only companions. We greeted him with a "Who in the world are you?" and after a few minutes' conversation, left him to his solitude and employment.

A wide plain extended from the cliffs to the sea; this plain gradually narrowed after passing a sandy projection into the sea, called Ras Aboo Zeneema. Aboo Zeneema is the occupant of a sorry-looking tomb that stands upon the little cape. After passing two points, where the cliffs hardly gave us room to advance between them and the sea, we came to a third projection, that quite put out of our heads the idea of passing dryshod. The Bedawin said there was a road over them, which some took and found a difficult pass, but the most of us made the outside passage, the camels going knee-deep in the water. This promontory was about a mile in extent, after which we came upon a broad plain, where the mountains retired for some distance. Here we encamped, without doubt in the neighbourhood of the encampment of the Israelites "on the Red Sea." We cannot suppose they went down Wady Ghurundel to the sea, for if so, they would have been compelled to retrace their steps, as Jebel Hummâm prevents a progress southward by the beach. Mr. Bartlett found that the case, and had to return inland by Wady Useit, before he could gain the position we now had upon the seashore. As they could not have gone down Wady Ghurundel, so Wady Taiyibeh is the first way they could have taken to the sea, and this is moreover the most direct route to Sinai, for which the Israelites were tending—for intervening hills and mountains prevent a *straight* course to Sinai. It was then the same course that we took, that was taken by the Israelites, and from the water in Wady Taiyibeh, it is probable that its mouth was the exact site of their encampment, which may have extended along the stream up to its source. This would just be a good day's journey for the host. We took a little more than seven hours to perform it, which, to the large numbers of the Israelites, encumbered with baggage and accompanied by women and children, would be at least a ten hours' journey.

When approaching the sea, the Arabs put gunpowder into the camels' nostrils, as a preventive against sickness by inhaling sea air—whether the camels acquire bravery by so often smelling gunpowder, our worthy escort did not say. When we reached the sea, Hassan, my swarthy leader, ran down, and having filled his mouth with the salt water, returned and squirted this also in the unfortunate proboscis of my beast. It was this fear of injury to their camels' health that induced the Bedawin to wish an encampment away from the sea,—but we couldn't spare the sea breeze and were almost rabid for a bath, and therefore gave our firm opinion that sea air was perfectly innoxious to beast as well as man. Hence, we encamped just above the ripple of the water, and listened to its song more devotedly than a lover ever listened to the voice of his mistress. That evening we had a delicious experience of the cooling qualities of the Red Sea. We had been roasting in a heat of about 115° (Fahr.) all day, and found the water richly invigorating. The sea was of a deep blue, and the opposite mountains of the Egyptian coast, about twenty miles distant, also wore a soft blue colour. We saw several sharks moving in the water, and the large blue *sting-galls* abounded, as near Ayun Mousa. In the night, one of our party discovered a hyæna before a tent, and the next morning a number of fowls were missing. The tracks of the hungry thief were all that he left for our satisfaction.

Leaving the sea, we passed over the sea-plain diagonally, crossing the bed of Wady Nukhl on our way, and entered Wady Nusb. The limestone region was now ceasing, and porphyritic formation commenced. Winding up the wady, we made a grand approach to the dark mountains of porphyry. The scenery was now sublime. High cliffs of the dark granite rose before us, and on every side were the desolate cliffs and defiles of Arabia Petræa. We here met some Arabs we had sent the night before for water. They brought the pure rain-water from the mountains, and we drank deeply. It was our first palatable draught for a week. The wady was studded with acacias and colocynth vines. That morning we came to our first mountain pass, called the Pass of Buderah. It is a height of about five hundred feet in perpendicularity, and scaled by a zig-zag. We dismounted, allowing the camels to go up unburdened. This height fairly blocks the road like a cross wall, and is one of the thousand odd formations abounding in the Sinai peninsula.

From the summit was a strange view of the particoloured mountains and winding defiles, and a small glimpse of the blue sea was obtained. The camels toiled up the rocky path, and we resumed our journey through wild rock scenery. At length, we reached the junction of Wady Mokatteb and Wady Maghara; our route lay through the former, but we made a short excursion up the latter, to see its curious sculptures. We very soon saw some inscriptions and Egyptian hieroglyphics on the rocks to our left. Passing these and going a short distance beyond the mouth of Wady Ghennee (which comes in from the right and is full of acacias), we reached the principal sculptures. They are situated high up the cliffs' side, near the seeming mouths of quarries, and are reached by some rough climbing. The sculptures consist of Egyptian bas-reliefs and calendars, some bearing the cartouches of very early kings, Suphis or Cheops among the number. They were, undoubtedly, carved when these quarries were worked by the Pharaohs, and bear additional testimony to the power and taste of those early monarchs. I here give an *exact* copy of one of the inscriptions in this wady—

Returning to Wady Mokatteb, we passed on to a large opening of about one and a half miles square, surrounded by red mountains, conspicuous among

THE STRANGE WRITING.

which was the Jebel Nebbee on its south-east corner. We passed along the west side of this plain, and found multitudes of inscriptions along the bases of the cliffs. Having encamped just beyond the plain, I copied several of the inscriptions. They were some in Greek and some in the strange character of Wady Maghara. Rude figures of camels were interspersed, and many crosses, thus +.

I here give some of the inscriptions, and can affirm them in every particular *exact*.

IWB

APCENIOY

KANAΘ . . . . .
OYCAφ . . . . .

†CEPΠ . . . .

ΠP

I offer no hypotheses regarding these strange and innumerable inscriptions, but content myself with remarking, that the Greek letters seem to destroy any supposition of *great* antiquity, unless the Greek inscriptions were placed there in imitation of previous carvings. But the whole matter is in process of investigation, and will, doubtless, be in a few years as little of a wonder as a Roman coin or a Grecian statue.

From Wady Mokatteb we entered Wady Feiran. About ten miles from the entrance, we came upon the oasis of El Husmee, its well, palm trees, and little garden enclosures rendering us as noisy as children with delight. A little farther, the hill of Feiran, or Pharan, came in sight, where stood the desert city of the Christians, now a collection of crumbled and crumbling ruins. Winding around this hill, that stands immediately in the centre of the wady, we hailed with joy a vast palm forest before us, and the gentle murmurs of a rippling brook. Our whole souls were roused in delight; we shrieked in enthusiasm, and felt intoxicated with the unexpected sight. We had known that Feiran was an oasis, but had thought of it as of Ghurundel and Useit—a few bushes, two or three palms, and a muddy pool. But here was the softest green sod, a large forest of waving palms, gardens of richest luxuriance, streams and fountains of refreshing coolness, and the warbles of a thousand birds. We lay upon the grass as if we had never before seen a blade, and we ate the fruit of the gardens with unexampled avidity. It was, indeed, the realization of romance. The novelist would need but a full and truthful description of this oasis, to give the highest colouring to his page, and a truthful narrator would be liable to suspicions regarding either his veracity or sanity.

Huts are seen in the various enclosures where the tillers of the soil reside. We saw but few,—among them some filthy women. This wady is the principal abode of our guides—the "Welad Said" section of the Sowalha tribe—and is highly praised, as is reasonable, by these wanderers. Besharah always spoke of Wady Feiran with a glistening eye and spirited accent. He said there was nothing like it, and I was inclined to agree with him when I encamped amid its verdure. I here give a brief description of the valley and its ruins, with a rough sketch of its form.

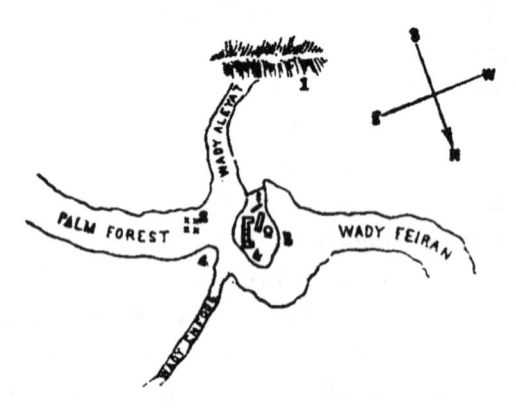

1. Mt. Serbal.
2. Encamping Ground.
3. Ruins of Public Buildings.
4. Ruins of the Town.

The ruins, as seen in the sketch, are principally situated on a mound that juts out into the basin formed by the junction of several wadys. The southeast side of this mound is precipitous, but the other side can be ascended. One portion has, at the base, the remnant of a thick stone wall, probably erected to prevent the wash of the hill by the rains, as also to answer purposes of defence, there being none on the precipitous side, where these reasons did not operate. This wall is built of large stones, and fastened by mortar. The buildings upon the mound are almost utterly ruined: the largest is upon the south-east portion of the hill overlooking the precipice. It appears to have been the cathedral and bishop's palace. The material of the structure is crude brick, mingled with stone. Several red sandstone pillars lie prostrate among the remains, and, probably, others are buried beneath the rubbish. These pillars are exceedingly plain, lacking the slightest ornament, are of no established order, and are eighteen inches in diameter. Near by, a circular wall seems to mark the remains of a baptistery. Several other buildings of lesser size occupy the mound, and were probably all dedicated to religious uses. Surrounded by a wall, they constituted a fortified sanctuary, to which the inhabitants of the Christian settlement might fly to escape the fury of the surrounding tribes. Opposite this mound, and situated on the point between Wady Feiran and Wady Enfoos, are the remains of the town itself. On my inquiry of the Arabs regarding the builders of this town, they frankly owned that the Hawagees, or Frank Christians of a former period, were the original framers and inhabitants of these structures. The houses are plain stone buildings, with low doors; some with one room, and others with more. The Arabs have converted some of them into store-houses, covering the tops of the rooms with a roof of palm-trunks, and fastening the wooden doors with rude wooden locks. Though it would not demand great ingenuity to enter these safes, yet, in some points, Arab honour is so staunch (forced to be so by a knowledge of their own interest) that the corn or other property here stored is as secure as if within the vaults of the Bank of England. These rude houses are apparently built without mortar, and are, consequently, much dilapidated.

The basin and wadys are here bounded by high cliffs, in whose sides are caves innumerable, the former abodes of anchorites, who deemed their future enjoyments of heaven capable of an expansion proportionable with the compression of their present earthly joys. Their knowledge of heaven was probably as profound as their acquaintance with earth. Where the hills are less perpendicular, their sides and summits are covered with small stone structures, whose purposes baffle my imagination. They are about eleven feet long, and six feet wide, and built of large stones, without mortar, but well filled up with sand and gravel. The interior is just large enough for one person to lie comfortably, being about seven feet by two, the walls and roof being two feet in thickness. What causes the surprise, is the fact that these buildings are entirely closed on all sides; if they were tombs, how came the bodies out? If the bodies had been abstracted, no one would have built up the tombs again in perfect symmetry and so hermetically sealed. To test the matter, I chose one of these buildings that was in all respects in a perfect state—the sides, ends, and roof were entire and as nicely fitted as if built by a modern professed mason; not a crevice could be seen anywhere, and not the slightest sign of its disturbance since its erection. I found it no easy task to unroof it by casting the heavy stones over the sides. After considerable labour, I removed the roof, and found (as in all the rest) nothing. Not a bone, or any trinket, or anything that could tell of the former presence of a body within There was no writing upon the interior or exterior. What these curious and multitudinous structures were, I am utterly at a loss to imagine; but that they were tombs, I unhesitatingly deny. The Arabs were as ignorant as myself. All they knew was, that these structures were built by the Hawagees. I saw no others in the desert like them, but in this district of Wady Feiran they are seen on every side, and all of exactly the same construction. Sometimes two or three would be ranged in a row under one continuous roof. There can be no doubt that they appertained to the Christian city of Pharan. The only mystery is their purpose.

Besides these strange erections, there are small ruined chapels seen on various elevated points; these are built in the same rude style as the houses below.

Feiran, or Pharan, is said by some to possess the same name that it held 3000 years ago; and an English nobleman applies the words of Habbakuk (" God came from Teman and the Holy One from Mount Paran ") to this spot. But I greatly dubitate in these conclusions. The first mention of Paran in the Scriptures is in relation to Ishmael, who (it is said) dwelt in " the wilderness of Paran." There is nothing in the context to fix the spot. It may have been near Mount Sinai, or it may have been near the Dead Sea, as far as this passage is concerned. The next mention of Paran is in Numbers x. 12, and xii. 16. By comparing these two passages and the intervening account, we find that the wilderness of Paran was reached by the Israelites after leaving the wilderness of Sinai, and that several encampments intervened between the Holy Mountain and this wilderness of Paran. We also see that from this wilderness of Paran the spies were sent out, and (Numbers xiii. 26) to it they returned, even *to Kadesh*. Now, from the attempt of the children of Israel to go up into Canaan from Kadesh, when they were defeated at Hormah, and the mention of Mount Hor as one of their nearest encampments to Kadesh (Numbers xx. 22), we learn that this Kadesh must have been near the southern extremity of the Dead Sea, in the vicinity of both Mount Hor and Palestine. Therefore the wilderness of Paran must have been in that vicinity. Again, in Deuteronomy i. 2, we see that Kadesh is eleven days from Sinai, while Wady Feiran is but two at furthest.

We can see no connection, therefore, between the Wady Feiran of the Sinai region and the Paran of Scripture.

The theory of Dr. Lepsius, regarding the identity of Rephidim and Feiran, present, to my thinking, stronger claims for belief. We are told that Israel left the Red Sea and encamped in the wilderness of Sin. Dr. Robinson places the wilderness of Sin along the Red Sea, consisting of a long tract of beach. This seems highly improbable from the words of Moses, that Israel *removed from* the Red Sea, and encamped in the wilderness of Sin. Supposing the Israelites took the most direct route to Sinai, for which they were aiming, I would place the wilderness of Sin in the neighbourhood of the Pass of Buderah, where our Arabs obtained water for us, and where there was probably a plenty (standing rain-water) in the earlier season in which the Israelites passed. *Dophkah*, the next mentioned station, would be somewhere in the Written Valley (Wady Mokatteb), and Alush would be sought in the same wady, probably at the large fine plain or basin above-mentioned, which would form one of the best encamping spots for a vast host in the whole Sinai region. The name *Alush* (crowds) seems to point out some extensive place of concourse. Rephidim would thus fall about seven miles north of the oasis of Feiran, while Feiran itself would be the settlement and headquarters of the Amalekites, the ancient Bedawin. After the defeat of the Amalekites, Israel would naturally take possession of their green oasis, and thus extend the name of Rephidim (Refreshings) to this place. This hypothesis harmonizes the fact of running water being present at Feiran, with the condition that Rephidim had no water, except what was brought by miracle from Horeb. Cosmas, 1300 years ago, pronounced Feiran to be Rephidim.

Pharan is known to have been a city as early as the fourth century, and was probably composed of Christians who had fled from persecutions in Egypt or Syria. It was a bishopric, and continued so to be for 700 years, when it seems to have been absorbed by its neighbour settlement at the convent of Mount Sinai. For the last six centuries, at least, it is not likely that any Christian has dwelt in this spot, though the traditions of the Arabs still refer the ruins to their real builders.

Mount Serbal is a conspicuous object from Pharan. It rises in jagged sugar-loaf peaks, but a few miles from the ruined city, at the extremity of the branch Wady Aleyat. The peculiar characters seen in Wady Mokatteb exist in various places between Pharan and the foot of Serbal, and are also carved on the very summit of the mountain, yet in the *immediate* vicinity of the ruins I could find none. Serbal is supposed by Dr. Lepsius to be the real Sinai,—but the worthy Doctor seems to have been led to this theory by the mere desire of opposing others. The fact of the nonexistence of any plain large enough for the Israelitish encampment, whence they could all see the mountain, is sufficient objection to the theory, and the vast array of testimony for the present Sinai in *tradition, the great plain Er-Rahah*, and *the steep front of the mountain* requiring bounds about it lest the people should touch it as a wall, completely throw the Prussian savant from his equilibrium. He deserves to be wrong for the wanton demolition he has made among the beautiful tombs of Thebes. We accuse Mohammed Ali of Vandalism in injuring Egyptian monuments, and here is a German *literatus* who has deliberately set hammer and axe at work among the finest remains of Egyptian art, and made a wreck of their greatest beauties.

But we'll drop Dr. Lepsius, and turn to bid adieu to this Paradise of the Bedawee, where brooks and gardens, fruits and flowers, the pasturing goat and the rural employments of the Arab have so ministered to our joy, and which render our departure so reluctant. We wound amid the palms, saluted the men who were tilling the fertile soil, and gazed quietly upon the tropical foliage that surrounded us. At length the palms grew fewer, the foliage less luxuriant, and the sward was thin and ragged. Still further, and vegetation ceased; we were again in the desert. We were still, however, in the Wady Feiran. In thirty-five minutes from our encampment, we passed two hills of yellow mud, about fifty feet high, and in a quarter of an hour more entered among a series of like hills, which skirted the

wady (which was here greatly widened) for a long distance, even to the mouth of Wady Sheikh, up which we turned. There must have been three or four miles of this curious and unusual formation, which seems to point out the existence of a former lake. I drew, (as I rode) a plan of this section of the wady.

Though the Bedawin cultivate the oasis of Feiran, yet they do not live there; a sort of slaves called the Jebeliyeh, (supposed to be the descendants of the servants Justinian sent to the Sinai convent), occupying the little huts of the wady. The Bedawin, however, dwell in the vicinity, and as we passed along to Wady Sheikh, our conductors were constantly meeting their friends and relatives. Their greeting was peculiar— no boisterous "How are you, old fellow?" but a silent striking of wrists, and then a low and indistinct muttering. This method of salutation certainly wore a solemn air, but had not the first token of proceeding from any joyful emotion. I would not give a "thank you" for a Bedawee friend, if it was but for the reserved and formal expressions of friendship they practise. Amid such etiquette, a friend is as desirable an object to meet as a funeral. But we saw one greeting that showed decidedly more sense. Hassan, my camel-leader, suddenly caught sight of a female face by the side of a small copse; instantly he handed me the halter, and in a twinkling I saw him and his fair attraction in a perfect shower of kisses. There was no reserve or solemnity there, but all was as gay as a wedding. Hassan resumed the camel-rope with many a look cast back upon the copse, until we had left it out of sight; but from that time till we parted at Akabah, Hassan's sweetheart was a favourite subject of jest. In vain the persecuted youth declared it was his mother. We laughed at his attempt to elude our jokes, and Hassan blushed through his swarthy skin.

On entering Wady Sheikh, the smiling Besharah bade us a temporary farewell. He was about going to his tent-home further up Wady Feiran, and would rejoin us when we left the convent. In Wady Sheikh we noticed more Sinaitic inscriptions. At the distance of three and a half hours from the oasis of Feiran, we reached Dr. Robinson's route again at Wady Sebeh, having been three days upon a more western road. Dr. Robinson found his route from Wady Taiyibeh to Wady Sebeh about twenty-five hours. Our route was twenty-four and a quarter hours. There can be, therefore, but little difference in their respective distances.

From the junction, an inclined plane brought us to a quasi pass, by which we came in full sight of a large chaotic-looking plain, at the other end of which rose the dark mass of Jebel el Fureia, the boundary of the interior sanctuary of Sinai. Our course was directly over this open tract, amid risings and ravines that were awful in their desolation. I had never looked upon so solemn a scene. Jagged peaks, cliffs, and defiles, rock and sand, all thrown in a promiscuous assemblage, made us think of old Chaos, where no living creature breathed away the silence. For two hours we toiled among this sea of rocks, with nothing upon which to turn the eye except the most desolate and stern features of Nature. We then descended into Wady Solaf, a mighty defile that cuts through this horrible wilderness. Crossing this deep ravine, we mounted its southern bank, and were soon at the extremity of the dreary expanse, at the base of the gaunt Jebel el Fureia, and the commencement of the Nukb Hawy, a pass of more than Alpine grandeur and wildness. This pass is the immediate entrance to the sacred plain of Sinai. It lies between Jebel el Fureia and Jebel es-Surey. The way at first is bounded by lofty cliffs, and mounts steeply among huge masses of detached rock and vast quantities of smaller stones.

Then it gradually becomes less difficult, and takes the appearance of a glen, with sandy path, and tufts of herbs growing about its side,—then palms of stunted growth, and a well (or pool of rain-water) refresh the eye. Thus on and on we wind and climb for nearly two hours before we reach the summit of the pass. Now and then a camel would give out, and require a removal of its load; at times the loads would remove themselves, and some breakage ensue. The riders had dismounted at the commencement, and trudged up the pass on foot. There was a huge rock upon the side of the path, that resembled a toad to the life. It seemed the Cerberus of the spot. We could scarcely relieve ourselves of the idea of its veritable existence, for in so wild, so strange, so unearthly a place, we would not have wondered at anything.

We again noticed the Sinaitic inscriptions upon the rocks along the Nukb. On reaching the summit of the pass, the high mountain walls still rising precipitously on either side, we all looked eagerly upon a frowning height before us, still two hours in advance. It was a dark high cliff of porphyry, that ended heavenward in jagged peaks, and seemed a mighty flame transformed to rock. We looked long and silently—we looked with beating hearts and burning thoughts—it was Sinai! The laugh and jest were thrown aside, and we felt awed before the sacred mountain, where the Almighty had displayed his glory to man. We thought of the words that fell on the ear of Moses on that very mount, "Put off thy shoes from off thy feet, for the place whereon thou standest is holy ground." The same solemn words now sounded to our hearts, and we felt this was indeed holy ground, where Jehovah had appeared to Israel, clothed in all the terrors of the God of Justice, and where again he had disclosed him self to his prophet Elijah, in the still small voice of the God of Mercy.

The descent of the south side of the pass is but trifling, compared with the ascent of the northern. In descending, our ears caught the grateful sound of falling water, and we turned our eyes towards the point whence the sound came. A beautiful cascade was leaping among the cliffs upon our right, yielding us the most delightful welcome we could have desired. We shortly passed a fountain, and were now upon the great plain Er-Rahah, where Israel had encamped before the mount. Ascending a slightly inclined plane, we reached the water-shed, and saw, by the side of the dark Sinai, in a retired ravine upon its left, the walls of the renowned convent which, for more than 1300 years, has kept solitary watch in this rocky wild. Our course was directly towards these walls, and in an hour and twenty minutes from the summit of the pass, we entered the narrow and difficult defile in which the convent stands. After twenty minutes of the roughest travel, we reached the building, which, with its gardens of loveliest green, was an unspeakable luxury to our eyes, that had been all day wearied with desolation.

The Desert of Sinai.

THE CONVENT AND ITS INMATES—ASCENT OF JEBEL MOUSA AND SUFSAFEH—WALK AROUND THE MOUNTAIN—DEPARTURE FROM SINAI—MONKISH TREATMENT—DESERT GROWTH—THE GULF OF AKABAH.

THE convent presents, in exterior, a plain wall of dusky stone, here and there supported by irregular buttresses. Before a window in the eastern wall projects a portico, from which is lowered a hook, by which the visitor is introduced to the monkish hospitality. Our camels were all collected beneath the walls, and there was a busy time in unloading and entering our baggage. The ladies were taken in by a doorway in the back of the convent, while the gentlemen were hoisted as luggage into the midst of a crowd of monks within the window. When all were safely entered, our Bedawin salaamed us, and wound down the ravine on their return to Feiran, after an agreement to be in readiness for our further travel after four days' interval. On the north-east corner flies the red flag of the convent, having on it the design of the burning bush.

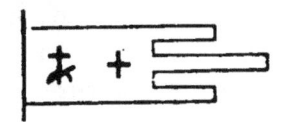

We were shown comfortable, clean rooms, that looked out upon the convent garden, which, with the help of our own beds, were most admirably suited for our sojourn. But one monk seemed to care aught for us, and he appeared to fill the office of waiter or chamberman to the establishment. The rest passed us as if we were old residents; indeed our whole stay in the convent differed nothing from life in our own house. No deference was shown to us, and we showed none in return. We found the monks not at all attractive, rather dirty, and apparently illiterate. The convent is an irregular square, built on the debris, at the very foot of Mount Sinai. As this debris is inclined, the walls upon the mountain side are more elevated than those upon the opposite side, though their height from the foundation appears the same, about thirty-five feet.

There are three entrances—the pulley-window above mentioned, which is about twenty-five feet from the ground; the low doorway on the mountain side by which females enter; and a subterranean passage upon the north side, which leads under an open space to the garden. From some miniature port-holes a few pigmy cannon peep out, whose report would frighten the monks as much as the Arabs. Within the walls is a confused mass of buildings, differing in height, architecture, and in exposure; moreover, corridors and wooden staircases innumerable, terraces and railings, court-yards and crooked passages, so promiscuously huddled as to defy the most skilful draughtsman to attempt a sketch of its plan. There is the workmanship of Justinian's age, in close companionship with yesterday's repairs; and by the side of the Greek church rises the minaret of a Mohammedan mosque!

The church is pretty but tawdry, abounding in embroidered hangings, mosaic floors, tables inlaid with tortoise shell and mother of pearl, old-fashioned gilt pictures of saints, and other bright ornaments. Over the niche at the end of the church is a very old mosaic of the Transfiguration. In a coffin, just within the choir, are the head and hand of St. Catharine, which were duly displayed to us amid clouds of incense and a quantum of chanting—the monks and a Greek servant of our number devoutly kissing the old skull. The coffin was of sculptured white marble, richly covered with satins. After being supplied all around with pewter rings taken from the tomb, (for which good silver coin was substituted), the lid was shut down, and the incense and chanting rapidly subsided. This St. Catharine was an Alexandrian virgin, who was martyred in the reign of the giant Emperor Maximin. about the year 236. By some peculiar concatenation of circumstances, her body was found upon the mountain, now called by her name, in the neighbourhood of Sinai. The holy monks, who even at that early period had a sort of monastery here, piously laid her bones in their chapel. These relics seem to have got into Justinian's convent afterwards, and they are still the principal articles in the relic line of which the convent boasts, though a crowd of holy bones besides these are to be seen in the charnel-house.

We waited to hear the Greek service performed, and found it formal, uninteresting, and irreverent, at least as far as its performance at Sinai was a specimen. Behind the church is the chapel of the Burning Bush. We entered in stocking feet from the church, and found it a carpeted room, hung with scores of gilded portraits of old saints. The bush (identical, on the word of a monk!) is still seen growing without the walls of the church.

We also attended service in the mosque. This mosque was built to get the right side of the Arabs. The service was conducted by my Ibrahim; the congregation was composed of our other Moslem servants. Ibrahim made a capital Imâm, and the solemn guttural voices of the responses in the dusky twilight had a far more solemn effect than the misnamed Christian jabber to which we had listened in the church.

The library of the convent is full of old Greek tomes and some valuable manuscripts, which, I fancy, the monks seldom trouble. On the shelves I found a familiar-looking volume, in the shape of Stephens' Incidents of Travel, which must be worse than Hebrew to the brethren, who probably find a consolation for their ignorance of its letter-press by enjoying the engravings.

The refectory is a plain room, with arched ceiling. A long table extends down the apartment. This table is furnished with drawers at every seat, where the holy brethren place their surplus provision after each meal, from which stock they draw as hunger dictates. At one end of the refectory is an altar and pictures of very forlorn aspect, and on the side of the room is a pulpit, from which some member of the fraternity mingles mental food with their physical nourishment during their repast. Near the pulpit is a set of book-shelves, where the literary dishes are preserved. Several cruciform lamps hang from the ceiling—these are ornamented with what appear to be ostrich eggs.

The cells of the monks are commodious but shockingly filthy, and send forth an odour most forbidding. In one we saw a brother one hundred and two years of age, and in another one of one hundred and five years, both hale, and polite in their salutation. A greater curiosity of longevity was the monk described by Stephens; he was one hundred and twenty years old, and had been more than seventy years in the convent! Though in decided dotage, he did not appear older than a man of eighty. The pure, dry air of this Sinai region must be the cause of this longevity: it is not seen so greatly among the Bedawin, because of their hardships and condition of semi-starvation; the monks, well provided with food, have no drawback to their vegetation, and seem only to die because weary of so long a life.

The charnel-house in the garden is a doleful spot. Placed in the midst of the loveliest foliage, it deepens in horror by the contrast. Bones and skulls, remnants of a dozen centuries, are piled on all sides; some of peculiar sanctity are placed in baskets and labelled. One skull and breast-bone thus placed was labelled "St. Stephen." It was the fragment of some old dirty monk, probably, who had said more Kyrie eleesons and pater-emons than his fellows, and obtained his reward in the honours of posthumous saintship. His bony neck still was hung with the rosary which he had worn while in life. The souls of his prayers had fled, leaving the beads of the rosary as their forsaken bodies, which kept fit company with his silent skeleton. Some of the honoured dead were laid out in long boxes. Among these were the remains of two Persian princes, and in the box that held their bones were the iron chains they wore when on their pilgrimage to Sinai. Iron collars and pilgrims' staffs, that had of old been inseparable companions of ignorant humanity, were now resting peaceably with the wrecks of that humanity. In spite of the incense which was burnt profusely by our attendant monk, the effluvia from the bodies was very offensive, and we gladly exchanged the noxious vapours of the charnel-house for the odorous groves of almonds and olives that graced the garden. There is a rough gardener's house and a white stucco well-temple within the enclosure. Besides the almond and olive trees, are grape vines, apple trees, cypresses, and other trees of greenest leaf; and beneath these grow various sorts of grain and vegetables. All this verdure springs from soil brought on camels from the valley of the Nile!

The convent of Mount Sinai was built by Justinian, in 527; but a chapel erected by the relic-gatherer Helena, is said to have stood there for two hundred years previous. Of course, the building has received repairs and alterations innumerable, the last of which were made by Kleber, during the French invasion of Egypt. Its strength, as well as the sanctity of the spot, has doubtless prevented its attack or capture by the Arabs. It is now, in part, a Botany Bay for misbehaving friars of the Greek church. We saw one monk who had been transported thither for calumniating the Patriarch of Constantinople; another had been a notorious murderer. We may thus be prepared for a little laxity in their morals, which otherwise might reflect unhappily upon the Greek church. The brethren (who numbered, at our visit, twenty-five) seem to spend their time in sleeping, lounging, praying, and making date preserves and araki. The date preserves are a compound of dates and almonds, well compressed and enclosed in leather envelopes tightly sewed. The araki is a strong intoxicating liquor made from the date, and well affected by the monkish community. Several times in the twenty-four hours the monks assembled at services, to each of which a sounded triangle served to summon the worshippers; most unpleasantly to us, this noisy instrument would discourse its music every night at 1 o'clock, when service was probably held as penance for the sins of the day. The servants of the convent are the Jebeliyeh, whom the Bedawin will not recognize as of the same race, and who are, as before remarked, thought to be the desendants of the Christian servants sent originally to the convent by Justinian. They are similar to the Bedawin in colour, language, and religion (or non-religion), with whom they have probably intermingled.

The 20th of April, 1849, was to me a memorable day,—a day spent in investigating a locality of the most thrilling interest, a locality which, if any part of earth may be esteemed sacred, may lay justest claim to that title. Two monks acted as our guides, and six Arabs of the Jebeliyeh carried our provisions, our Bibles, and our writing materials. We issued from the back door of the convent, where the ascent commenced immediately over the debris of the mountain. Very soon, the path became a rude sort of staircase of large stones, facilitating the progress, which, however, is still fatiguing, and conducts the traveller up a steep defile, or water-course. In seventeen minutes we reached the Fountain Mayan el Jebel, one of the sweetest springs on earth, retired in a small cave, and girt with softest green. We drank of the refreshing cool water, and then continued the weary ascent. In another half hour we gained the chapel of the Virgin—a rude stone hut, containing a corresponding rude painting of the Virgin. Five minutes further, we passed under a stone gateway, where the path is just sufficiently wide to allow one person to pass at a time. Still five minutes further, is another such gateway. These were formerly spots where the monks took tribute from the ascending pilgrims. Just beyond this second gateway is the tall cypress of Mt. Sinai, surrounded by a stone wall, and near it is a cistern of rain-water and a small pond. Nails and spikes are driven into the tree, at intervals, to facilitate climbing. The tree is about eight feet in circumference at the distance of five feet from the ground. It stands in a small basin, well fitted to receive the winter rains.

Not far from this is the chapel of Elijah, another rude structure of stone, with two apartments; one is said to have been Elijah's sleeping-place! At length, after a climbing of an hour and a quarter, we reached the summit of Jebel Mousa, the highest peak of Sinai. Two rude stone buildings occupy the summit, bearing the lofty titles of mosque and church, in spite of their insignificance. Of course the monks would testify on oath that the church is built *exactly* upon the spot where God gave the tables of stone to Moses, and the Mohammedans would do the same regarding the mosque. That God gave Moses the tables of stone here is highly probable; but the northern peak of Sufsafeh is undoubtedly the spot where "the Lord came down in the sight of all the people" and orally delivered the law; for, from Sufsafeh, the great plain El Rahah is clearly seen below, while from *this* summit not a portion of it is visible. We spent an hour on the roof of the little church-entitled hut, and there read the law of God. The view was sublime in desolation. On all sides rose the dark jagged peaks of the mountains of Horeb—a tempest-tossed sea of rocky cliffs, possessing not one blade of verdure that could relieve the eye.

Anxious to reach Sufsafeh, as the most probable site of the giving of the Law, we left the summit of Jebel Mousa, and passed down the peak to the backbone of the mountain that ran northward to the other height of Sufsafeh. Close to the summit of Jebel

Mousa is a small cave, just sufficiently large to contain a prostrate man, and having in its side a small window-like opening. This (say the infallible monks) is the cave in which Moses lay when God revealed himself to him, as "the Lord, merciful and gracious." Further down the peak is shown the print of Mohammed's camel's foot, which was wont to use mountains as stepping-stones in travelling on the earth! In fifteen minutes from the summit we again reached the cypress. Continuing thence north-westerly along the uneven back of the mountain, over huge masses of rock, and through little green spots where brooks rippled by, we reached (in about half an hour from the cypress) another rude stone hut, which our guide termed "the Chapel of John the Baptist," but which is called by Dr. Robinson "the Chapel of the Virgin of the Zone." The little chapel which Dr. R. calls the "Chapel of John the Baptist," (and which we had passed nearer the cypress,) my guide termed the "Chapel of Gregorius." From *our* "Chapel of the Baptist" the ascent was excessively steep and rough, up a fearful defile of monstrous rocks—then came the last climb, almost perpendicular, exceedingly difficult, and not without danger; this brought us to the summit of Sufsafeh, in one hour and twelve minutes from the cypress tree. This extreme difficulty of access (while the other peak is very accessible) makes me think that though Sufsafeh was probably the spot where the Lord descended in the sight of the people, and gave the Law, yet the other summit was the site of the frequent interviews between God and Moses; it may be objected that, at the time of one of these interviews, "the sight of the glory of the Lord was like devouring fire on the top of the mount *in the eyes of the children of Israel.*" But we suppose this fire enveloped the whole summit, including both peaks, and then the children of Israel below could have seen that which appeared about Sufsafeh; and if the appearance of flame extended to a great height, they could also see that above Jebel Mousa.

In this hypothesis, the little basin, where the cypress stands, will be the spot where Aaron, Nadab, Abihu, and the seventy elders of Israel beheld the glory of God (See Exodus xxiv. 9, 12). From Sufsafeh, the whole plain of Er-Rahah was seen at our feet, and a large part of the broad Wady Sheikh, abundant room for the encampment of all Israel. For the rest, the view was as from Jebel Mousa, wild and grand to fearfulness. No spot on earth could have been selected so awfully impressive and so exactly adapted to the promulgation of God's law—the stern, unyielding law which declared, that "the soul that sinneth, it shall die!" These rugged mountain precipices of blackened rock seemed to frown a blasting curse on man, and echoed hoarsely the mighty thunders of Heaven which proclaimed a law too holy for human nature to endure. Thus did Nature yield her correspondent terrors at this display of Divine justice and power. So, at Olivet, when a risen Saviour was ascending to present his successful intercessions at the throne of God—to add the last link in that chain of mercy that bound the sinning race of man to Heaven's throne, in spite of the broken law of Sinai—then was Nature smiling in her loveliness,—the olive and the fig grew green upon that beautiful mountain,—fields of yellow grain and many-coloured flowers waved cheerfully on Olivet, and the soft scenery of Palestine greeted the delighted eye. When we look upon the dreary peaks of Sinai, the Mount of Olives must form the background; then can we bear the sight and even touch the awful mountain. On this hallowed summit I wrote a copy of the law of God; and while my pen was tracing the words on the very spot where first they had been uttered, and that by God's own voice, the thunder crashed above my head, and a hundred cliffs took up the echo. A thunderstorm on Sinai! We were overpowered with the coincidence, and felt as if the voice of God had not yet died away from that sacred height, but muttered still the terrors of the law.

After a long and unspeakably delightful stay upon Sufsafeh, we descended the mountain by a more direct route, and reached the convent in an hour and five minutes. The next day we took the same monkish and Arabic escort, and made the complete circuit of the Holy Mountain. We passed down the rough Wady Shueib, in which the convent stands, to the great plain, then westward along the face of Sinai (which is here a mountain "that can be touched" while the person stands upon the plain) to the western side. Wady Ledja here enters the plain, and at its mouth are two pretty gardens belonging to the monks. Turning up the wady, which is an exceeding rough defile, we soon reached a huge detached rock, evidently fallen from the cliffs above. This is called by the monks "the rock of Moses," and the mark of water is piously shown upon its face. This mark appeared to us a vein in the rock. In an hour and forty-three minutes we reached the deserted convent, El Arbain, or "of the Forty," so called from the murder of the forty monks who once inhabited it; the legend is some four hundred years old. A fine garden or tree-conserve surrounds it, where grow poplars as well as many kinds of fruit trees, and pretty brooks murmur pleasantly among the verdure. A few Jebeliyeh attend to the garden, but no monks reside here. We had intended the ascent of Jebel Katherin, but as the monks assured us that we would not have time for the ascent that day, we reluctantly gave it up and continued our circuit of Sinai. Keeping on, therefore, along Wady Ledja, we reached the southern extremity of the mountain, which we found here bounded by gravel hills, over which a rough way conducted us to the convent wady. We reached the convent in two hours from El. Arbain, having found the entire circuit of the mountain a walk of three hours and forty-three minutes.

The time fixed for our sojourn having transpired, we were busied on the morning of the 23d April in preparation for departure. The camels were heard groaning before the walls, the Arabs were vociferating as usual, and we were making our last arrangements with the monkish landlords. At length we were let down by the pulley, and greeted enthusiastically by the merry-faced Besharah. He kissed me over and over again, and rubbed his gray wiry beard against my cheek most pitilessly. We found sixty camels in attendance, and on inquiry, learned that these were to accompany us for that day's journey only, and in the evening a choice should be made by the Sheikhs of those desired for the remaining way to Akabah. At a quarter past two, we re-commenced our camel-riding, amid reiterated cries for "backsheesh" on the part of the Jebeliyeh, and proceeded down the defile. At its entrance upon the plain is an Arab cemetery, of no pretensions. From it our guides had taken sand on our way to the convent, and placed it upon the camels' heads, as a charm of some sort. The plain was covered with the red wild poppy, which we were told was good food for the camels. Entering the great Wady Sheikh, (which here runs eastward, and then bends around by a large curve to the spot where we had before seen it,) we rode slowly on past the cliffs of the companion-mountains of Sinai, and, in two hours from the plain, reached the tomb of Sheikh Salih, who is said to have been a Syrian prophet. From him the wady derives its name of "Sheikh." The tomb is a square stone building, with a pyramidal roof. The coffin within is surrounded by a wooden partition, and covered with rags of various colours. I followed our Bedawin into the tomb. As they entered they kissed the door-post; they then prostrated themselves before the coffin, kissed it, and muttered a prayer; then taking up a handful of the sand from within, they sprinkled it upon their own heads and upon the heads of the camels, and even treated us to a small shower. A short distance beyond this tomb we encamped for the night. On encamping, Hassan, one of our Egyptian servants, an excellent fellow, was missing. No one had seen him on the march, and we were at a loss to imagine the cause of his absence. While thus perplexed, we saw Hassan enter the camp, followed by a monk. The poor Egyptian was bleeding badly from the head, his back was much bruised, and his elbow and knee were severely cut. Some Jebeliyeh of the convent had also arrived with Hassan, and I immediately inquired of them the cause of his wounds. Their story was this: that the monks had been dissatisfied with our pay, and took advantage of Hassan's being the last in the convent, to extort more money from him. He had emptied his pockets for them, but still they were unsatisfied, and finding no chance of obtaining their satisfaction in cash, they took it out in belabouring most unmercifully the unfortunate servant, and nearly murdered him, before their fun was complete. Hassan confirmed this story, and shortly after became delirious. I straightway accosted the monk, and finding his statements most manifestly false, and bordering on impudence, I walked him out of the camp, and bade him be aware that the insult offered us by his convent would be duly reported to higher authority. Poor Hassan had his wounds bathed in brandy, but recovered slowly. Every day his forlorn appearance on his camel would excite our sympathy, for his obliging disposition had won our hearts. A Christian convent was the last spot whence an attack had been expected in the desert, yet we found better treatment among the wild Bedawin, than within the walls of the would-be sacred monastery.

A great number of Arabs gathered about our tents that night, and we feared mischief, but Besharah assured us that they were all Towarah, and were friendly; thus encouraged, we slept none the worse. The next day brought us out of the Sinaitic region to a small pass called Ojret el Furas, where some heaps of stone were the remnants of rude fortifications constructed by the Bedawin in some ancient battle. We had passed (near Wady Sheikh, from which we turned soon after the morning' start) a small garden enclosure watered by the slightly brackish fountain of Aboo Suweirah, and again (much later in the day) had passed over a wide opening that was filled with large acacias, of the size of full grown apple trees. From Wady Orfan we had looked back upon the Sinai group, to which we were then bidding a final farewell. The two cliffs of Um Lauz and Um Alawy stood as sentinels before the sacred region. The first part of the day's journey was among high porphyritic cliffs, which gradually changed to low and rounder hills,—mountains, however, bounding the prospect on all sides. The next day's experience bore testimony to the truth of the words of Moses in calling this region, after leaving Sinai, "that great and terrible wilderness" (Deut. i. 19). Dr. Robinson terms it a "frightful desert." It was a waste of limestone and sand, fearfully dreary, and which, in a hot sun, must make the journey almost intolerably oppressive. Fortunately, we had a cool, cloudy day for the passage, and were enabled to support the trial. In two hours from Ojret el Furas, we passed Sinaitic inscriptions, with rude carvings of camels and goats, exactly the same as in Wady Mokatteb. This rebuts the idea of their existence only *west* of Sinai. Two hours further, a very peculiar fort-like rock is situated in the centre of an expansion of the wady (Wady S'kah), and on it are more of the rude carvings of camels. This strange rock bears the name of "Huzaybet Hejaj." Near this I saw two ravens and a vulture. The day before, I had seen a beautiful green bird, of the size of a ground-thrush. These, and the singing birds of Wady Feiran, were the only kinds we saw in the desert. Of quadrupeds, we had only found the hyæna and the gazelle, unless we mention the lizard. Of trees, the *Tuhl* and *Seyal*, both *acacias*, were the most frequent. They are of diminutive and scraggy growth, much resembling in size and shape small apple trees. The Seyal has the smoother bark, and from it is derived the gum Arabic. The *Nakhl* or *Palm* is seen only by fountains, and generally appears of stunted growth. The *Dôm* Palm I only observed in Wady Taba, on the Red Sea, opposite Akabah. The *Nebbek* grows in Wady Feiran, and produces a palatable fruit resembling a light-coloured cherry, and having an apple taste. This fruit is dried and ground by the Arabs, and then used like flour. Of herbs, the Desert of Arabia Petræa has a plenty, scattered in the various wadys, where they are supported by the annual income of rain. Of these, the *Turfa* or *Tamarisk* is the most abundant, a pine-like bush, from which the Arabian manna is obtained. In the Great Wady el Arabah, between the Dead and Red Seas, is found a plant called *Ertah*, very much resembling this Turfa. The *Retem* or *Broom plant*, is also of frequent occurrence, a very similar bush, being the *juniper* of our English Bible, under which Elijah rested. The *Abeitharan* and *Rimth* are two similar low, straggling shrubs of very strong pitchy odour, and resembling some of our winter-greens. The *Sillee* is a short shrub that bears green thorns at the extremity of each twig. The *Umrara*, found in the Arabah, is a thorny plant, and bears a flower like clover. The *Turbeh*, a small shrub with flowers like Forget-me-nots, abounds in the Arabah. All these above-named plants are eagerly eaten by the camels. Then there are the *Address*, having gray leaves and a button-like flower, with thorns projecting from the flower; the *Sakkaran*, with a flower like the morning-glory; the *Ussher* or *Mulbeiny*, resembling the laurel or magnolia (found in Wady Ghuraleh); the *Salla-Mekka*, a low shrub with leaves like those of the locust tree; (it bears a bean which is used as a purgative, and is exported for that purpose); the *Hemath*, having the taste of sorrel; the *Murkh*, a tall bush; the *Guzzooly*, a coarse grass; the *Goordhy* (eaten by camels); the *Dahamee;* the *Sabbah;* the *Adam*, and the *Handal* or *Colocynth*, a vine. These are the principal growth of the desert; the names were given me directly by the Arabs on the spot, and immediately recorded. A great peculiarity of most of these herbs is their strong flavour, which seems to be particularly pleasing to the camel. It was upon them that our camels lived entirely; they grow immediately out of the sand, in the beds of water-courses, and are detached from one another, thus contributing but little to relieve the barren aspect of the ground.

After passing over the dreary tract above described, we entered among the mountains that skirt the sea, a part of the same range that bound the Dead Sea on the west, and run uninterruptedly for two hundred miles to the extreme southern point of the Sinai peninsula. These mountains form the western boundary not only of the Dead Sea but also of the great valley of the Arabah, and of the Gulf of Akabah, thus constituting the grand bulwark of the highlands of the desert of Et-Tih. Where we entered this range, the height of the mountains was probably a thousand feet. We passed along Wady Ghuzaleh to Wady Wettir, the whole way lying amid these noble heights. The last mentioned wady is a large drain to the desert, and down it we journeyed to the sea. Some of the scenes in Wady Ghuzaleh were remarkably wild; on all sides rose precipitous cliffs of a dark reddish-brown, capped by a lighter coloured stratum, and here and there a steep inclined plane, of red debris, marked the course of some winter torrent from its source among the bleak summits, and a few stunted seyal trees appeared in the dry bed, sustained by the yearly flow. In Wady el-Ain, we saw palm trees and water just before its entrance into the Wady Ghuzaleh, in which we were travelling. This water passes along the latter wady, and is filled with a green water-moss, which probably accounts for its bad taste. It runs in quite a large stream.

Both Ghuzaleh and Wettir, and especially the latter, abound in fine bold scenery. One pass in Wettir was remarkably grand, being exceedingly narrow, and sided by stupendous cliffs of the dark rock. When we reached the sea, we could scarcely discern the other shore from the quantity of sand that filled the air, yet we could look with strange feelings upon the sea that once bore the navies of Solomon, and was whitened by his merchant-fleets on their way to Ophir and the Indies.

The Desert of Paran and Akabah.

SEA-BEACH—ISLAND OF KUREIA—AKABAH—SHEIKH HOSSEIN—
CONSULTATIONS—DESPONDENCY—DELAYS—DEPARTURE.

AIN EL NUWEIBY is a pretty palm grove and fountain belonging to the Terabin, and situated an hour north of Wady Wettir, upon the shore. Here Sheikh Suleiman was killed when conducting Dr. Fisk, an account of which is given in the work of Dr. F. The sheikh's tomb is situated some distance up the inclination that extends from the mountains to the sea. It is a small rude stone tomb, about eighteen inches high within, and hung (as usual) with rags. The Arabs who went up to it muttered prayers and threw stones upon the tomb, and some placed sprigs of herbs upon it. For two days we skirted the sea—the beach abounding in shells and coral. One projecting rock, El Wasileh, was shown us, as a former look-out of great importance to the Bedawin to watch against surprise from hostile tribes. At Abu Suweira we passed a few palms, some bushes, and a brackish spring. The deep blue sea and the tall cloud-capped mountains of the opposite coast formed an untiring scene of beauty. A slight haze gave the other shore the appearance of softest green, and we eagerly nursed the delusion. We could see the palms of Hakl, a little station of the pilgrim caravan, close by the water on the other side, about nine miles distant. We picked up a large variety of shells; there were the large conch-shells and scollop-shells, and an immense variety of smaller species. White and red coral abounded, from the latter of which some have derived the name of the sea. A host of small shell-fish were actively coursing over the sand, and among them crabs from one to five inches in length. There were also remains of lobsters, well bleached. The crabs had deep round holes in the sand, down which they would precipitately tumble at our approach; the sand thrown out of these holes formed little cones, and presented a very odd appearance. Several trunks of palm trees were thrown up by the waves. A thin pudding-stone formation close to the water appeared often upon the beach, and small fragments of a gray granite were seen, but whence they came is a problem. There was scarcely any seaweed upon the whole shore, a want that rendered the beach of peculiar neat and clean appearance. Swallows were skimming the water and cutting the air in all directions, snipe chirped and ran along the edge of the sea, and crows here there found some booty worthy their attention. We noticed the tracks of some very large birds, showing a foot of five inches in extent when spread; and the jackals had also left *their* footprints along the sand. The mountains, 1500 feet in height, sometimes approached the sea so nearly as scarcely to allow space for our passage, and again would retire for a distance of one or two miles. The level of the beach would here and there be interrupted by the high inclined planes of the descending wadys. The only occasion of our leaving the sea between our arrival upon its shore and Akabah, was about eight hours before reaching the latter place. For two hours we travelled *behind* projecting mountains, *before* which there was no passage-way (at least so the Arabs affirmed). In this back road we crossed two severe passes, where our camels laboured with great difficulty, and where we were very fearful of their complete exhaustion. On reaching the sea again, Akabah was in sight, on the opposite shore, near the head of the gulf. A long row of palm groves by the waterside marked the spot. We shortly came opposite the islet of Kureia or Graya, situated about a quarter of a mile from the shore, in a small bay, and crowned with a ruined fortress of crusading days. Opposite Akabah, we found low mud hills as outworks in front of the mountain range. Turning the corner of the sea, we passed along its head, on a pebbly beach about three miles long. The beach becomes sandy nearer Akabah, and here the mounds of Elath or Ailah are passed. Turning again at the north-east corner of the sea, and advancing southward for five minutes, we reached our encamping ground beneath the palms, between the castle of Akabah and the water.

Akabah consists of this castle, some dozen miserable huts, a long array of palms, and some poorly managed gardens. These gardens are cultivated by a sort of Jebeliyeh, who form the principal population, and an Egyptian governor resides in the castle, though Egypt has but slender rule in this wilderness. The Alawin appear to be the dominant Bedawee tribe in this region, and their head-quarters are in the mountains east of the great valley of the Arabah—the Scriptural mountains of Seir, now called "Es-Sherah." The castle of Akabah is said to have been built by El-Ghoree, one of the last independent Memlook Sultans of Egypt, about the year 1500. It is an oblong quadrangle, containing an open court. On each corner is a tower, those on the east corners being round, and those on the west octagonal. On the north side is the gate, of imposing character, ornamented with two round towers. A series of chambers, one story high, ranged along the interior of the walls, form the accommodations of the edifice; and over them, upon their roof, are erected wretched huts as additional house-room. The material of the fortress is a light stone, each stone being about a foot square. The walls are about twenty-five feet in height—somewhat higher on the east side. A bulwark of four feet in height surrounds the top, and in this are cut loop-holes. On the east and north sides the stones of every alternate layer are painted red, presenting the striped appearance of some of the Cairo mosques. Two sorry looking cannon seem to be the entire artillery force of the castle, and these would require the combined powers of the whole garrison (who, in my reckoning, numbered five men and their families) to discharge. The interior of this formidable fortress is ricketty and filthy beyond belief. Women, children, and cattle are mingled together in a sea of pollution. I hurried through them to reach the battlements, and as hurriedly made my escape, feeling as if some gaunt pestilence was at my side. Before the castle are a number of dirty mud and stone huts huddled together, where vegetate the squalid citizens of Akabah. There are, perhaps, a hundred of these characters, of mixed Bedawin and Egyptian race.

The castle is entirely behind the palms, and has no trees in its immediate neighbourhood. From this northward extends a range of mounds at the termination of a high inclined bed of a wady that comes down from the eastern mountains, here a mile or two distant. Are not these the mounds of *Ezion-Geber?* The mounds of *Elath* are seen at the head of the sea. Elath means " Strength," and was probably a stronghold to guard the navigation of the sea. Solomon used it as a port (2 Chron. viii. 17); and after him we find Jehoshaphat mentioned as building ships at the neighbouring town of Ezion-Geber (2 Chron. xx. 36). From the fact that Elath is not mentioned here, it is probable that it was one of the fenced cities that Shishak had previously taken, (2 Chron. xii. 4), and probably destroyed. Again, we are told (2 Chron. xxvi. 2,) that Uzziah rebuilt Elath, and again made it a city of Judah. Then the Syrians obtained possession of it in the reign of Ahaz. After this, we hear no more of this city in Scripture—it probably fell into the hands of Pharaoh Nechoh, in the days of Josiah, and then followed the regular round of subjection to Babylon, Persia, Greece, and Rome. Under the latter empires, it became "Ailah." Then came Moslem rule, and the episode of the crusaders. Under Moslem power it soon dwindled to non-existence, except in its confused ruins.

So much for Elath—but where is Ezion-Geber? No one pretends to say. We know it was close to Elath (Deut. ii. 8; 1 Kings ix. 26; 2 Chron. viii. 17), and probably in Solomon's and Jehoshaphat's days, it had superior advantages to Elath as a port.—(See 1 Kings ix. 26; 2 Chron. xx. 36.) Josephus, in narrating the fact of Solomon's construction of ships at Ezion-Geber, states that the name of the place in his day was Berenice; but this statement throws no light upon its present position. As it existed as late as the days of Josephus, and was an important city, we must find its mounds as we do those of Elath. Now the only mounds near those of Elath, and "on the shore of the Red Sea," are those of Akabah; the conclusion is, therefore, probable, that Akabah occupies the exact site of Ezion-Geber.

Akabah was the limit to which Besharah and the Towarahs were to conduct us. Their territory extended no further, and here we were to entrust ourselves to the great Sheikh Hossein ebn Agad, and the fierce Alawin. We had despatched a messenger to seek the Sheikh in his mountain fastnesses, and patiently awaited his arrival. Meanwhile we retained the Towarahs in our service by a bribe, that we might have some one on whom to fall back in case of too extortionate a demand on the part of Hossein.

We arrived on Saturday, and Sheikh Hossein at Monday noon. Meantime, we suffered under the hot sun of Akabah by day, and listened to the chirping of a myriad crickets by night. Bathing in the sea was a great luxury, but then we had to watch sharply against sharks. Not a boat disturbs the sea, but the fisherman pushes out on a raft of palm logs, and so sits by the day beneath a broiling sun. True, I did see boats, and such as I did not expect to see in this retired spot. They were small toy-boats, with which the children played, and were probably importations from the Nile, brought by the few Egyptians who here dream away life. Fish abound in these waters, and sea fowl are plentiful. The afternoon of our arrival, a large body of Tiyahah and other Bedawee tribes passed, with a booty of 1000 camels, gained in a contest with a tribe at three days' distance from Akabah. A few wounded warriors appeared among their number, and the camels were smeared along their necks with streaks of blood. It had been a regular plundering expedition, in which the Tiyahah, Terabin, Haiwat, and Haweitat were co-partners. This Arabian method of accumulating capital has been practised since the days of Chedorlaomer. The victors respectfully salaamed us as they passed, and went on their way to the division of the spoil.

I noticed the custom of scooping a hollow in the beach-sand, about three feet from the sea, and from this procuring *fresh* water. I tried the water, and found it entirely free from salt. This phenomenon is accounted for by considering the water thus derived not as proceeding from the sea, but as filtered from the mountains through the intervening sand.

A few Amran, Wady Mousa, and Alawin Arabs were seen wandering among the palms, presenting a far wilder appearance than our mild Towarah.

The messenger whom we had sent for Sheikh Hossein had left Akabah two days before our arrival there, having been dismissed on his errand while we were among the Sinai mountains. We had, therefore, expected that the Sheikh would have arrived by the time of our arrival. We were much disappointed at his non-appearance, for we feared detention in the great heat. Sunday came, and no Sheikh yet appeared. Some told us that Sheikh Hossein had killed a man of the Wady Mousa tribe, and dared not go among them with us. Others said he was afraid of the combined tribes that had just passed us. Still another report was, that the mighty Sheikh had been giving a grand feast to these tribes. Others surmised that he was dead. Amid all these sayings, we remained perplexed. Ibrahim had already fallen under the great heat, prostrated with a burning fever. His piteous groans and lamentations that he should never again see his beloved Cairo, were heart-rending. I now felt that I had been foolish to venture into the desert. I feared that the ladies must soon give way before the hot climate, and a host of imagined ills beset my path. Hossein's delay added to my anxiety. It might be treachery was afloat, and I shuddered at the thought of our helpless condition. At length, a council of deliberation was held, at which the Egyptian Sub-Governor was present, (the Governor himself being absent,) and we here concluded to remain till Tuesday morning, in expectation of the Sheikh; if *then* he had not arrived, we should start for Hebron direct, omitting Petra, with our Towarah. A Sheikh of the Wady Mousa Arabs was present, who offered to take us on to Petra; but we knew that if he took us through the Alawin territory, it would be at our peril, and we declined his offer.

To our great joy, at Monday noon, Sheikh Hossein arrived, and was a half hour at the Governor's preparing himself for an interview. We arranged a tent for his reception and the gentlemen of the party there assembled. The Sheikh made his appearance in a flowing robe of scarlet, and attended by the retinue of a prince. We piped and coffeed him—the usual oriental preliminary to every business—and, through poor, sick Ibrahim, as interpreter, opened negotiations, by informing him that we had received the letter sent by our English friend to the British Consul in Cairo, and were prepared to proceed under his escort to Petra, upon the terms that he (Sheikh Hossein) had therein promised. The Sheikh here interrupted us by whispering to Ibrahim that there were entirely too many bystanders for the present transaction of business, and proposed a postponement until a more suitable opportunity; at the same time declaring (as a soft lining to our impatience) that his promises to the British Consul were truth itself. The cunning old villain was anxious to arrange matters with us in privacy, that he might swindle his tribe out of their due, by foisting upon them the belief of an agreement with us for a less price than the reality, the surplus serving as a bounty for Hossein's own coffers. His notorious rascality and the actual sequel made us thus uncharitable in our surmises.

A few hours afterwards we again met his Highness in the tent. Now he was unattended, and we hurried on to our desired topic. But sheikhship must always be propitiated by pipes and coffee; and, accordingly, we had to stifle our impatience until the due amount of introductory tobacco, mocha, and sherbet also had been received. This entirely spoiled our secrecy; for the fragrance of the coffee and the Latakiyeh proved an irresistible bait to the outside barbarians, and one and another slipped in, unbidden, to assist in our deliberations. But the Sheikh seemed fearful of stretching our long suffering to further limits, and accordingly expressed himself ready to hear our requests. Thus summoned, I rose, and repeated my former demand, whether he was willing to conduct us safely to Hebron (via Petra) for the sum mentioned in the letter to the British Consul. To our real surprise, the pompous gray-beard unhesitatingly assented. These terms were 240 piastres (twelve dollars) per camel for the whole distance to Syria. The next point was the *number* of camels. Here we struck the first rock. I informed Hossein that we wished twenty-five. He objected peremptorily, and assured us he would see us all in the bottom of the Red Sea (or some equally forcible expression) before we should stir northward with less than thirty-two, the number with which we arrived. I gave him my reasons for the alteration in numbers—that *then* we had *three* Sheikhs, but *now* were to have only *one;* hence two camels were to be deducted. Again, several water-casks and boxes were to be left behind—this would further diminish the number; and lastly, several of our camels had had hitherto but half a load—hence there should be still greater diminution. But here the Sheikh had us completely. He triumphantly appealed to the written promise, and we found, too truly, that there the number of camels to be furnished at Akabah had been determined to be the same with the number contracted for with the Towarah at Cairo. Fortunately, we had really contracted for twenty-nine at Cairo, the rest having been added from necessity after the contract was drawn. We showed the contract to the Sheikh, and then appealed to the assembly if the deduction of two Sheikhs ought not make a deduction of two camels. The appeal was successful, and, forced by public opinion, the Sheikh agreed to be satisfied with twenty-seven.*

The next subject was the route. He consented at once to take us to Petra, and allow us to remain there two days; but to conduct us to Hebron was impossible. There was the great bugbear of a quarantine there, and no Alawy was fool enough to put his neck in such a noose. He would, however, take us to Dhahariyeh, a frontier village, six hours from Hebron. To this we were forced to consent, though we afterwards discovered it was a trick formed to compensate for his want of success in making a *private* arrangement with us, for his hope of spoil had been entirely cut off from that source.

The next item was the amount of daily travel; this was to be as many hours as we chose, except for the two days among the Petra mountains, in which, from the difficulty of the path, the Sheikh was to determine how long a journey his camels could endure.

The last clauses of the contract provided that *good* camels should be furnished, that particularly easy animals should be obtained for the ladies, and that "backsheesh" should be dealt according to our option.

---

*Afterwards changed to *twenty-eight*.

A verbal assent having been given to these particulars, the Governor's scribe, duly equipped with his stylus and ink, and provided with a sheet of coarse brown paper, commenced immortalizing the contract in black and white; but here a Syrian, one of our servants, interfered, determined to draw up so lawyer-like a document, that the Sheikh could find no loop-hole of escape. The astounded scribe, on whom all the literary labours of Akabah had hitherto fallen, demurred resolutely at this infringement of his right. Was he, the honourable Secretary of the Gubernatorial Court of Akabah, to yield his powers to a dog of a Syrian, and that, too, a servant? Indignation was most righteously his, but perseverance was as certainly Giovanni's. A compromise was effected, by which Giovanni agreed to do the duty and hand the fee to the high-minded secretary—a compromise which seemed to show that the honourable penman placed a higher estimate on the gain than on the honour of his office. After all was satisfactorily arranged, I produced the silver, and counted out to the Sheikh the two-thirds of the price, the rest being payable at Petra. He here slipped in his claim for forty piastres per camel as his own fee. As this was in his proposals to the British Consul, it was immediately paid; and now was closed our great business arrangement with the redoubtable Sheikh of the Alawin, to which we had looked forward as to some mighty Slough of Despond. The arrangement was sufficiently satisfactory—the fulfilment was still somewhat doubtful.

The Governor of Akabah now put in his claim on our treasury for four hundred piastres (twenty dollars), for having sent two dromedaries after Hossein. I asked him why on earth he had sent two, for I was wholly unaware that the rule of three proved that two dromedaries could reach a given point twice as fast as one—and we had only required one. He made no explanation, and I handed him one hundred piastres, telling him I could only pay for one, and this hundred was ample pay for that. He utterly refused this, and I at length soothed him with two hundred. Sheikh Hossein now thought it his turn to propose an appendix to the day's arrangements. He did so in the modest request to give his son Mohammed (who was to be our leader), a pound of coffee and a pound of tobacco daily! We laughed the old man out of this notion, and he beat a retreat to the ladies' tent, where he urged upon them the expediency of each furnishing him with a pair of pantaloons, declaring solemnly that this was his regular tribute from the English ladies who before had visited his country. The ladies assured him that such a gift to a gentleman was highly improper in their country, and they could not insult him in such a manner. The unfortunate Sheikh had to give up the hunt and pocket his disappointment.

Our Towarah had promised to wait for our starting on Tuesday, before they should leave; but to our surprise, we saw them making ready for departure, and Besharah came to make his farewell. I told him I could not wish him peace, if he acted so ungratefully, after our kindness; but he insisted it was not his fault —he would be very glad to stay and do everything in his power for us; but his men were paid and wished to be off, and he was afraid to remain alone. All this was merely a scheme for renewed "backsheesh," and our circumstances were such that we were forced to offer the Arabs the desired reward for remaining. But Tuesday came, and no camels or Alawin (as promised by Sheikh Hossein) were to be seen. The Towarah were now very impatient to depart, and I therefore thought best to make a clean breast to Besharah. I took him to a side tent, and frankly told him how we were circumstanced; that we feared treachery from Hossein, and wished his Towarah to remain as our escort in case circumstances would require our retreat from Akabah. I thus trusted to his honour, and he replied by the odious and unceasing "backsheesh." I was fairly disgusted. I told him he was an ungrateful fellow, and that I had largely fee'd him during the route. I then recapitulated the various presents he had received. He seemed to have some conscience left, and withdrew his demand.

Meanwhile we were roasted, toasted, and broiled beneath the burning sun of Akabah, the mercury keeping up manfully among the hundreds. We imagined the approach of all sorts of diseases, and even fell into a melancholy; home almost sank beneath our mental horizon, and frightful deserts, with savage Arabs, filled our desponding vision. We had studied Akabah till every stone was familiar, and we had pondered so vehemently on Solomon's navy at this Ezion-Geber, that the thought of the Israelitish fleet was a painful incubus upon our minds, for life at Akabah had few incidents to divert our weary spirits.

Sheikh Hossein would now and then form some relief. The Sheikh was an immense consumer of tobacco and coffee, and never seen without his pipe or coffee-cup. He called himself fifty years of age, but another fifteen might be added without endangering the truth. His flowing scarlet robe was always a conspicuous object among the palms, and report says it was a gift from Linant Bey, (Mons. Linant), the companion of Laborde. He has six sons and two daughters. He is quite tall, with a wild but artful face, and is regarded with the greatest deference, not only by his own, but by the neighbouring tribes. A dispute having occurred between the Syrian Giovanni and one of the Towarah, it was referred to Hossein as judge. He acted the umpire with immense dignity, and gave a final decision.

The Governor's daughter, a dirty little child, in faded finery, sometimes honoured our tents with a visit, on which occasions a score of ragged Akabans would look wistfully upon the heiress apparent, as if ardently desirous of the high rank that could be conferred by the possession of her hand.

Tuesday was waning, and still no Alawin arrived. We therefore sent for Hossein and told him our determination to go the other route with the Towarah, unless the camels should be forthcoming that evening. The Sheikh courteously assented to this arrangement, and moreover affirmed that in that case he would return all the money already paid him, and pay us an additional sum for our disappointment! He added, that he could swear to us of the certain arrival of the camels that night.

True enough, as the shades of evening were gathering over Akabah, a hundred wild Alawin on fleet dromedaries came rapidly down the sand-hills, and poured into the palm grove, by the side of our encampment. They maintained a solemn silence as they entered a large enclosure of palms, and afforded us one of the most romantic spectacles we ever witnessed. Their swarthy visages and Bedawee garb, the multitude of camels, the dim twilight, and the green palms, formed a scene of indescribable interest. We almost shuddered to think of putting ourselves into the hands of these fierce sons of Esau. They wore the Bedawee kefiyeh in place of the turban of the Towarah, and the match-lock of our old escort was

ARRIVAL OF THE EDOMITES.

transformed to the more certain flint. The Alawin were evidently a higher order of Bedawin than the Towarah, and we conceived a degree of respect for them that no Arab had before inspired. Many of them bore a stick of the same shaped handle as is seen in the Egyptian sculptures as held by the deities.

They sprang from their camels, and our future guide, Mohammed, with Salim, brother of Hossein, came forward and shook us each by the hand, touching their lips and heart. The rest prepared food for the kneeling camels, and as darkness spread, bivouac fires enlightened the grove, and threw an additional charm on the strange scene.

That evening Hossein, Mohammed, and another Alawy Sheikh, took coffee with us, and promised to start in the morning, as soon as we should select our camels. Our Towarah were again bribed to wait another day, and see us off. Besharah even consented to go with us to Dhahariyeh, in order to comfort Ibrahim, who was greatly attached to him; but on second thoughts he gave up the idea, probably not being overanxious for so close proximity to the Alawin.

True to his word, Sheikh Hossein's corps of camels and Edomites were all in readiness at an early hour, and the scarlet-robed monarch was busying himself among his forces, determining who should go and who should stay. His pipe was ever in his mouth, and a cloud of smoke continually surrounded his head. Twenty-seven good camels were selected and loaded, our Towarah assisting as experienced hands. As it turned out, Hossein added two camels beyond the contracted number. As soon as I perceived this, I called the old nabob, and told him that this wouldn't do—that such a method of obtaining money was not capable of success. The magnanimous chieftain astonished me by assuring us we should not be at a single para's expense beyond the amount contracted.

Mohammed, our young leader, was also clothed in a robe of scarlet cloth, with a gown of Brousa silk beneath—his head was covered with a gay silk kefiyeh, bound by a rope of camel's hair—and his bare legs stood out of a rusty pair of huge boots, of Frank workmanship, the gift of some past traveller.

Edom.

THE ARABAH—MOUNT HOR—PETRA—ITS WONDERS—DEPARTURE.

At half-past seven o'clock on Wednesday morning, May 2d, we quitted the grove of Akabah, and parted from our good but begging Towarah. We took our way over the sand-hills to the North, leaving the mounds of Elath on our left. The Great Arabah was here about six miles in width, and directly across we saw the difficult pass of Akabah, that gives name to the palm grove and castle we had left. Joseph Pitts, to whose remarkable effort of authorship we have before referred, seems to have experienced the weariness of this pass; his quaint words are these:—" About ten Days before we got to *Cairo*, we came to a very long steep Hill, called *Ackaba*, which the *Hagges* are usually much afraid how they shall be able to get up. Those who can will walk it. The poor Camels, having no Hoofs, find it very hard Work, and many drop here. They were all untied, and we dealt gently with them, moving very slowly, and often halting. Before we came to this Hill, I observed no Descent, and when we were at the Top there was none, but all plain as before." He then profoundly adds, " We passed by Mount *Sinai* by Night, and, perhaps, when I was asleep; so that I had no Prospect of it !"

It is well known to everybody that an immense depressed plain or valley extends from the Dead to the Red Sea, a distance of about ninety miles. This valley really commences beyond the Dead Sea, northward, and even beyond the Sea of Tiberias, at the foot of Mount Hermon, forming an entire length of 230 miles. It is called in the Hebrew Scriptures the "Arabah" (ערבה), which signifies "a sterile region," and the portion of the plain between the Dead and Red Seas is known to this day among the Arabs by the same name. The word "Arabia" is derived from the identical root. The valley varies in width from five to fifteen miles, and is bounded by rocky cliffs or precipitous mountains. It has been supposed by many that the Jordan passed through the whole extent of this plain previous to the destruction of Sodom and Gomorrah, and emptied itself into the Red Sea. This theory has been stoutly opposed, and the discovery of the great depth of the Dead Sea by Lieutenant Lynch, has given confidence to the opponents. They place Sodom and Gomorrah in the great south bay of the sea, which is only a few feet in depth, and this portion, they imagine, was first overflowed at the destruction of the cities, while the major part of the sea, lying north of the peninsula, had ever been the reservoir of the Jordan's waters. There is certainly a great plausibility in this conjecture, but a statement in Genesis makes me believe that, although the north part of the sea was probably existing from the earliest period of the world, yet the Jordan flowed through it (as through the Sea of Tiberias) to the Red Sea. The statement in Genesis is contained in the 10th, 11th, and 12th verses of the 13th chapter. Here Lot is described as lifting up his eyes and beholding "all the *plain of Jordan.*" Then he "chose him all the *plain of Jordan,*" and "pitched his tent *towards Sodom.*" As Sodom must have stood at the south extremity of the original sea, and as by the manifest signification of the text, Sodom was either *in* the plain of Jordan or upon its very borders, the conclusion is very urgent that the Jordan must have again made its appearance south of the sea. In that case the Red Sea could have been the only receptacle of its waters. I saw nothing in the character of the Arabah to militate against this belief, though a scientific investigation might raise new objections. Such an investigation should be undertaken as a proper sequel to the expedition of Lieut. Lynch. At the same time the real level of the Sea of Tiberias should be decided, and then the exploration of the Jordan valley might be considered complete.

To return from this Jordanic digression.

The Arabah, during our first day's travel, was well sprinkled with seyal and turfa trees, and many varieties of herbs, which gave an appearance, at a distance, of a cultivated plain. On approach, the intervals of sand or gravel between the trees and bushes dissipated the welcome illusion. The surface of the plain was slightly uneven, and here and there was broken by the descending beds of side wadys, which boldly projected almost to the centre of the Arabah in huge inclined planes, whose summits were among the lofty cliffs. At one point we passed a small hollow that bore marks of having retained the waters of the winter rains until recently.

We had only been four hours from Akabah, when Mr. Mohammed informed us he was about to halt for the night. It was then a half hour before noon, and we were highly amused with his cool effrontery. On asking the reason of so absurd a desire, he said he was himself willing to proceed, nay, rather anxious to continue the march, but it was *customary* (the old song) to stop at that point, and his Arabs wished to conform to the time-honoured habit, for beyond we could find no browsing for the camels. We said nothing in reply, but ourselves and servants kept resolutely on our way, and the rest deemed it prudent to follow. The excuse about the browsing, we found, as expected, a Bedawin hyperbole; we had learned to place a just estimate on an Arab's words, and always laid our course accordingly, as the mariner is guided by the magnet (though it never tells the true north) by making a due allowance for its variation.

The mountains on either side were lofty and savage —especially did the craggy summits of Mount Seir, upon our right, present a forbidding aspect. Our escort was now composed of thirty armed Alawin, which, with our own party, completed the number of forty-three souls; a Gaza merchant, a forlorn negro, made the forty-fourth, and we thus considered ourselves sufficiently formidable to oppose a stout defence in case of attack, for the Arabah is a noted field for marauding parties, as it is a sort of neutral ground and boundary of several tribes. The curious formation of the Arabah, the unfrequented character of the route, the wild nature of our Alawin, the apprehensions of attack, and, moreover, the Scriptural associations of the region, all combined to fill our minds with intense interest and excitement. While at Akabah, and when perplexed amid the difficulties of our future route, I had accidently opened my Bible to this appropriate passage, " Who will lead me to the strong city? Who will bring me into Edom?" and my spirit had taken courage at the reply that is appended, " Even thou, O God!" This question and answer were ever in my mind as we toiled along the arid plain of the Arabah, and most fully was its purport accomplished with us, though in so different a manner from its original design and fulfilment. We felt the continual presence of the Guide of Israel through this desert of Israel's wanderings, and by his merciful hand were led safely to the termination of our projected journey.

At 3¼, P. M., of our first day, Mohammed again proposed a halt. There was still an hour of our day's quantum remaining, but as Ibrahim was fearfully sick with his fever, we consented to pitch, and so did about twenty-four miles from Akabah, by the side of an extensive salt marsh, now nearly dry, but thickly encrusted with salt. This marsh occupies the centre of the Arabah, and appeared to us about two miles in length. We had found our new camels much stronger and of quicker gait than those of the Towarah, making three miles to the hour, instead of the two and a half miles of our old carriers. The Alawin themselves, though showing less civilization than the Towarah, behaved respectfully and obligingly. Indeed, on our whole journey to Hebron they acted most unexceptionably, always complying with our requirements, assisting us in every way possible, and entirely avoiding the wearisome begging that so cancelled the good qualities of the Towarah. Especially was Mohammed an example to sheikhdom: he mingled the indefatigable benevolence of a philanthropist with the gallantry of a finished beau. So delighted were we with the youthful chieftain, that we sent back from Hebron to his father a most complimentary epistle regarding his son's excellencies, that must have been a pleasant draught for the old man's pride.

Our second day from Akabah was very hot, and the reflection from the sand exceedingly annoying. We kept close to the eastern mountains, in order to skirt the salt marsh, and then our route again lay nearly in the centre of the plain. The Arabah now grew wider at every mile, and we found ourselves (just north of the marsh) among reddish sand-hills that were sprinkled with tufts of herbs. This character of the ground continued throughout the second day, the sand-hills appearing about twenty or thirty feet in average height. An hour and a half north of the marsh, a large inclined plane, the mouth of a wady, of this peculiar red colour, comes over from the eastern range, and here appeared to us to be the watershed of the Arabah. The table-land of the watershed continued a mile or two, and then there was a perceptible gradual descent northward. The elevation of the watershed seemed to us to be no obstacle whatever in the way of the Jordan theory. Finding a large quantity of rain-water standing in pools a little further to the north, we halted and refreshed ourselves. We found it comparatively cool, and of good taste. The delight experienced at finding such a reservoir in the burning desert is utterly unappreciable by those at home. The quenching of the severest thirst acquired among scenes of verdure or the objects of civilized life, cannot give the flush of enjoyment that pervades a desert-weary pilgrim at the sight of a brimming pool. In the former case, the very sight of surrounding objects forms a pleasure to the spirit, and serves to break the force of the joy of quenched thirst; but in the latter case, the transition from a choking dryness to full satisfaction in its removal is immediate. No attractive scenes let you down easily to the fulfilled desire, but in an instant you make the exchange of unalloyed misery for perfect satisfaction.

Another hour brought us to a little wady within and parallel to the Arabah—a wady within a wady. It was only eight or ten feet broad in some places, and its banks were about six feet high. Mohammed called it Wady Heimah. The mountains now on either hand appeared to become lower, those on the east retiring, and a new link of lower sandy-looking hills occupying the old line of their front upon the great wady. The mountains behind became more pointed and broken—those on the west, though apparently lower, retained their former appearance of steep, regular, dark granite cliffs. That evening we encamped in Wady Ghurundel, which runs out from the eastern hills down (it is supposed) to the Wady Jeib—a large wady that drains the Arabah and empties into the Dead Sea. In the cool of the evening we walked out from the camp to examine a ruin near the foot of the cliffs, for we had encamped close under the eastern range. The ruin is of a stone building, of small dimensions, and was originally, it is probable, a station erected by the crusaders. It is on a hillock by the side of Wady Ghurundel, just after it issues from its mountain-dell. We walked up the narrow defile, and soon came to the brook of Ain Ghurundel and about two acres of coarse grass, six or eight feet high. A dwarf palm bush and other trees grew around; but the palm tree, mentioned by preceding travellers as standing at the mouth of this dell, was no longer there, having been blown down in the past winter.

The next morning we found a heavy dew was on our tent, the first we had noticed in the desert. As usual, we were on our way by six o'clock, and soon reached a ridge of sand-hills, varying (we supposed) from fifty to three hundred feet in height, that ran slantingly across the Arabah. These hills effectually prevent any water at the south from flowing directly into the Dead Sea, but from our previous observation regarding the watershed, we had no doubt that between that watershed and these hills all water ran down to the west side of the Arabah, and then bent around these hills to the Dead Sea. These hills do not touch the eastern range of mountains, but are connected with it by an elevation of the desert, which is an effectual barrier to the passage of water. It was over this we passed. Some plantations of fine wheat (Arab. "Zerra") were seen towards the centre of the Arabah. These were owned jointly by the Alawin and Haiwat tribes, some of which latter were seen with their camels busied about their grain. Several came out and saluted our escort. Multitudes of large storks were hovering over this attractive portion of the desert, or standing amidst the crop. The whole Arabah is covered with tracks of large birds, and probably they are made by these storks and the vultures, which were also seen in great number. At eleven o'clock, Mohammed rode up to my side, and pointing eagerly to the north-east, exclaimed, "Jebel Neby Haroun! Shoof! Shoof!" I looked, as he pointed; a wild sea of desolate summits rose before us, and, slightly more conspicuous than the rest, was the mountain-top where the first and greatest high priest of the Jewish ceremonial laid aside his robes of office, and yielded his breath to Him that had given it.

It was at the foot of these mountains that Israel had rested, while Moses, Aaron, and Eleazar, "went up into Mount Hor in the sight of all the congregation," and here the tribes had mourned for thirty days. We now commenced mounting over sand-hills, gaining finer views of the Arabah, and the desolate extent of western mountains. The way was rough and stony, and led us into the mountains of Seir. About noon, rocks of most fanciful shapes arrested our attention, on one of which was a ruin (probably of a crusading guard-house), admirably posted for observation of approaching enemies towards Petra. There appeared to be remnants of another on the other side of the road. The way grew wilder continually. But Hor rose directly before, and on its summit the white tomb of Aaron shone brightly in the sun's rays. At two P. M. we encamped at the mouth of Wady Abu-Gesheibeh, on an open inclination, looking down upon the broad Arabah we had left. In the afternoon, we suddenly saw our Alawin spring to their guns, and make quick preparation for battle. They had detected some moving figures among the bushes below our camp, and in an instant they were off to meet the supposed enemy. A moment's suspense, and the imagined foe proved to be a few Aiziyeh from the vicinity of Hebron. Thus was all our pomp of warlike preparation completely fruitless, and in place of trophies, our brave defenders only brought back to camp a half-dozen mouths to feed. These Aiziyeh were on what we should call a Quixotic adventure. One of their tribe had been missing, and supposed to have been slain by some members of a tribe twenty days to the south-east of our camp. These valiant six were on their way to revenge his death. Not only did such an operation resemble the search after a needle in a hay-stack, but the attempt seemed about to terminate in a certain capture of a Tartar. But they were more experienced in these matters than we, and very probably in the end they obtained the satisfaction that would have exactly suited some home-fools—either the death of an enemy or their own fall. The latter sort of satisfaction has ever been a problem, and unfortunately it puts the receiver entirely out of the power of instructing us with an analysis of the pleasure, so that we must ever be in darkness on that point.

During the night we stationed sentinels, as we had entered a region that bears an indisputable title to insecurity. Almost every traveller, who has penetrated these fastnesses, has found a hornet's nest, and we were not sufficiently sanguine to expect an exception from the usual entertainment.

On leaving our camp, (the fourth day from Akabah,) we immediately struck into Wady Abu-Gesheibeh, a beautiful narrow ravine, where tall oleanders in full flower lined the way. The rocks exhibited faces of a mahogany hue, and stood out in a thousand strange and frowning positions. In a half hour we reached the foot of the Great Pass of Abu-Gesheibeh, that conducts to the rock-hewn metropolis. Then came two hours of severe climbing up the steep and winding ascent, the camels halting, slipping, and disarranging their loads; and we, on foot, encouraged in all the toil by the view we should obtain from the summit, and by the near proximity of Petra. The camels leaped like goats from rock to rock, and found a footing where a mule would have been seriously disheartened. It was a wild sight,—the swarthy Bedawin and laden camels toiling up the mountain-side, now hidden by projecting crags, and now brought into full relief upon some lofty rock. The poor beasts groaned pitifully with the severity of the labour, and their lamentations were mingled with the cries of the Arabs, who were urging on their faltering footsteps. We hastened forward to the summit, and turned to enjoy one of the grandest views we had ever beheld. The vast expanse of the Arabah lay at our feet, and beyond extended the high western desert. There, before us, was the fountain of Er-Weibeh, on the western skirt of the Arabah. This was the Kadesh-barnea of Israel, and to it and beyond it over the grim mountains lay our future route to the Land of Promise. Immediately around us was a tumultuous sea of mountains, and turning, we looked upon the dark peak of Hor surmounted by its whitened Wely. We could not gaze enough upon this wonderful landscape, and with reluctance left our post of observation to descend the eastern side of the pass. This side was much less in height, the valleys and ravines of the whole region of Seir being greatly elevated above the Arabah. On reaching the base of Mount Hor, we alighted and sent on the dromedaries and camels, intending ourselves to pass over the mountain into Petra, while the caravan made the circuit. We were accompanied by four Arabs, two being the Wady Mousa Sheikhs who had joined us at Akabah. One of these Sheikhs was a nephew of the notorious Abu-Zeitun, who had caused all the trouble with Irby and Mangles, and afterwards with Dr. Robinson. This nephew was as ugly in visage as his illustrious uncle had been in heart. His head resembled a naked skull, and with his Bedawee rags gathered about his person, he only needed the pale horse to appear exactly the King of Terrors. He endeavoured to make himself particularly agreeable to us,—a result, however well meant, certainly of impossible attainment. In three-quarters of an hour we reached the top of Hor, after a rough and rapid climb over a steep and rocky side, now and then broken by short levels. Just below the very pinnacle is a basin of considerable dimensions. Of course the height of the mountain is not to be determined by the forty-five minutes of our ascent, as our point of starting was a valley raised an immense height above the level of the sea. The summit of Hor is very small,—scarce larger than to serve as a platform for the tomb of Aaron. This tomb (though of *Hor* antiquity) is a modern building, of about twenty-six feet square and twelve feet in height. In one corner rises a small white dome. The material is the stone of the mountain, coated with plaster. The roof is flat, and forms a grand observatory. The interior is arched, like the crypt of an old English cathedral, and the roof is supported by one massive column in the centre and one against the wall forming a pilaster. The centre column is hung around with rags, as is also the tomb itself, which is a stone box-like structure, (of the usual shape of Moslem tombs,) situated near the entrance door, and ornamented with Arabic inscriptions. At the furthest end of the building from the door is a stairway leading to the vault beneath. Over the tomb are suspended a few ostrich eggs, to which one of our friends' servants, a mischief-loving Greek, tied a card of a Smyrna Hotel, with his own name duly emblazoned thereon. It was a novel place, on the dreary peak of this distant desert mountain, to advertise an inn, and it is highly probable that the Smyrniote card appeared to the simple Bedawin the mystic talisman of the Frank.

The view, like that from the top of the Pass, was remarkably extensive and soul-stirring; but from this point two objects were in sight that had not caught our vision before—Petra and the Dead Sea. Of Petra, little was seen, but that little was the beautiful Ed Deir, its fine façade perched strangely on the side of a distant cliff. So unbecoming this wild place was the finished temple, that in spite of our knowledge of its existence, we were startled at its presence. It was as if, while wandering through a savage forest, our eyes should suddenly fall upon a fair and noble lady arrayed in all the drapery of a court. We looked earnestly and thoughtfully upon the distant enchantment, and longed to reach the mysterious City of the Rock.

The extreme south of the Dead Sea lay northward. On its eastern shore rose the mountains of Moab, and our Arab guides pointed out the lofty Kerak. The large Wady Jerafeh ran into the Arabah from the south-west over against Mount Hor, forming a conspicuous object in the view. We spent twenty minutes upon the summit, and then descended the eastern side. We could see our camels like mites in the distance below us, wending their way towards the opening of Wady Mousa. We found the descent exceedingly steep and broken by rocks and gullies. In a half hour we gained the valley. Another half hour of rough surface among rocks brought us to excavations, on either side, in the limestone and sandstone cliffs. These were the suburbs of the city. A short distance beyond, we turned a projecting mountain, and Petra, the ancient, mysterious Petra, burst full in view, —a large retired basin, surrounded by lofty cliffs of dark rock, that were honeycombed with the dwellings of the Edomites. One lonely column stood before us. We soon reached the spot, and found the column attended by fallen brethren; all, however, of a late period. The path was still excessively rough and broken. On all sides the artificial caverns looked down upon us, some of them apparently inaccessible in the lofty cliffs. In five and a half hours from our previous encampment, we quietly pitched in the centre of the deserted city, by the dry bed of the stream that almost equally divides the site of Petra. Petra consists of a large basin among the mountains; this basin is of very irregular surface, and is surrounded by cliffs of red sandstone. It is almost completely shut in by these natural walls. The story, however, of its being accessible only by one route, is false. Dr. Robinson entered by one way and left it by another. We entered and left it by a third. The Sik ravine appears to be the only way of entering Petra by a path level with the general surface of the basin, the other routes bringing one into its solitudes over hills and mountains. The ravine, opposite the Sik, through which the same stream flows, is said by the Arabs to be impassable. Our entrance was made over the southern hills.

We saw much pasture on the limestone hills that lay behind the basin, which reminded us of the Downs of England. Even the red sandstone cliffs supported on their summits and on their ledges a growth of grass and cedar trees. The oleander was plentiful, ornamenting the wild scenery with its gay flowers. The basin itself contains the few remains of *buildings* that Petra boasts, its tombs and temples being for the most part rock-hewn, and as lasting as the mountains themselves. These remains are an embankment of *masonry* along a part of the steep sides of the brook's channel, probably the pieces of a former bridge—a ruined triumphal arch, bearing some fine traces of the chisel in its ornaments, and which was composed of a main and two side passages—and a fragment of a palace, called among the Arabs by the ridiculous name of "Kasr Pharon," or "Palace of Pharaoh." These remains are of a light freestone. The columns, before mentioned, may be added as the relics of *stone and mortar* Petra, and all these must find a date among the reigns of the later Roman emperors. It is *rock-hewn* Petra that is of gray antiquity, and even then it is not the façades of beauty that tell of the days of Solomon, but the plainer caverns of the rugged cliffs. The carved work of Petra betrays the chisel of the Roman artist. Our first visit (after a brief rest) was to the high temple of Ed-Deir, whose distant grace we had viewed from the summit of Mount Hor. This was the most remote object of sight from our encampment, and we therefore deemed it wise to make our first examination *there*, lest a sudden departure (so common to sojourners at Petra) should entirely defraud us of the visit. We proceeded along the southern bank of the stream, passed the ruins above mentioned, then crossing, took our way northward, along the extreme edge of the basin, close under the cliffs. We soon entered a charming ravine, filled with oleanders; turning westward into a branch ravine of like wildness and beauty, we ascended its bed by steps cut in the rock, and well worn by the rains of centuries. We were a half hour in this romantic scenery, winding among the rocks, before reaching a small grassy plain, on which fronted the object of our search. It looked placidly yet nobly over the vast scene before it; a frowning front would have been ungrateful, for Time had not touched a feature of its face. It had been born amid a thronging population; that host had entirely passed away, and the silence of desolation now surrounded its neglected beauty; yet it wore the same smiling aspect with which it had greeted the crowds of former ages. It had felt no change amid the changes of succeeding centuries. An undying cheerfulness had impressed its quiet existence, that imitated the glory of the ceaseless sun, who casts his rays alike upon the grave-yard and the tournament. We sat long and thoughtfully before it, and could have gazed a year and have been unwearied.

But our time was precious, and we were forced to occupy our moments in *seeing*, and leave *thinking* to a day of less excitement. The temple, façade and all, is carved entirely from the rock, and its ornamental front is, perhaps, a hundred feet in height. A close and critical examination of this façade detracts from its general effect, by exposing its great architectural errors both in design and execution. The broken pediment, which is seen also elsewhere in Petra, is an uncouth conceit, but partially relieved by the round and ornamented tower intervening between the fragments. The capitals of the columns are, moreover, exceedingly rude, the friable nature of the stone probably forbidding any delicate workmanship. The interior is a plain bare-walled excavation, of very moderate dimensions for the height of the façade. At the furthest side from the doorway is a large niche, elevated slightly above the floor, and reached by two small flights of steps, one on each extremity of its base. The walls, though bare of *original* ornaments, are adorned by the names of travellers, for this is the only " Livre des Etrangers " that Petra now possesses. A hundred names are here seen, a majority of which seemed to belong to our fellow-countrymen of the Western World. We could find the record of the visit of only one American lady before us, who had penetrated the innermost recesses of Bedawee life. In front of Ed-Deir, though not obstructing the view from its entrance, are craggy rocks, thoroughly pierced with excavations. One, higher than the rest, vies with Ed-Deir in size, having at its extremity a tasteful niche, decorated with fine bas-relief rosettes and female half figures holding cornucopias. Above this excavation are the relics of a superstructure, from which is a commanding view of Petra, Mount Hor, and the Arabah. This was, doubtless, a prominent watch-station, when there was " wisdom in Teman," and when fierce Edom, in its " terribleness and pride of heart," dwelt in the clefts of the rock. We looked down upon the forsaken city, and thought of the condemnation once uttered against it and now fulfilled. " Thy terribleness hath deceived thee and the pride of thy heart, O thou that dwellest in the clefts of the rock, that holdest the height of the hill: though thou shouldest make thy nest as high as the eagle, I will bring thee down from thence, saith the Lord." " Also Edom shall be a desolation." " No man shall abide there, neither shall a son of man dwell in it." " Edom shall be a desolate wilderness." " I will make thee (Mount Seir) perpetual desolations, and thy cities shall not return." These were the words of the prophets of the Most High, spoken when Edom was rich in her prosperity, her commerce extensive, her armies invincible, and her fields fruitful. How sad the contrast! Now hear the lamentation! " There is Edom, her kings, and all her princes, which with their might are laid by them that were slain by the sword: they lie with the uncircumcised and with them that go down to the pit." If ever man can be impressed with a sense of his own insignificance, and the power of his God, it is when, standing above the forsaken caves of Petra, he looks upon the inspired page, and then upon the desolations of the surrounding scene. In descending to the encampment, we retraced the romantic path, winding witchingly among rocks and bushes, now bringing before us a glorious view, and now shutting us completely in a narrow fissure. At the bottom we entered several caverns. In one, about a hundred yards from our path, we found a large number of skulls and bones, and rags, of the same appearance and odour with the mummy cloths of Egypt. Others contained rude stone sarcophagi. Some had the door-posts and lintels carved ornamentally, but all the interiors were plain and of coarse workmanship. A fine fig tree full of promising fruit grew in the pathway from Ed-Deir.

On returning to our tents, we paid to the death-Sheikh nephew of Abu-Zeitun (who professed to be

Grand Sheikh of Wady Mousa) the ghufr or tax which Sheikh Hossein of the Alawin had represented to the British Consul as a fixed price. This ghufr was 100 piastres (five dollars) for each visiter, and twenty piastres (one dollar) extra for each one who had ascended Mt. Hor. This was a total of forty dollars for our party. We considered the Wady Mousa tribe as having perfect authority to demand this, as much as the government of any civilized land to demand a duty on its imports. We cheerfully paid the amount, and the Arabs received it with an expression of thanks, almost the first I had ever heard a Bedawee make. We paid our Alawin (who accompanied us to Ed-Deir) four piastres (twenty cents) apiece for their trouble. They showed some symptoms of grumbling, but our inimitable young Sheikh Mohammed nipped the murmur in the bud. The distance between Ed-Deir and our encampment was just an hour. Our next visit was to the imposing array of façades upon the eastern side of the basin. One of these has received the name of the "Corinthian tomb" from travellers; but *why* is a mystery, for it could scarcely have been a place of sepulture, or else the tombs of Petra were the most conspicuous objects, which is not at all likely. And I looked in vain to find any Corinthianism in its architecture. The façade closely resembles that of Ed-Deir, and was, without doubt, sculptured at the same late date. It is much defaced by the action of rain upon the soft sandstone. Within, it has large stone stalls against the back and one side. In one of these stalls is a low stone counter, holding three sunken basins, like those seen in the little "bottegas" of Pompeii.

Next to this façade, northward, is one of immense dimensions. It exhibits above its carved portal's row upon row of relieved columns, extending to the top of the cliff. The capitals of these columns were of the same rude and unseemly shape as those of Ed-Deir.

The whole rank of façades on this side are raised high above the level of our encampment, a lofty ledge forming platforms before them. One of these excavations (about sixty feet square) had three niches in the back wall, and three upon the sides, like chapels to a cathedral. Masonry is seen occasionally where a corner needed a finish, or where a cornice was wanted. In one I found a fragment of a "London Times!"

Beyond the columned façade (still northward) is a fine front, at the acute angle formed by a small ravine. This face is turned not, like the others of the row, towards the basin, but towards the north. It bears a Latin inscription beneath its pediment, which puzzled my curiosity to decipher. I endeavoured again and again to climb by a column, but my zeal couldn't furnish me with foothold. I then struck up the ravine, intending to *come around* the inscription, if possible. Some distance behind the edifice, I found means of climbing the cliff, and, on reaching the top, hurried forward to the façade, thinking a triumph already gained. I reached the huge urn that ornamented the summit of the pediment, but my discoveries advanced no further in this direction. The inaccessible inscription was far below me, and an attempt to climb downwards to its level, would have made me an occupant of some grim Petran tomb for a longer period than was desirable. I felt like Tantalus, the water rising to my lips, and I unable to drink. In order to aid my energies, I had concocted ideas of wonderful revelations of Petra history, and accurate delineations of Edom life, all derived from my most profound research among the inscriptions of Mt. Seir, and now all my glorious theories were to be stifled at the birth, just because a pediment chose to be an *impediment*. I wrote the whole Idumean race fools, for carving inscriptions where nobody could read them, and crawled down the cliff again, as sulkily as a whipped schoolboy. The ravine was wildly beautiful, and put me in better humour. I stood again in front of the façade, and endeavoured to read the mysterious words. At length, by selecting the most advantageous position, and studying carefully the long array of letters, I brought off the following as the meagre result of my labours :—

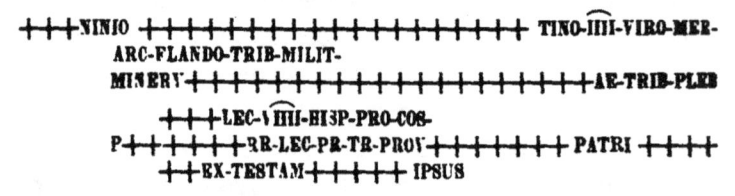

++++NINIO +++++++++++++++++++ TINO-IIII-VIRO-MER-ARC-FLANDO-TRIB-MILIT-
MINERV++++++++++++++++++++++AE-TRIB-PLEB
+++LEC-VIIII-HISP-PRO-COS-
P+++++++RR-LEC-PR-TR-PROV++++++++ PATRI ++++
++EX-TESTAM+++++ IPSUS

Laborde saw this inscription, and supposed he found in it the name of Quintus Prætextus Florentinus; as he mentions no use of ladder, spy-glass, or other help in reading the inscription, either twenty years had greatly defaced the letters, or his powers of sight must have been remarkable, for with a great far-sightedness and persevering labour, the above was all I could decipher.

Southward from this principal row of façades, the celebrated Sik ravine enters the basin, between a projecting hill and the eastern cliffs. On the interior of this projecting hill, in a retired spot, well fitted for the drama, is the rock-hewn theatre. An audience, when witnesses of some well-wrought tragedy, in so wild a scenery of nature, must have kindled with no common enthusiasm. There is no stage on earth more adapted to the graver subjects of the drama than this mountain theatre of the Idumean desert; yet, for more than a thousand years its seats have dwelt untenanted, and the gaunt cliffs have greeted it as a brother in desolation. We strove to imagine it the haunt of busy man, who had retired temporarily from his labour, and would again return to make vocal those solitudes with the sounds of earnest, vigorous life. But we could not enjoy this anticipation, for the forsaken stones bore the impress of the prophet's sentence. " Perpetual desolations," "perpetual desolations" was written on every wall and seat of rock that man had wrought to fulfil his purposes. The noble theatre of the mighty Petra was " a habitation of dragons and a court for owls."

Above the rising rows of semicircular seats, were private boxes, hewn from the rock, where the nobles of Petra had sat untainted by the vulgar gaze. Passing on up the ravine, we struck eastward, and soon reached the Khasné, the gem of Petra. This is a façade of exquisite workmanship, of the same general style with Ed-Deir and the so-called Corinthian tomb, but of far more beautiful detail. It is carved where the rock is of a soft rose-colour, which adds greatly to its ravishing beauties. Its lower columns are Corinthian, of delicate execution. One is missing. Above the centre columns is a rich pediment, sparkling with rarest chisellings. Above these, other columns support a broken pediment and the intervening tower, as in Ed-Deir. One urn surmounts all, which is well chipped by bullets, for the suspicious Bedawee looks upon it as a coffer of old treasure, and seldom passes without sacrificing some powder and lead in an attempt to gain the prize. Hence the name of *Khasné* or *Treasury* is attached to the structure. Several bas-reliefs on pedestals ornament the front, between the columns. Each of the two on either side the grand doorway is evidently a centaur carrying off a female. These bas-reliefs are much injured by the rains. There is a vestibule or porch behind the centre columns, having a doorway in the furthest wall, and one upon each side. The first leads to the main chamber, a plain square excavation; the last two conduct to side chambers, also plain, with the exception of a niche with a grooved floor, that ornaments the side of one. The purpose of the grooved floor to the niche is difficult to decide. The ravine in which the Khasné stands is in reality not the Sik, though, as containing the stream, I have called it by that name. The Sik proper enters this ravine at right angles, directly opposite the Khasné, which must have been sculptured in that position purposely for the effect on approaching from the Sik.

The Sik is one of the most wonderful passes to be found on the earth. Its walls of rock rise two hundred feet over the traveller's head, and between these frowning heights there is scarce a pathway for the camel. In this remarkable ravine the oleander grows luxuriantly, and here and there a green vine clambers along the rock from some slight hollow, where a little earth had gathered. In many places the projecting cliffs almost meet above your head, and noon wears a twilight robe. For two miles this strange and awful pass winds through the heart of the dark cliffs, ere you arrive again in the full blaze of day. Picture the sensations of an ancient citizen of Rome on arriving at this Idumean metropolis. He enters this wild ravine, and feels as if approaching the gates of Orcus. The dark and savage defile appears unearthly, and with his wonder at the novel scene is mingled the sense of desolation. The proximity of the haunts of man is inconceivable, and the Roman of the third century moves on, breathless to know the issue of his strange pilgrimage, when a gleam of sunshine reveals before his astonished vision a temple of the fairest hue and rarest ornament—so lovely in so wild a spot, that it seems a spirit from a higher world alighted for a moments' rest ere it takes flight again for a fitter home.

So admirably have the architects of Petra adapted their works to the natural scenery of that surpassing site.

In a half hour along the dark defile, we reached the spot over which a light arch sprang from cliff to cliff, under which, on either side, was a niche flanked by pilasters. Here was probably the gateway of the city, and here ten men could have made effectual resistance against an army. On returning through the Sik, I found a fragment of a frieze containing a part of a Greek inscription. All that was intelligible were the letters Μ Ε Φ Ο. Traces of pavement remain along the Sik, and a rock-hewn gutter, along which the waters of the winter rains had been conducted, in order to allow a passage for the inhabitants through the defile. On our return, the Khasné burst upon us again, and drew from us expressions of admiration and astonishment, as if it were now beheld for the first. I doubt if the world contains a more enchanting sight than this rosy temple of the rock. Its colour, its position, its material, its delicacy of chiselling, and the wild flowers that grow before its portal, all render it a fairy miracle of loveliness.

Opposite the theatre, the rocks are cut into caverns, of varied ornament. Some bear a remote resemblance to an Egyptian pylon; others are topped by a curious staircase ornament. These seem of older date than the grand façades, and may probably have been the tombs, temples, or dwellings of the ancient Edomites.

We had intended remaining two days in Petra, but

the fierce-looking Arabs of Wady Mousa became so numerous in our camp that we deemed it prudent to leave, after a sojourn of twenty-four hours. They had not molested us; but we had seen the principal points of the wonderful city, and were content to waive a more minute investigation, to obtain a release from anticipations of a brush with our savage neighbours. So at noon of the day following our arrival, we were wending back by our route of entrance, over the rocks and hills, and towards the great pass. We left, fully impressed that the Khasné and Ed-Deir, as well as the fine structures on the eastern cliff, were never tombs, but temples. The elaborate staircase to Ed-Deir and the niche in its wall, the position of the Khasné and its style of ornament, and the apparent signification of a part of the Latin inscription, are some of the reasons for this impression. As we toiled among the inequalities of the path, we saw that " thorns had come up in the palaces of Edom, and nettles and brambles in the fortresses thereof." It is a wonderful accomplishment of God's word that renders Petra an uninhabited city. The caverns stand ready for occupants, but the Bedawee studiously avoids them, and makes his home beyond the confines of the abandoned capital, by the valleys and hills that lie eastward.

Edom and the "South Country."

THE PASS OF RUBEIYA—THE ARABAH—SAND-STORM—KADESH—SUFAH—RUINS.

In about two hours from our encampment, we turned from our former route and commenced the descent of the Pass of Rubeiya, further north than Abu Gesheibeh. This was the worst of all the passes we had seen, and its scenery put Switzerland to the blush. There was the usual amount of camel groaning, the loosening of loads, and the cries of the Arabs, and at a distance of four hours from Petra, we halted (about two-thirds way down the pass) in a little retired hollow that bordered the rough path, and offered just sufficient surface for our tents. The Arabah was spread out before us, and the summit of Mount Hor, with its white wely, appeared over intervening heights. We were struck with the mingling of limestone and red sandstone that marked the whole Petra region. The former generally supported a growth of thin pasture. A black millepede, of eight inches in length, was frequent, but was unlike the other branches of the family with whom I was acquainted, in being very slow in its movements.

Our second day from Petra was spent in crossing the broad, sandy, hot Arabah. Directly across, it was here about ten miles; but by our course, slanting greatly to the north, it was at least twenty, if we call the main mountains of the western side the boundary of the plain. More strictly, the Arabah is hereabouts divided into two descriptions of surface: the eastern portion is a comparative plain, running directly to the mountains of Seir, while on the west, a hilly section occurs before reaching the high mountain barrier of the western desert. We only gained this hilly region on the evening of the second day, after a most fatiguing journey. The day was very hot, and a scorching *khamseen*, like the breath of a furnace, blew in our faces. This raised the loose sand of which this part of the great plain is composed, and filled our eyes with the minute particles. As El Weibeh, which we reached in nine and a half hours, is a great rendezvous for marauders, we were compelled to journey a half hour beyond. A ten hours' camel ride can never be very agreeable, even amid all the luxuries of the earth, but over the Arabah in a khamseen, it savours of the bitterness of the Inquisition. We had just encamped, when the wind violently increased, and a vast cloud of sand was seen to blacken the air on its approach. We thought of the pictured horrors of the Simoon, which we had often imagined, and we quailed. We took shelter behind our tents, and the Bedawin rolled themselves up in their garments to a total disappearance. I was some distance up a side wady, examining a small ruin, when I saw the great cloud whirling onwards. I rushed precipitately to the camp to seek a refuge, and be present in case of danger. I just reached the tents as the storm burst upon us. Though it was early in the afternoon, yet there was the dimness of twilight about us. Our eyes, ears, noses, and mouths, and every nook and crevice of our boxes, were filled with the fine sand. It lasted but a few minutes, and we were relieved for the time from any anxiety; but in the evening we enjoyed another similar gust, which strained our tent ropes as if to bursting. The gale continued violent all night, and we slept in our clothes, through fear of losing our houses.

A short distance from our Rubeiya encampment, we had left Ain Taiyibeh on the left; supposed by some, with much probability, to be the *Mosera* of Deut. x. 6. Shortly after this, we had entered and passed through a wady of very singular formation, a part of the descent of Mount Seir. It was a winding gully, bounded by cliffs of a light clay. Down its centre runs a long rocky ridge, on which is the path for the camels. This ridge is barely wide enough for the beasts, and the traveller, thus mounted on this narrow summit, feels as moving along the ridge of a sloping roof. This wady bears the name of Gunaty, which is most appropriately pronounced *Go-naughty*. This descent had brought us fairly into the Arabah, and straightway all the caravan was formed into a compact body, lest stragglers might be cut off by marauding parties. Scouts were duly despatched in all directions, and the scarlet-robed Mohammed, taking a spy-glass from one of the party, mounted a sand-hill and amused himself by bravely telescoping the whole plain. However, we met no enemies but the khamseen. The path was marked by many parallel camel tracks, as if the route was much frequented. Heaps of stones marked the road where any uncertainty might have arisen. A hare, with ears erect, bounded before us over the sand. Four hours from our encampment, we had seen a dozen or more hewn stones, probably brought from some neighbouring post of the crusaders, and here placed to mark the road. An hour and a half further, we passed down into a wady (another wady within a wady) running N. W. It is called Wady Muthely, and rises a short distance east of the point where we entered it. In a quarter of an hour, we reached its junction, with Wady Jereida which enters from the north-east. This junction is a mile wide. The united wadys are called by the name of Jereida, and down this we kept, its boundary sand-hills completely hiding the rest of the Arabah from view. Turning northward, and cutting off a small corner, we entered Wady el-Jeib, the great drain of the Arabah, in seven hours and fifteen minutes from our Rubeiya encampment. We crossed El-Jeib very slantingly northward, taking an hour and three-quarters for the passage. Mounting its western side, we gained El-Weibeh shortly after three in the afternoon. Here are three springs, a large quantity of coarse grass, a dozen or more palm bushes, and other verdure. Two springs (the more southern) are near together, but the third is a considerable distance to the north-west. The natural taste of the water in the two former was very unpleasant, and in the latter the low state of the spring and the abundance of weeds caused a taste equally disagreeable. The camels, however, all drank heartily. This spot is supposed by Dr. Robinson to be Kadesh-Barnea, and his arguments are plain and powerful. I take this occasion of adding my testimony regarding the wonderful precision of Dr. Robinson's great work. I had his books and maps constantly by me while traversing Arabia Petræa and Palestine, and examined them with more critical scrutiny than it is probable they ever before received. With such admirable opportunities to form a correct estimate of the "Biblical Researches," I unhesitatingly assert my belief that a more minutely precise work was never written by man. We were daily and hourly put to new wonder at its elaborate perfection; and in all differences between the statements of the Arabs and those of Dr. Robinson, the latter would invariably prove correct.

I have mentioned a ruin which I was visiting at the time of the sand-storm. This was about a half mile from our encampment up the Wady Hazoo. Our camp was at the mouth of this wady, (which comes down from the west,) where is considerable verdure, caused by the waters of Ain Hazoo. I strolled up the wady, and found plenty of coarse grass and acacia trees, with a very small stream of brackish water running among them. On a clay hillock of perhaps thirty-five feet in height, and in the centre of the wady, was the ruin, a stone building of rude workmanship, about fifteen feet square; it was a capital look-out, and I suppose may be referred to the days of the crusaders.

In the Arabah we had seen several very large lizards (Arab. "Dhab"), of dusky brown colour, and about eighteen inches long. While in Wady Wettir, before reaching Akabah, we had found one of a gay green hue, and like size.

The next day from Ain Hazoo, we were busy in traversing the hills that form the transition between the lower portion of the Arabah and the high western desert. Our course was not direct to the western mountains, but slanting northward in the direction of Hebron. The hills were of sand, of gravel, and of flint, and among them we crossed several wadys running down to the Jeib. In these wadys grew many seyal trees. Vultures were soaring over our way, and some beautiful gazelles bounded before us. In two hours and thirty-five minutes from Ain Hazoo, we reached the brackish water and slight verdure of Ain Mureidhah. In about three hours after, we ascended the steep pass of Ghurar, which may be called the limit of the Arabah, though even yet a high ridge stood before us, which we were to scale before reaching the table-land of Judea. A half hour took us up the steep, which was followed by a short descent beyond. Then came a sea of gravel and sand-hills, till we crossed the broad Wady Figreh, and reached the foot of the pass of Sufah about half-past two, eight hours and a half from Ain Hazoo. The whole scene was now most dreary, reminding us of the approach to Sinai. The truncated cone of Jebel Madurah lifted its light-brown form on our left—the mountain ridge of a thousand feet in height rose forbiddingly before us, and behind we looked upon a broken wilderness. Three passes in this vicinity scale this mountain-wall: that of Yemen, an apparent gash in the cliffs, was several miles at our left; Sufey was nearer upon our right; and Sufah, with which we had to contend, lay not very temptingly in our course. The theory that makes El-Weibeh the Scripture Kadesh naturally places Hormah at this spot, and Sufah becomes a corruption of Zephath. (See Numbers xiv. 45, and Judges i. 17.) We thought it no wonder that the Amalekites and Amorites had been a little too much for Israel in this spot. I shouldn't have liked to have seen a single Amalekite dispute our passage, or I fear, fagged as we were with the tedious and laborious ascent, we should have not been sufficiently courageous to have denied his authority. We dismounted at the foot, and struck directly up a steep smooth rocky surface, while the camels took a more circuitous path. The heat (half-past 2 P. M.) was intense, and the ascent was pure climbing, and this pleasant work lasted an hour and a quarter, when we flung ourselves down on the summit, thoroughly exhausted, and determined not to stir a step further forward that day. We had never suffered so before. Well is the pass called Sufah (pronounced Suffer.) Our frames were wearied beyond measure, our throats were parched with thirst, and the heat had fevered our systems. We drank and seemed to find no satisfaction, and threw ourselves prostrate under our tents, gasping for breath. The thermometer showed a heat of 97° Fahrenheit in the shade of the rocks, but it was in the *sun* that our fatiguing ascent had been made.

The ruins of Ibrahim Pacha's fort was close to our encampment, on a slight elevation above the small level on which we had pitched. Though Ibrahim Pacha made use of this building, I doubt not it existed long before he passed by with his army. The ruin bears marks of an age at least as distant as that of the crusades. The view hence was similar in character to that from the heights of Petra. The Arabah lay far below us, bounded by the mountain range of Sherah. Immediately beneath us was the sea of sand-hills we had crossed since leaving El-Weibeh. The Ghor at the south of the Dead Sea was visible upon our left, and to the right was the peculiar Jebel Madurah, a striking feature in the view. This Madurah is detached from all other mountains, and rises from the plain as we may imagine the tower of Babel on the plain of Shinar. The Arabs have a story of a city formerly there, and it is highly probable that so fine a site once held a fortress. There was but little fodder for our camels where we had encamped, but we were too weary to think of advancing. The poor beasts had not for two days had much picking, and had all that day travelled slowly in consequence. It was, therefore, with great regret we were forced to deny the patient creatures still longer. We were encamped as on the top of a house, precipices on almost every side, and our tents gathered within a very small compass.

Yet there was a *funniness* in such a lodging place, and the view was so grand, comprising so vast an extent of desert stretched out as a map before us, that we enjoyed our encampment on Sufah with uncommon zest. The repose after our fatigue was no small ingredient of our delight. There, on that dreary summit, as a suitable spot, we reviewed our desert tour, and joyfully anticipated our arrival in two days among scenes of civilized life. No Israelite ever coveted a sight of Canaan more than we. We had found desert journeying, in spite of its romance and novelty, a wearisome task, and Hebron wore, in our minds, a hue of perfect loveliness that we never before had attached to anything earthly.

We had become very much interested in Mohammed, and each evening we held long chats on every conceivable subject on which an Arab is capable of discoursing. We urged upon the young Edomite the advantages of foreign travel, and recounted descriptions of other countries, as baits to his curiosity; but Mohammed was a Bedawee all over; to our queries whether he ever would visit other lands, he gave a most significant "La! la!" (No! no!) and, pointing to the grim mountains of Esau, he said that *there* was his home, and why should he leave it? His ideas of the world beyond the desert were as dark as his face,—even old Besharah had more correct conceptions of Frankdom, for he had made a formal application to us to use our influence in making him Consul of England and America for the Sinai peninsula!!! But Mohammed was above such mean distinction. He had rather a poor opinion of anything or anybody that didn't live among sand and rocks, and was fairly disgusted when he heard that we had no camels in our country. I tried to give him some comprehension of steamboats, railroads, and magnetic telegraphs, but I was compelled to desist, lest the dignified Idumean should fairly write us madmen. He listened with a credence worthy of an auditor of the "Arabian Nights." His knowledge of civilization was not much more extensive than such as was derived from occasional visits to Hebron, and, consequently, the world beyond the desert was to him a confused mass of governors and quarantines. No marvel, the independent warrior saw little attraction out of his wilderness.

The next morning we left Sufah, passing a few small stone buildings near the path, and for an hour descended very gradually over a rough way to the green plain of Et-Teraibeh, that spread out to another low range of heights before us. The green of the plain made us believe we were fairly out of the desert, but it was really but the transition state we were now entering. The verdure was a thin growth of wild barley and wild oats, from among which the scarlet anemone here and there lifted itself. Crossing this plain, the pass of Murzeikah led us up the low range of heights. The ascent was but of twenty minutes, and sufficiently gradual, but the heat of the day and the confined character of the ravine, together with its dazzling limestone, rendered it very exhausting. We soon saw our first Judean ruin. It was Kurnub, situated on a small hill, nearly a mile to the left of our path. Dr. Robinson supposes it the *Tamar* of Ezekiel.

The hills now became greener and more rounded, and the larks were singing about us; we were fast leaving the wastes of the desert. We were entering the land which for 1500 years held the most wonderful people that ever dwelt on earth, and which had borne the footsteps of the incarnate God. The Land of Promise—the land given to Abraham, Isaac, and Jacob —the land of the Redeemer—the land of Comfort and

Hope, was now ours to tread,—we were at its portals, and we entered with the Bible in our hands.

Mohammed had called us aside, and told us if we would give a little for the extra trouble, he would not care for his father's orders, but carry us direct to Hebron instead of Dhahariyeh. Of course, this had been old Hossein's own trick to derive an increase of remuneration, the Hebron quarantine having been a good tool for his purposes. We pretended to exceeding verdancy (as our interest was greatly at stake, owing to the difficulty of procuring animals at Dhahariyeh to take us to Hebron), and told the young Sheikh we would gladly do so. He told us to say nothing (as if he was engaged in a profound exercise of cunning), and he would take the Hebron route. This relieved us of some anxiety, and for the additional distance our model Sheikh was satisfied with a small premium.

In Wady Ararah (Aroer of Robinson), we passed several dam-like structures, of undoubted antiquity, built, probably, for purposes of irrigation, when all this land was so richly fertile as to merit the epithet of "flowing with milk and honey." In this wady we passed some more ruins upon the right and left, to which the Arabs gave the name of El-Kuzeir. It may be the site of Gezer (Joshua, xii. 12, and 1 Kings, ix. 15, 16, 17,) which must have stood in this vicinity. The ruins consisted of small stone buildings, greatly dilapitated. A solitary Dhullam Arab and his camel appeared near the spot. Shortly after, we came to the first wheat field; and after a hot, fatiguing day, we encamped for the last time in the desert, in a tributary of Wady Milh. Some imposing ruins appeared eastward. I ran to them, (perhaps a half mile) and found but the remains of an Arab cemetery. The most conspicuous ruin was of a sort of mosque-tomb, which distance had greatly helped to magnify in my imagination.

Judea.

THE FRONTIER—MAON AND CARMEL—HEBRON—QUARANTINE—
JOURNEY TO JERUSALEM—POOLS OF SOLOMON—GARDENS—
BETHLEHEM—ENTRANCE INTO THE HOLY CITY.

The next morning we were off early, panting after Hebron. The "hill-country of Judea" lay before us. In twenty minutes we arrived at the wells of Milh—two strong-built monuments of ancient Palestine. Their curbs are of fine white marble, grooved by the friction of ropes. In all directions around these wells were strewn quantities of unhewn stone, the materials of a former settlement. We had passed Kurnub at a distance, and El Kuzeir was somewhat removed from our path, but here our route lay directly among the remnants of a town of Judah, of undoubted scriptural antiquity. Here, it is highly probable, Abraham and the two succeeding patriarchs had often watered their immense flocks, for they dwelt, we know, in this vicinity. After them, perhaps, no descendant of the father of the faithful had visited these refreshing waters, until Caleb and his colleagues, while traversing the country between Kadesh and Hebron, rested here, we may believe, from the fatigues of their desert journey. Thirty-eight years thereafter, Joshua, as commander of the host of Israel, had swept this southern land with the besom of destruction, and the children of Judah became the fixed possessors of the soil. Yet this frontier station must have felt the force of the frequent invasions of the surrounding nations. The Mesopotamians, the Moabites, the Midianites, the Amalekites, and the Philistines, had severally seized upon the outskirts of Judah, and these wells had often satisfied the thirst of these hostile tribes. Still, under the Judges, the enemies were again and again repulsed. During the administration of the holy Samuel, the land was comparatively free from these marauders; but when Saul became the first monarch of Israel, the Philistines seem to have attained their greatest vigour, and his whole reign was spent in warfare with these pertinacious foes. Under David and Solomon, this frontier enjoyed its longest period of rest; but the sins of Rehoboam brought up a greater enemy than the land had ever before known, in the person of Shishak, King of Egypt. Then, again, this southern border enjoyed a long period of quiet through many reigns, while the sins of Judah were visited by incursions of enemies upon the north. In the reign of Hezekiah, it is probable the Assyrian hosts of Sennacherib spread themselves over this region; for we hear of them at Lachish, in the south of Judah. Under Manasseh the Assyrians were again troublesome; and Josiah found in Pharaoh-Nechoh another Shishak. The land was now so enfeebled that the Egyptian conqueror even named its monarch, when Nebuchadnezzar, the great autocrat of Babylon, snatched the prey from Nechoh's hands, and for seventy years a foreign sway afflicted the country of David and Solomon. Then came the return of the captives, by order of Cyrus; but, both under the Persian and Grecian empires, this border could have seen but little peace, situated as it was between the great provinces (and afterwards independent sovereignties) of Egypt and Syria. Even the

Roman power could not entirely arrest the incursions of the Arab tribes. Rome gave way to Moslem might, and the last thousand years have witnessed the weakening influences of the Prophet's sway.

No marvel, then, that ruins mark the former sites of cities in this border-land. We thought of the various nations whose representatives had slaked their thirst at these old wells during the past three thousand years, and speculated on the wonders that the future might reveal in this neglected spot.

This Milh is supposed by Dr. Robinson to be the Bible *Moladah*, not from etymological but from historical testimony.

From Milh we struck north-easterly past the hill of Kuseifeh* to the range of heights before us. Kuseifeh showed extensive ruins on our left, and among them two columns were conspicuous. In three hours from Milh we were gently ascending among the hills, and shortly after saw gladly the first ploughed field—then came another and another—flocks of sheep and goats, with tending herdsmen, were now first seen—the desert was fast passing away. A horse next caught our attention —this too was the first of its kind we had seen since leaving Egypt, and as it passed by our camels, we laughed loudly at its pigmy appearance. It bore a Jehaly Arab, armed with a lance of unreasonable length. Near by was an encampment of Jehalin, the black tents clinging to the hillside. El Kuryetein, the ruins of a considerable town, was passed upon our right. Is not this the Kerioth of Joshua (xv. 25)? Here were many Jehalin, the Abrahams and Isaacs of the day, with their flocks, herds, and camels. A steep ascent of thirty-five minutes brought us to the summit of the

---

* Perhaps this is the *Ziph* of the Southern country of Judah (Joshua xv. 24.)

heights, and we were now in the hill country of Judea. A fine view of the mountains of Moab presented itself, though a range of intervening sandy heights completely shut from view the basin of the Dead Sea. We continued along an elevated ridge for an hour, the path being almost on a level. We thought of Abraham, who looked from a point only a few miles further north upon the smoke of burning Sodom. The dense cloud of vapour lifting itself from behind those dreary hills must have formed a scene peculiarly impressive to the mind of the patriarch. Several deep cisterns, with small and well-like mouths, attracted our attention along the road. Each had a huge stone rolled into the mouth, so large, however, as to prevent its falling into the cistern;—this custom brought forcibly to mind the sweet pastoral scene of Jacob and Rachel, which occurred by "the great stone that was upon the well's mouth." Descending slightly, we passed the ruins of Maon and Carmel—the former upon a conspicuous hill, and the latter further north and more extensive. The principal ruin at the latter is the large castle, which is placed by Dr. Robinson in the Herodian age, and its pointed arches are supposed to be a modern repair of the Saracens. Its arched roof is in ruins. About the remains a few Arabs were feeding their flocks, and some of their number had climbed to the top of the walls to gaze at the passing strangers. East of the main ruins is a natural amphitheatre, formed by the hills, in which is a large reservoir of water, from which some shepherds were busily engaged in drawing. Of course we could not look upon these ruins and these rural scenes without deep emotion, and a vivid recollection of the story of Abigail, the Carmelitess. "There was a man in Maon, whose possessions were in Carmel." His dwelling was on the loftier height of Maon, while his farm lands lay in the more fertile region of Carmel, a few miles northward. David had been hiding at Engedi, near the Dead Sea, some fifteen miles to the east of Carmel, and getting knowledge of a sheep-shearing (always a time of merriment) that was taking place on the farm of the wealthy Nabal, he despatches a commission to the Carmelite to ask a participation in the joy. They naively remark that they had " come in a good day," but their hints are of no avail, and they bring back word to David of their disappointment and insult. Then comes the preparation for revenge on the part of the young Bethlehemite, and the propitiatory conduct of Abigail. The laden asses and the fair escort meet the youthful warrior, and his revenge gives way to love. Nabal dies, and Abigail becomes the bride of David. This romantic yet truthful story threw an indescribable interest over the spot. We felt we had reached enchanted ground, and the delight of past scenes was forgotten in the superior enjoyments of the Land of Promise.

At Carmel we saw the first cows, of a very small breed, and shortly after discovered several yoke of oxen before the ploughs. These ploughs were of rude construction, but had one improvement I had not expected to see in Palestine,—this was a tin tube running down behind the coulter, and into which the ploughman cast the seed as he ploughed. The character of the surface, with its beaten path, its rocky ground, its thorny thickets, and its fertile patches, brought to our minds the parable of the sower. The flat rocks are in many places hollowed to receive water, and at these hollows the flocks are watered. On our left we saw Jutta, and about it were the first trees we had seen in Palestine. This Jutta is, of course, the Juttah of Scripture, and most probably the town where Elizabeth lived and was visited by the Virgin Mary.* It was pleasant to look at that cluster of trees, and think of the events, so quiet and yet so fraught with wonderful results to man, that had there transpired.

"Um el-Amad" (the mother of the pillar) was another field of ruins on our right, and soon after Tell Zif, a mound, rose near us, behind which were the ruins of Ziph. The abundance of ruins that a traveller beholds on entering the Holy Land, while it astonishes him, clearly testifies to the former fertility and populous settlement of the country. After passing Tell Zif, we entered the Hebron hills, and for an hour wound among them; the hills were not lofty, and were separated from one another by very narrow valleys. The face of the country all day had resembled that of the downs of England, though much more stony, the soil often appearing very rich. Shrubs grew plenteously, but trees were seen only in a few instances. We had left the plains of wild barley, when we ascended from the level of Milh, and entered the hill country of Judea. I was glad to escape from the almost interminable tracts of wild barley, for its long sharp beard constantly pierced my slippered feet, when I walked, and rendered me a cripple. We had found the hill country (as before said) of a different growth. Cultivation had touched it here and there, and even where no tillage was seen, the wild growth was shrubs and bushes. Such, too, was the general appearance of the hills of Hebron, as we slowly wound among them, till, upon turning a corner, we suddenly saw one of the most transporting sights we had ever witnessed. It was the

---

* St. Luke's words are,'Επορεύθη εἰς πόλιν 'Ιούδα'' (went to a city of Judah). This sense is frigid, and Reland well conjectures 'Ιούτα; the paragraph will then read, "she went to the city of Juttah." This emendation is followed by many distinguished commentators.

Vale of Hebron. Fields of all shades of green lay stretched out before us, and the hill-side smiled with vineyards, green fig trees, olive orchards, and pomegranates. We shouted with inexpressible ecstacy. The last trace of the desert had faded away, and we were again in the world—the world of life and beauty. Another turn brought the gray stone town before our eyes; it rested sweetly along the eastern hill, and we thought it the fairest object on which he had ever gazed. We kept along the pathway, which follows the base of the western hills, and met many women and girls who had come out from the town. One peculiarly beautiful face called out our exclamations, for since leaving Italy we had travelled through lands of feminine ugliness.

Passing along the front of the town, we looked up at the large mosque, the main building of the place, and saw with interest the two pools by our side, one of them "the pool of Hebron" mentioned in Scripture. Turning to the left into a little alcove in the hills, a beautiful green sward lay before us, and here we pitched our tents, in full view of the interesting town. A new, clean looking building, resembling a miniature model of the Sinai convent, stood behind us, and from this issued a deputation to meet us. They stood at a respectful distance, and in a most undignified manner took to their heels if we attempted to be neighbourly. This deputation was composed of several lazy Turks and an Italian doctor. They informed us that persons arriving from the desert were considered in Hebron as infected; that the building so clean and new behind us was the quarantine, and that we were respectfully invited to take up our lodgings therein for the space of seven days. We replied that we regretted that the authorities should be guilty of such folly as to reckon persons infected who had been more than a month on the free, open desert,—that we should, however, obey the powers that were, by remaining stationary for a week, but as to entering a house, in which we knew not how many unpleasant bedfellows rioted, when we had tents in plenty, and a delicious green lawn whereon to encamp, was a thing too preposterous for the honourable delegation to demand. The delegation received our reply with becoming gravity, but entirely demurred from our last position. The building had been erected for travellers, and into it travellers must go. We turned to our Arabs and told them to have the tents pitched as soon as possible, and the delegation were struck dumb by our impudence. We knew their great desire to have us within four walls was to derive increased pecuniary benefits from our sojourn; and we knew, also, that any attempt to force us into the building would place our compellers in a like state of quarantine with ourselves; we therefore stoutly resisted, and had no fear that they would long insist on the matter. It was as we anticipated. The green lawn was, for the time, consecrated to the goddess Hygeia, and we held undisputed sway over this territory. None of the *profanum vulgus* were allowed to come within a respectful distance of our new possession, and we were as proud as the lunatic who fancies himself a king in his cell. Two or three Hebronites entered into our service as "guardians," (a name adopted by the Turks from the Italians, and used throughout the Levant,) to perform various tent duties; and two or three others remained without the infected district, as our messengers to the town for eatables, &c. Two sleepy looking Turkish soldiers, in baggy trowsers, guarded our camp, to prevent our sudden departure; but two muskets without holders would have proved as effectual an obstacle, if we had desired such an issue. However, we could imagine them as guards to our royal selves, and as part of the appurtenances of our green domain.

On each side of our encampment was a Moslem graveyard; behind, the terraced hills rose beautifully, well stocked with olives; and before us was the town, lying along the opposite hills. On the evening of our arrival we paid our Sheikh Mohammed the remaining one-third of the money of the contract, and 500 additional piastres, ($25,) as including both "backsheesh" and extra pay for making Hebron instead of Dhahariyeh the end of his route. He was perfectly satisfied, and thanked us heartily. Though our caravan had consisted of thirty-three camels, yet we paid only for twenty-eight, and not a murmur resulted. This was according to old Hossein's word at Akabah. In all things the Alawin and their sheikhs had treated us with kindness and honour, and we formed a far higher opinion of their noble qualities than we had of the begging, tricking, though good-natured Towarah. I had ridden from Akabah on Sheikh Salim's favourite camel, and a fine animal it was. When I first mounted, Sheikh Salim came up and kissed the petted beast, and then turning to me, said, "As you care for me, care for him." The incident had made a deep impression, shewing what kind feelings may dwell in a Bedawee's heart.

The next morning, after paying Mohammed, I paid the camel-men only five piastres (twenty-five cents) apiece, the *leaders* of our camels receiving twenty piastres ($1.) Notwithstanding the small amount, they were all grateful, and not one asked for a present, excepting a semi-fool of the party, who begged a *kefiyeh*. Mohammed kissed us on both cheeks at parting, and we warmly returned his salutation. We were so pleased with the Alawin, that we could not refrain from complimenting them in the most approved manner, and we gave them loud and cordial huzzas as they left us, the next morning after our arrival, to regain their beloved home in the desert. They looked nobly as they rode off with flying kefiyehs, Mohammed with his scarlet robes conspicuous among his brethren. A quarantine guard on horseback preceded them, to conduct them beyond the bounds of Hebron.

We were joyous in the extreme at having left the desert. A great weight of anxiety was removed from my mind, and I breathed freely. We had undergone fatigue, heat, and thirst, such as we never before had experienced, and our route had been through a land where attack was most to be feared. With all this, we had reached Hebron almost in perfect health, and in the highest spirits. We had all grown perceptibly thin since leaving Cairo, but did not view that as a subject of regret. In the place where Abraham had often lifted up his voice to God, it was no small privilege for us to review our desert journey, and raise our voices in thanksgiving to the same great guide and Saviour.

Hebron lies, as before stated, on the eastern side of the valley and on the slope of the eastern hills. The valley is only a quarter of a mile in width, and in some parts less than that. The town may be divided into three distinct portions; first, the main town, which lay immediately before our encampment, and which covered the hill-side nearly to the summit; secondly, a smaller cluster of houses further north, and extending only one-third the height of the hill; and thirdly, a small quasi suburb on the *west* side of the valley, just south of our encampment. All the houses are of gray stone, and are built in the usual Syrian style, like square boxes, generally surmounted by a small dome.

About the centre of the main town is the celebrated mosque, consisting of a large oblong enclosure, with square tower-like minarets on the N. W. and S. E. corners. The walls are of immense stones, of darker hue than the houses of the town, and adorned with plain pilasters. Along the top of this wall is a battlement of lighter colour and evident modern erection. This wall (as seen from the opposite hill) merely encloses a court, at the south extremity of which is an edifice, closely resembling a country methodist steepleless church. It appears to be plastered without, and has a façade higher than the roof. This building is, of course, the mosque proper, and here is said to be the cave of Machpelah, where Abraham, Isaac, and Jacob and their wives lie buried. The large bevelled stones of the wall must be of great antiquity, and may with reason be referred to the days of Jewish glory. The cave of Machpelah must certainly be in this neighbourhood, and may as well be supposed beneath the mosque as elsewhere; only, in that case, we must consider the town as somewhat moved from its original position, as the mosque is not now in anything corresponding to *a field* of Ephron the Hittite.

Between our camp and the town, just at the foot of our green slope, was the large pool, a well built, rectangular basin of masonry one hundred and thirty-three feet in length, with a descent of stone steps at its eastern corner. It was over this pool that the hands and feet of Rechab and Baanah, the murderers of Ishbosheth, were hung.

For five days we had Hebron, its mosque, its pool, and its surrounding olives, whose ashy foliage covered every hill, before our eyes, and not a feature in the scene escaped our scrutiny. We spent our time in reading the small stock of books we had completely worn out with reading before, in writing letters and journals, and in watching the noticeable occurrences in our vicinity. Quoits and leapfrog were not despised, and in the latter, we worked wonders before the eyes of the Hebronites.

We had sent to Jerusalem to seek a release from quarantine at the hands of the English Consul, but in vain. The only compromise we could effect, was to have our *seven* days interpreted in the Eastern manner, to wit, the *part of seven* days. Our quarantine was, therefore, really to be but of five and a half days duration. Indeed, this was all that had been intended by our quarantine authorities at the first, but we were too tenacious of the Frank system of reckoning to understand.

The first night in our Hebron camp, we were entertained by a wedding festival. We could see the glare of the torches in the town, and hear the monotonous and loud cries of the multitude. We could detect no instrumental music. The song seemed to consist of two responsive dirge-like choruses, each of six syllables, and repeated without abatement, and apparently by the same voices, for hours. It was a most wearisome and doleful jubilee.

The next morning we witnessed a long funeral procession pass into the burial-ground at our side. A number of women, veiled in white, preceded, and a melancholy dirge (the twin of the wedding song) accompanied the solemn march.

For four successive days there was a new funeral procession that issued from the town, and deposited a human wreck among the tombstones of the cemetery. In each case appeared the white-veiled women, always apart from the men, and the dismal chanting was an unfailing accompaniment. The bodies were borne on biers, and reminded us of the scene before the gate of Nain.

Every day (apart from the funeral processions) scores of these white-veiled females would come and sit among the tombs, resembling a flock of pigeons alighted. From a near view of their faces when their veils were withdrawn, we had great doubts regarding the depth of their sorrow. The grave-yard is, rather, a "ladies' exchange" at Hebron, where the fair Syrians assemble to talk scandal over the dead,—as fit a place for such employment as was ever used.

At night, the whole vale echoed with the howls of dogs and jackals roaming after prey. This recalled the words of David regarding the iniquitous—"They return at evening; they make a noise like a dog, and go round about the city."—(Psalm lix. 6.)

Abd-er-Rhaman, the notorious Arab, now Governor of Hebron, often stopped, in passing, and spoke a few words to us. They were always of the same import, begging our camel rope-nets. His gubernational dignity was no obstacle to his grasping propensities, even though begging was the means, and a few ropes the end. We refused the official beggar again and again, but he never wearied of asking. He was a man of, apparently, sixty-five, with a cunning eye, and a mouth in perpetual movement; probably a habit obtained by having been often made to eat his words. He dressed in the Bedawee cloak, and, with his ragged retinue, was a complete "loafer" on horseback. His brother and son sometimes accompanied him in his passages to and from the quarantine establishment.

Our tents having been pitched upon the grass, and every night bringing heavy dews, we found a dampness in our natural floors, exceedingly disagreeable, and the very opposite extreme from our *desert* experience.

The tents every morning were almost dripping with moisture, and our beds and bedding nearly in a similar state; yet, to our surprise, we managed to quit Hebron without cough or catarrh. Long tracks of two inches wide were worn in all directions through the grass by the large black-bodied, red-headed ants, and myriads of these industrious creatures were constantly seen traversing these paths of their own formation. The multitudes of these busy animals, and the regular character of their miniature roads, were incredible, and formed a subject of our astonishment the whole time of our quarantine. We were visited during our stay by several Jerusalemites. Among others, the Secretary of the British Consul arrived, and Mr. Meshullam, whose neat little hotel in the Holy City is well known and praised by every late traveller in Palestine, brought us the latest European news.

We thus remained stationary for our allotted term, enjoying the pleasant prospect of the sweet scenery of the vale. The figs, vines, and pomegranates, we were never weary in viewing; and they clustered about this retired spot so witchingly, that we felt the " happy valley" of Rasselas was here realized.

The afternoon previous to our full liberty, we walked, under the guidance of our guardians, to Abraham's Oak, a half hour north-west of Hebron, along the vale, there considerably enlarged. The road was a rough mule-path, and, in some parts, exhibited specimens of a break-neck pavement. On each side were vineyards and olive orchards, each vineyard having its lodge in the centre,—a plain, square, stone building, " the tower" of our Lord's parable. The round hills were laid out in terraces, supported by stone walls, and here grew all the mingled verdure of fig and apricot, vine, and pomegranate, and olive. Frequently the gray rock jutted out from the fertile soil: this was the "stony ground" of the sower. We passed several wells and springs upon the way, and at one we rested and drank, remembering the incident of Jacob's well, when the wearied Jesus rested upon its brink. The spreading old oak was visible at a distance, and a venerable aspect it had. Its boughs stretch out not more than seven feet above the ground at their extremities, forming a delicious bower for a noon-day siesta. The least circumference of the trunk is twenty-two feet nine inches, and the circumference of the foliage is more than 250 feet! A large grim owl was sitting among its branches, enjoying the twilight of his position, and appearing like a guardian spectre of the tree. The oak is well supposed to have an age of at least five hundred years, though tradition has made itself as ridiculous as usual, in declaring it the very tree of Abraham. Yet it was under such a tree, and in this neighbourhood, that the patriarch entertained his heavenly guests. A well stood near the old oak, and we could fancy that thence the water was drawn to wash the feet of the angel visitants. Not only did we think of Abraham in this interesting spot, but the spies of Israel were present to our minds; for here Sir Moses Montefiore had obtained a bunch of grapes nearly a yard in length, such as those spies had borne "between two, upon a staff," to the camp of their brethren, as tokens of the land's fertility. We were, indeed, in the country of Eshcol and Mamre.

After returning to the camp, we mounted the hill upon the west of the town, behind our green lawn. We ascended over terrace upon terrace, and through a thick orchard of aged olives. On the summit, we found the ruins of a Saracen fort, of one hundred feet square. Many of the rooms were entire, and the stones in some parts of the walls were uncommonly large. The pointed arch, the gingerbread ornaments and flat domes were abundant—the remnants of two good sized columns, a mill partly ruined, and fragments of staircases, were all that was noticeable. From the summit of a tower that rises within, and higher than the walls, we could perceive that no other ruins existed on this hill. A large olive grew amid the ruins, telling of their state of dilapidation for a long period. At length the morning of our freedom dawned. The Italian doctor came and scrutinized our faces, and not being able to find any great paleness or other marks of disease, pronounced us well, and gave us "pratique." Poor Ibrahim, who was still grievously sick, though recovering, was passed over in the examination, he having been enjoined to *look well* in spite of his malady, for we had no idea of having his fever magnified into some contagious disease for the sake of the quarantine fund.

Horses had been provided for our journey to Jerusalem, and we mounted them with new sensations, after a months' experience of camel-riding. Sending on our luggage, we made the first use of our liberty in visiting the town. We entered at the south, and first visited the mosque; a hundred jealous, scowling Mussulmans, watched our survey, to forbid our entrance within the holy place, and we had to rest satisfied with an outward examination. A covered fountain of slight pretensions stood near the walls, but this and the fact that no pilasters were to be found on the back wall, were all the additional discoveries we made. Leaving the mosque, we passed through the bazaars, dark arched ways, like the crypts of a Saxon church, though now and then a gleam of light from some opening in the stone, or a brief space of leafy roof, where vines grew over trellises, gave some relief to the dismal character of the marts of business in Hebron. We noticed two factories of water-skins—the skins stuffed and sunning on the tops of the low houses, looked like the mutilated bodies of their former possessors.

We found Hebron not so clean in reality as it had been in appearance from our encampment. Its narrow lanes were full of oriental fragrance, yet it compared well with any town in Egypt. The population is estimated at ten thousand, one-third of whom are Jews. Judging from the size of the town, I should consider this far too high an estimate, though all rules fail in the census of an Eastern community.

Leaving Hebron at the north end of the town, we took the road to Jerusalem. The vale became gradually broader, but the hills wore the same appearance, round, rocky, well-sprinkled with olives, terraced naturally and artificially, and abounding in vineyards, the vines being so pruned as to resemble young fruit trees. Taking a more easterly valley, we did not pass the old oak. We soon passed the ruined village of Khurbet en Nusarah, and then another known as Ramet el Khulil. Beyond these, on an elevated position at our right, was the mosque Neby Yunus (Prophet Jonah), and the village of Hulhul. Here the Mussulman says the Prophet was buried. One hour from Hebron was Ain ed-Dirweh, a fountain, with many ruins in its vicinity—which Dr. Robinson suggests to be Bethzur (Josh. xv. 58), and Bonar supposes Sirah (2 Sam. iii. 26.) The latter opinion seems to have the best evidence, but both may be correct, the place having possessed two names. There are very few data in the matter.

Beit-Ummer is the name of a ruin upon the left of the road, opposite which is a stagnant pool of apparently ancient date. Then came Beit-Hagar and Beit-

Haran, so thickly scattered are the ruins of Judea. Our road now wound monotonously through a less cultivated district for two hours, when (in four hours and forty minutes from Hebron) we reached the Pools of Solomon, at the head of a deep wady running towards Bethlehem. These pools are three in number, situated at short intervals along the wady, and are formed of plastered masonry. All travellers unite in yielding to them a high antiquity, and perhaps there is no reason to object to their existence in the days of Solomon. They may be the "pools of water" which "the Preacher" made "to water therewith the wood that bringeth forth trees." The pools are of large dimensions, being respectively 582, 423, and 380 feet in length, and averaging 178, 205, and 232 feet in breadth. What is very curious, the highest pool has no regularity in its shape, no two of its sides being parallel, and the other two differ greatly in their breadths at different points. The configuration of the valley was probably the reason of this lack of symmetry. The highest pool was half full of water, the second held some, though half its bottom was bare, and the third held a little at the eastern end, forming a little marsh, where the frogs were vociferating in full chorus. The bottoms of the pools are very uneven, owing, I suppose, to the nature of the wady's bed. The sealed fountain, that aided in supplying the pools, is now filled up to the arch with rubbish. I descended some dozen steps, and found a small vestibule which had led into the blocked-up apartment. Through this vestibule the water ran down to the pools. Near by were the remains of an aqueduct that once brought water from El Khudr, or St. George, as a feeder to the pools. By the north side of the first and highest pool, stands a large, clumsy Saracen castle, filled, at the time of our visit, with filth and Arabs.

After a full survey of the pools and their neighbourhood, we abandoned the usual route to Jerusalem, and struck down the wady of the pools towards Bethlehem. It became quite a dell, and in a brief time, as we turned northward, a beautiful sight appeared—the vale beyond and below us was filled with the richest foliage and in finest cultivation; the hill-sides, being here very barren, added by contrast tenfold to the beauty of this little Paradise. Here, says tradition, Solomon had his vineyards, gardens, and orchards, that were watered by the stream from those noble pools. It was a charming spot for the monarch's pleasure grounds, and the tradition is a happy one, if not true. Mr. Meshullam, who was to be our host in Jerusalem, was the present lessee of this beautiful valley, and under his escort we passed among the groves and by the side of a gentle brook that fertilized the vale. The ruins of a village clung to the left hill-side. This spot is called by Dr. Robinson, *Urtas*, and is supposed by him to be the Etam of Scripture, the Etham of Josephus and the Talmud. The only name I could derive from the guides, was El Tos (the cup), and the shape of the verdant valley is sufficient reason for this title. East of this sweet spot rose conspicuously the flat-topped height of Jebel el Fureidis, which Pococke suggests may be Beth Haccerem; " blow the trumpet in Tekoa, and set up a sign of fire in Beth Haccerem." The site of Tekoa is ascertained without doubt a little southward of this mountain, and there is every probability of the truth of Pococke's suggestion. Certainly there could be no better place for a signal-fire in the whole country than this lofty and detached summit. As we approached Bethlehem, the reflection from the limestone became very painful to the eyes, the mid-day sun exerting its full force. The town was perched upon a steep hill before us, up which our horses climbed with the facility of cats. The convent was by far the most conspicuous building in view, and towards it we directed our way. Passing the well of Bethlehem (which Dr. Robinson found to be only an opening into the aqueduct), we soon reached the convent and dismounted. We found that the French Consul and a French bishop were on a visit, their horses standing before the door. This doorway is so low, that one entering has to stoop most respectfully. Whether this is so arranged to prevent Arab robbers from entrance, or to extort homage from the Moslem visiters, is a question. The church is a large handsome building, covered by a wooden roof, supported by four rows of Corinthian columns. Beneath this are all the localities of tradition run wild,—the grotto stable where Christ was born! the *white marble* manger where he was laid! and a silver star marking the place whence the star of Bethlehem received its lustre! Beautiful lamps and fine paintings surround these traditionary baubles, that profane the most wonderful display of Divine mercy to our world. There were numerous other spots of monkish legend pointed out, almost equally repulsive. The only good we derived from the convent was in considering it as the place where Jerome translated the Scriptures, and in enjoying the view from its roof. In this view we needed no tradition to excite our most reverential feelings. We looked over the unchanged hills and vales, where David had often strayed, a stripling keeper of his father's flocks, and a green plain below the town reminded us of the shepherds who, perhaps on that very plain, had seen the glorious host of heaven's messengers, and learned the welcome tidings of a Saviour's birth. We followed them, in imagination, up the hill to the town, and strove to realize their feelings in gazing on the new-born Jesus. Hither, too, had come the Eastern Magi, in search of the star-told Christ, and here they had exposed their offerings to the Lord of Glory. Here, too, had Herod, in his rage, caused the blood of the babes of Bethlehem to be outpoured. The thoughts of these events received new life upon the site of their transaction. The heavens had once rested upon this hill of earth, and had left the traces of their visit in the holy and joyous reminiscences that clustered in our minds. We gazed long and thankfully upon the interesting scenes about this hallowed height, and then descended to prosecute our journey to Jerusalem. On our way to the horses, many Bethlehemite Christians brought boxes and ornaments of mother-of-pearl to sell: these form a large trade in the town, and are carved with some skill. Bethlehem and Nazareth, the places of our Lord's birth and education, are both of Christian population, in the midst of a Mohammedan country; so curious has been the order of Providence in establishing this coincidence. Leaving Bethlehem, we passed down the northern slope of the hill, and shortly arrived at Rachel's tomb, a Moslem wely of the usual style, in a field to the westward of our path. It is a modern structure, but on the traditionary spot of Rachel's burial.

West of the tomb, on the eastern face of a fine hill, was Beit-Jala, embosomed in olives. The convent of Mar Elyas was before us, placed where the monks say the prophet rested on his way to Beersheba, and where they pretend to show the mark left by his sleeping body in the rock. We gazed anxiously upon its white walls, and urged our horses up the hill-side; but it was not the shining convent that gave us energy, and sent the thrill of eager expectation through our veins, but we knew that from that monastic height the eye might rest upon Jerusalem. The intensity of hope rendered us speechless, as we hasted along the stony path. Joy and awe were alike accumulating in our hearts as we neared the summit. The Past and Present were equally unheeded, for our whole thoughts were centred on the Future prospect. Onward, with increasing zeal, we vied in the ascent. The point was gained, and the Holy City lay fair and peaceful before our enraptured eyes. Not in the wild forests of the Western World, not among the huge wrecks of Egyptian art, not on the snow-clad peaks of romantic Switzerland, had any scene so riveted our gaze. The drapery of Nature in the land of the setting sun was richer far, the halls of Karnac had published the highest triumphs of the human powers, and Alpine ranges had yielded far nobler spectacles of earth's magnificence; yet here were all surpassed, for heaven threw its shechinah upon the scene, and clothed the hill of Zion with a robe of glory. The sweetest memories hovered, like fairest angels, over the towers of Salem. Past, Present, and Future all concentred on the oracle of God. There is Zion, the home of the psalmist-monarch; there Moriah, the mount of Israel's God; and yonder, green with its appropriate foliage, and graceful as a heavenly height, is mild and holy Olivet. They rise as beacons to the wearied soul, and all are bathed in the radiance of the Cross. The scene was grand, unspeakably. Our overflowing hearts sent forth their swollen streams of feeling in vocal rejoicing. We looked back upon Bethlehem—there was the cradle; we turned to Calvary—there was the grave. Between these two had Heaven and earth been reconciled. We paused awhile to drink deep of this first draught, and then spurred on to reach the city. As we passed towards the imposing walls, we thought how "beautiful for situation was the city of the Great King." The road led over the skirts of the broad green plain of Rephaim, where the Philistine host had encamped against the new-made monarch of Israel, and the gathering of whose rich harvests had furnished the evangelical prophet with a striking illustration of the overthrow of the kingdom of Jeroboam.* The village of Siloah appeared upon the declivities of Olivet, and reminded us of the "waters that went softly."† We were now upon a level with the city walls, when the deep ravine or valley of the sons of Hinnom intercepted our path. Passing down and along this valley eastward and northward, we thought of the fires that had here arisen upon Molech's altars, where Ahaz and Manasseh had burned their own offspring, and from whose scenes of blood and pollution the everlasting abode of the damned had received its title. Tradition has placed the scene of the awful death of Judas on the side of this appropriate valley. Skirting the dry and ruined lower pool of Gihon, which is but a dammed portion of the western valley, we crossed by the side of the old aqueduct, and ascended to the Jaffa Gate.

---

* Isaiah xvii. 5.   † Isaiah viii. 6.

18

Jerusalem.

POPULATION—JEWS—MOSQUES—BETHANY—SILOAH—GETH-
SEMANE—CHURCH OF ST. JAMES.

We delivered our quarantine certificates, and in another moment were within the Holy City. Here a new order of things presented itself—narrow dirty lanes and low crumbling houses were the contents of the formidable walls. The streets were paved with large stones, whose surfaces were as smooth as ice, and caused our horses to slip at every step. There was no uniformity either in the positions of the streets or in their surfaces, except a uniform avoidance of all symmetry or comfort. Pursuing a labyrinthine route, we at length reached the house of Mr. Meshullam, and found neat, clean, and comfortable accommodations prepared for our reception.

It would be folly in me, a passing traveller, to attempt a minute description of Jerusalem as it is, when the works of learned and thorough explorers of its condition are to be seen in every library of the civilized world. A few words upon its principal attractions to the Christian traveller are all I offer, ere I continue the narrative of our journey northward.

We spent ten days of soul-stirring enjoyment in the metropolis of the Promised Land, and, with our Bibles as constant companions, visited again and again its hallowed localities. The blasphemous traditions of

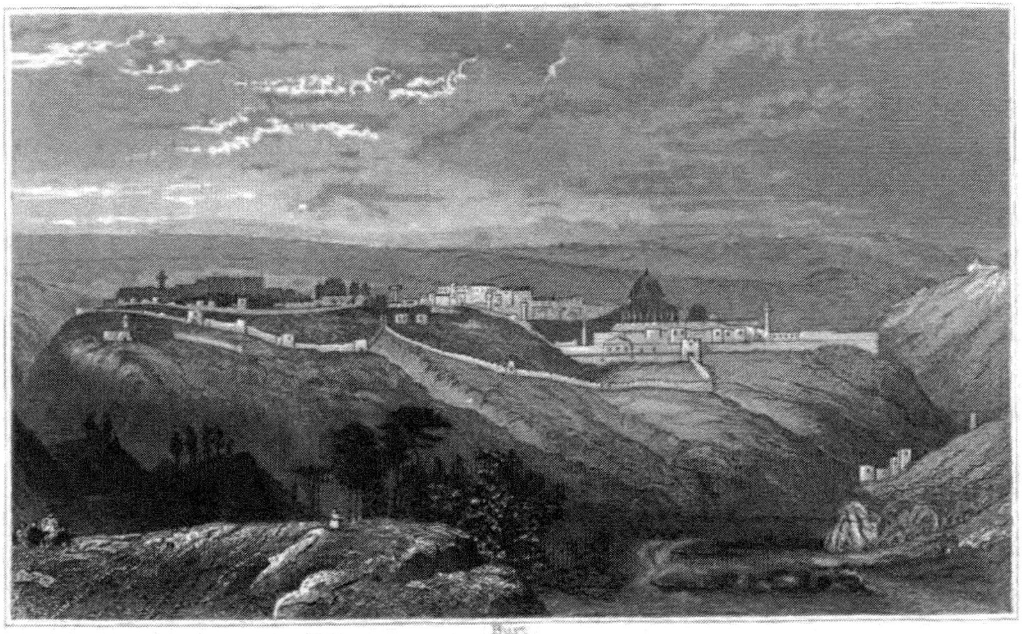

the monks, who even show the mark of our Saviour's shoulder where he leaned against the wall, and barefacedly exhibit the spot where the centurion, who attended the crucifixion, did penance, we flung to the winds; while the general situation and form of the city, its natural features, and the points of undoubted identity, claimed our earnest attention. But once did we visit the so-styled church of the Holy Sepulchre, and were disgusted at its tinsel and the profane mummery of the services. The sepulchre was a manifest absurdity, and the other exhibited localities bore the broadest seal of the father of lies. 'Tis all of a piece with the Via Dolorosa, Pilate's judgment hall, the pillar to which the Saviour was bound, and a hundred other such monkish fooleries.

Jerusalem is now said to contain a population of only 11,000, and yet certainly does not appear to be very thinly inhabited. One of my first causes of surprise was the small extent of the city; I walked leisurely the entire circuit of the walls in three-quarters of an hour, so that the circumference of the city cannot be greatly over two miles.* Now, as all sides of Jerusalem but the north are bounded by deep ravines, it is only at the north the city could have been extended, and here Dr. Robinson discovered traces of Agrippa's outermost wall. From these facts, and from comparison with modern cities, James Fergusson, in his work on the topography of Jerusalem, has conclusively shown that the testimony of Josephus regarding the millions that were in the city at the time of the siege, is utterly false. Fergusson states that under no circumstances could Jerusalem, according to his careful comparison of its size with other populous cities, have contained more than

---

* Dr. Robinson, by actual measurement, makes it about 2 5-11 miles.

35,000 or 40,000 inhabitants. The modern traveller will naturally find himself an advocate for this opinion.

The character of the present city is much like that of other oriental towns, the houses resembling square stone houses, and the streets narrow and filthy. The bazaars are miserably stocked, and do not possess the first attraction. It is estimated that 5,000 Jews reside within the walls. Their men wear a dark blue gown and tarbouch, with a turban of varied light blue and white, and their women carry a white veil over their heads and shoulders. They are principally aged persons, who have come from various parts of the world to lay their bones in the Valley of Jehoshaphat. They are the most bigoted of their race, and cling with desperate tenacity round the decaying ruins of their ancient city. In the Valley of Jehoshaphat, over against the temple-mount, the side of Olivet is almost regularly paved with their plain monumental slabs. Here thousands have been buried, according to their anxious wish, that there they might rise to greet the coming Messiah. Every Friday, the Jews assemble before the great outer wall of the temple-court, which yet remains, and wail their lamentable state. Here we found some seated, reading aloud, others rubbing their hands along the seams of the huge wall, and then kissing their withdrawn palms, and still others kissing the stones themselves. Well did the lamentation of the wailing prophet become these children of Jacob— "Our necks are under persecution; we labour and have no rest; we have given the hand to the Egyptians and Assyrians to be satisfied with bread; our fathers have sinned and are not, and we have borne their iniquities; servants have ruled over us; there is none that doth deliver us out of their hand. The joy of our heart is ceased; our dance is turned into mourning; the crown is fallen from our head; wo unto us that we have sinned! For this our heart is faint; for these our eyes are dim. Turn thou us unto thee, O Lord, and we shall be turned; renew our days as of old. But thou hast utterly rejected us; thou art very wroth against us."*

There are several synagogues in the city, one of which we visited, to see Israel worshipping in his own home. It was an affecting sight to behold these representatives of that down-trodden and despised people, collected from many different parts of the earth, and here united in the worship of their fathers' God; choosing, rather, to live beneath the oppression of Moslem rule, than forsake the land of their kings and prophets. Yet it was sadder to think of the cause of their sufferings, in the rejection of their Messiah in this very city. We looked upon their services with the ardent hope that ere long they may worship upon the summit of their temple-mount, in unrestrained joy, the Redeemer that they crucified. The synagogue was composed of four separate rooms, connected with one another, in each of which, on a raised floor, was a reader of the law, to whose rapid enunciation the congregation responded. The women sat in screened galleries or in the entrance-porch. The rooms were of simple adorning, but kept clean and in order.

The antiquities of Jerusalem, as far as art is concerned, are very few, so thoroughly have the sins of the Jewish nation been visited upon their darling city. Parts of the wall of the temple-area, with its attached fragment of the Tyropœon bridge, a few stones of the ancient city walls, a half dozen pools, the supposed tower of Hippicus, and the tomb excavations of the vicinity,

---

* Lamentations, chap. 5, verse 5, &c.

are nearly all the relics of Judea's capital. The traveller, therefore, will be disappointed who goes to seek in Jerusalem such traces of the past as he has seen in Rome or Athens, unless his faith overgrow his sagacity, and he follows the guidance of some stupid friar. In the latter case, as by enchantment, stirring antiquities will greet him on every side; the fresh masonry of yesterday will assume the frown of ages, and every pit or hillock of the ground will support a thrilling story. As we were obstinate skeptics in all monastic tales, it was our delight to seek in Nature's unchanging features the clearest memories of "the days of old." We loved to linger upon the beautiful sides of Olivet, and press the same ground a Saviour trod. From that height, sacred in the eyes of every Christian, the city lay spread out as a model—the mosque of Omar, with its large dome and immense surrounding area, appeared conspicuously. This is Moriah, and now no Jew or Christian can gain admission to the consecrated ground. Within the area, we could see the Moslems promenading or lounging by the fountains, or about entering the holy edifice with uncovered feet. Beyond this vast enclosure, which occupies a quarter of the city's area, were the confused houses of the town, prominent among them rising the towers of the citadel and the new Episcopal church. Between the city and our elevated position, was sunken the deep dry bed of the Kedron, to which tradition, Jewish, Christian, and Moslem, has given the name of the "valley of Jehoshaphat," in view of the evidently figurative language of the prophet Joel; and under the influence of this delusive hope that here the world shall receive its final judgment, the Jews have for ages sought, and still seek devoutly, a place of burial in the narrow valley. It was from such a position as that, which we often occupied upon the Mount of Olives, that our Saviour had wept over the blinded, self-destroying city, and predicted its present state of degradation. It was, moreover, upon the side of this hill that the Saviour had uttered his agonizing prayers, after the last supper had been eaten with his disciples. To this had come the traitor and his murderous band, issuing from the silent city, and with gleam of torch descending the steep banks, and crossing the Kedron, to bring pollution in the peaceful bowers of Gethsemane. Hence had gone the Divine Lamb to the slaughter. Another scene of startling interest had occurred upon this hill of memories. Over its lofty brow, and down its eastern inclination, the rock-worn path leads us to Bethany, still called by the name of Lazarus. Here grow the olive, apricot, and mulberry, and all the charms of rural retirement gather about the spot. A dozen simple houses form the hamlet, whither so often the Son of God had withdrawn, after a day of teaching in the bustling city. Here the two sisters had basked in the sunshine of his Divine countenance, and here the stupendous miracle of their brother's resurrection had been performed. The monks have not suffered this quiet place to escape the mocking hand of tradition, and the house of Lazarus, his sepulchre, and the dwelling of Simon the leper, are alike shown to the inquiring traveller. The first is a high ruin, in two parts, and the most conspicuous object in the place. The sepulchre is entered by a doorway under a hill, close to the village. On descending twenty or thirty steps, a rock-hewn chamber with niches is reached—this is apparently ancient. From this is entered another apartment, of arched masonry, which appears of modern origin. The highest interest of this rural hamlet was derived from the words of the Evangelist—" And he led them out as far as to Bethany, and he lifted up his hands and blessed them. And it came to pass, while he blessed them, he was parted from them, and carried up into heaven." Notwithstanding this plain testimony of Scripture, the *summit* of the Mount of Olives is confidently shown as the place whence our Lord ascended, and even his foot-prints are adduced as proof! The simple inhabitants of Bethany gathered about us as we pondered upon the events that had there been witnessed, but which were probably as unknown to these poor peasants as if they had occurred on the surface of another planet. After indulging in the reflections that such a place naturally suggested, we returned to the city around the southern limb of Olivet, entering the valley of Kedron near the tomb of Absalom.

There are four conspicuous tombs upon the side of the valley, and opposite the city wall. They bear the names of Absalom, Jehoshaphat, St. James, and Zachariah, but with what correctness of application it is difficult to decide. Absalom's and Zachariah's are very similar. They are both square-based, pointed-roofed structures, hewn out of the rock, the former being surmounted by mason work where the rock failed in height. They are both ornamented with Ionic half-columns, but in other details they differ. The other two tombs are excavations in the rock;—Jehoshaphat's was so cumbered with rubbish that I could not enter, yet from the outside it appeared to be a large cavern. The borders of its doorway were richly ornamented. That of St. James reminded me of those at Beni Hassan on the Nile—its front is supported by two Doric columns. It consists of several chambers, some of which have holes for the dead. The tomb is situated quite high on the cliff, and is apparently inaccessible when viewed from the front, but on passing to the side of the tomb of Zachariah, its entrance is seen, being a side passage through the rock.

Leaving these sepulchres and passing southward, we find other objects of interest in the valley of the Kedron. Beyond the corner of the city wall, we reach a double flight of stone steps that lead down to the cavernous source of Siloa's brook; here the pure cold water flows so "softly" that the current is barely perceptible. Hence it passes through the rock for 1750 feet to the "Pool of Siloam." The interesting account of Dr. Robinson's persevering exploration of this passage will be remembered by every reader of his "Researches." Opposite this fountain is the miserable village of Siloam, apparently clinging to the cliffs. Beyond this we reach the junction of the Tyropœon and the valley of the son of Hinnom with the Vale of Kedron. This junction forms a broad fertile expanse, where even yet are beautiful gardens, and where were of old "the king's gardens." They are watered by the stream from the Pool of Siloam. This pool is just within the Tyropœon. It is of small dimensions, compared with the others we had seen, and held about eighteen inches of water at the time. There were the remnants of six columns on its eastern face, and of two in a line along its centre. In the back, or northern end, is a cave, into which we entered, and by descending several steps inwardly we could feel the water flowing "softly" into the pool. We climbed down into the pool itself, and washed, remembering that here had one born blind received his sight by washing in these waters at the command of the son of Mary. Below the gardens is a well that bears the names of Job and Nehemiah. The well is 125 feet deep, and of excellent water. It is covered by a ruinous building of stone, and surrounded by stone troughs. Near by is a small pool, and a building attached. .This place is by many supposed to be En-Rogel, where Adonijah attempted to make himself king.* Retracing our steps a short distance, we enter the deep defile of Hinnom, and skirt the south of Zion; on the left is the steep side of the so-called Hill of Evil Counsel, where tradition has placed a meeting of the chief priests to take counsel how to put Jesus to death. All along its face are excavated tombs in the rock, some of them slightly ornamented, and among them is the plot of ground supposed to be the Aceldama of Judas. A large stone building now exists on the spot, the floor of which is on a far lower level than the external ground. This is the old charnel house of the Christians, but every way resembles a huge cistern. After passing the broad base of Zion, we turn northward, and find the valley broader and its level higher. Here is the great Pool of Gihon, occupying nearly the whole valley for 600 feet in length. This large pool was now dry, and grain was growing on its bottom. Beyond the pool, northward, the aqueduct crosses the vale. Still further on, we look up to the buildings of the citadel and the Jaffa gate. The valley (here the Valley of Gihon) now slants westward, and by following it beyond the north-west corner of the city wall, we reach the upper pool of Gihon, about half the size of the lower pool. Between the northwest and north-east corners of the city, we see the large cavern, in a detached cliff near the Damascus gate, which bears the name of the Grotto of Jeremiah, from some legend of sandy foundation. Beyond this, eastward, we again strike the steep bank of Kedron.

I have stated that the walls of Jerusalem never could have been of more extensive circuit, except at the

---

* 1 Kings i. 9.

north side of the city. There is an exception to this remark, for parts of Moriah (Ophel) and Zion at the south are now without the walls, which formerly must have been enclosed. Yet these excluded portions are comparatively small, and would help but little in magnifying the population of the city. On Ophel are no buildings, but on the outer part of Zion is the mosque of David, which the Mohammedans declare contains the Psalmist's tomb, and where Christians cannot enter. Here also is shown, by the still more credulous Christians, an arched and columned *upper room*, where our Lord ate the last supper! and nearer the walls is the Armenian convent, said to be the house of Caiaphas! It has a very neat court and chapel, on one side of which is a little box-like room, with blue tile walls, piously exhibited as the Saviour's prison! Near these buildings are the Armenian, American, English, and other cemeteries. The Zion gate leads into the city on the summit of this hill, and here, as at the Jaffa gate, we were always accosted by a number of wretched, loathsome lepers. These poor afflicted creatures live apart from the rest of mankind, and, it is said, intermarry and raise families of leprous children. They form one of the saddest spectacles of human misery we have ever witnessed.

The great mosque of Omar, it is well known, is forbidden ground to the Christian; and the extensive enclosure, or "Haram esh Sherif," which surrounds the sacred building, is equally shut against all but the true Mussulman. Notwithstanding this law of exclusiveness, many cunning Christians have penetrated within the holy precincts, and satisfied themselves and the world that the mysterious secrecy concealed no equivalent wonder. Drawings have even been taken of the interior of the mosque and its fellow-structure,

El-Aksa, while the deluded Moslems of Jerusalem suppose they are preserving most secret the contents of the sacred edifice. Of course all these Christian visits have been performed in disguise, for the known intruder would lose his life in the attempt. The architecture of the mosque has led Mr. Fergusson to consider it an originally Christian edifice, and hence he has broached the startling theory of its being the church of Constantine, over the Holy Sepulchre. He has adduced many plausible arguments for this novel doctrine, which certainly seems quite as capable of proof as the theory of the existence of the sepulchre at its monkish site. The only *near* views we could obtain of the mosque and its area were from the centre of an arched passage leading into it from the Via Dolorosa, and from the roof of the barracks, formerly the governor's house. This last point is at the north of the Haram, and overlooks the whole. From here Catherwood made the drawings for his celebrated panorama. A fine *distant* view of the Haram is had from the Mount of Olives, as before noticed. On one occasion I was attempting to make the shortest way from the Jaffa gate to that of St. Stephen, and on my passage was suddenly brought to a complete halt by the interposition of several threatening Mussulmans, who most unmistakeably desired a retrograde movement on my part. I at once saw my error. I was upon the verge of the consecrated soil, and these were its faithful guardians. I turned and sought another road to the gate, while the true believers who had saved the holy place from pollution greeted my retreat with boisterous laughter. At another time, in merely passing along the Via Dolorosa, opposite an archway that opened to the Haram, I was saluted by a shower of stones from some juvenile defenders of the faith,

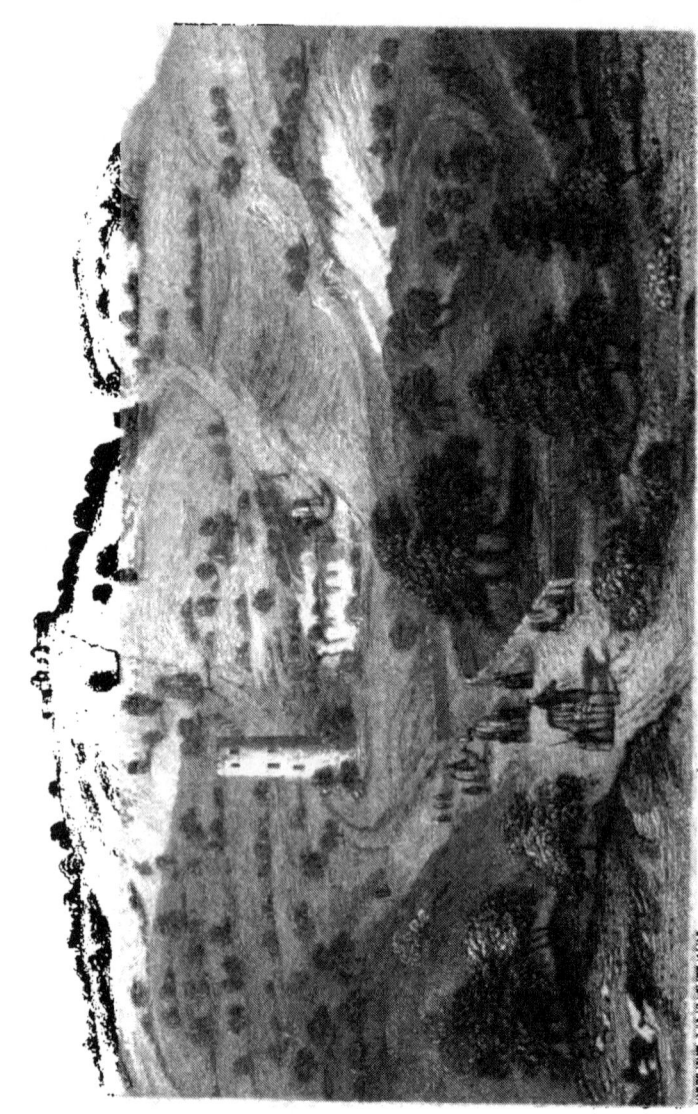

THE MOUNT OF OLIVES AND GARDEN OF GETHSEMANE.

who were evidently encouraged in their valorous piety by some older heads beside them. The spirit of "the Koran or the sword" is still existing, and only restrained from its old method of action by fear of consequences. However, the same spirit may be found without going to Islam; it is co-extensive with sin.

Gethsemane is pointed out by the monks at the foot of Olivet, where eight extremely aged olive trees are enclosed by a lofty white wall of 120 feet in extent on each side. This wall had been lately erected to prevent relic-seeking pilgrims from destroying the trees by breaking off fragments of bark or twigs as mementos of their pilgrimage. The wall has injured the beauty of the spot, and its division into vegetable patches has assisted to complete its profanation. On one of our visits to this enclosure, (admittance to which is gained by a little low door in one corner,) we found an odd visiter before us. Halil Effendi, a Turkish nabob, was sitting under the trees, talking gayly with the monks, evidently considering himself as good a Christian as the best of them. Although the monkish site of Gethsemane is of douthful truth, yet it was repugnant to our feelings to see the apparent levity of these visiters in a spot which some of them, at least, believed to be the scene of our Saviour's agony. But we had before learned the fact that the presence of the sites of the holiest events have no power in themselves to soften the heart, and we had seen those who professed to be peculiarly servants of the Most High, in apparently the most perfect thoughtlessness upon the spot where the most solemn memories should have filled their minds.

Once, in ascending the Mount of Olives, we noticed our guide, as we passed through the corn fields, "pluck the ears of corn and eat, rubbing them in his hands,"* vividly recalling the event in our Saviour's life that gave rise to the Pharisaical accusation of his profanation of the Sabbath. The summit of Olivet is now crowned by a mosque and filthy village, from which the Dead Sea was plainly visible, and to the north-west the mosque-crowned height of Neby Samwil was conspicuous. The Mount of Olives may include the summit upon the north and south, which are really parts of the same hill, and which altogether form the most graceful height I have ever seen. In gently rounded form, and in its colour of mingled green and white, it is unsurpassed.

One of the prettiest churches in Jerusalem is that of St. James, attached to the Arminian convent. A fine court lies before the entrance, which is, however, sorrily ornamented by some attempts in the fine arts. One picture of "Elijah ascending," with horses of eccentric breed, acts as a curious solemnizer of the feelings on entering a sanctuary. The general effect of the interior is very pleasant. A blue tile wainscot surrounds the church—the pulpit and canopy as well as the side-doors are of very fine work in tortoise-shell and mother-of-pearl; the floor exhibits some rich mosaic; here and there is spread a beautiful carpet, and some meritorious paintings adorn the walls. Though there is much of the usual oriental tinsel, yet it seems not to detract from the general effect of the church. There are a lightness and purity in the white roof and domes, that contrast well with the ornaments below.

During our stay at Jerusalem we experienced every kindness at the hands of Mr. Finn, the British Consul, Bishop Gobat, and Mr. Nicolayson, with their families,

---

* Luke vi. 1.

whose attentions are a subject of grateful recollection to every one who has lately visited the Holy City. Nor can we forget the obliging efforts of our host, Mr. Meshullam, in affording us all the assistance of his experience to increase the pleasure and profit of our sojourn.

The English church is a beautiful edifice, presenting more architectural elegance than any building in the city. It stands upon the northern portion of Zion, and, as the first Protestant church edifice in Jerusalem, seems to betoken the fulfilment of the prophecy, "The Redeemer shall come to Zion."[*]

---

[*] Isaiah, lix. 20.

Judah—Benjamin—Ephraim.

MAR SABA—DEAD SEA—THE JORDAN—JERICHO—START FOR THE NORTH—BETHEL—SHECHEM—JACOB'S WELL—JOSEPH'S TOMB.

On the 21st of May, we left Jerusalem on an excursion to the Dead Sea. Mohammed, a Bedawee Sheikh, acted as our guide, and at 2, P. M., our cavalcade issued from the Jaffa gate. Our path was rough, narrow, rocky, and winding along the hill-sides that border the Kedron. We were to spend the night at the Greek convent of Mar Saba, which is situated upon the sides of the Kedron, about nine miles below Jerusalem. For that distance, the Kedron is a deep-sunk, steep-sided ravine, and, near the convent, is remarkably wild and romantic. On our way, several fierce-visaged Arabs made their appearance in our path, and I involuntarily remembered him that fell among thieves in the neighbourhood. I was greatly relieved to discover that these new arrivals were our escort, who had been ordered to meet us at this point. A poor young German accompanied us on foot. Penniless, and almost garmentless, this youth had wandered as a pilgrim from his home in the fatherland to the distant scenes of the events of the Saviour's life. He had been robbed of some pittance by the Arabs, but yet had persevered in visiting the Holy Sepulchre and all the other traditionary points of interest in Jerusalem. He had been at Nazareth and Bethlehem, and now told us that the priests had instructed him to bathe in Jordan, and then he should be absolved from all his sins. The poor fellow, in this wretched hope, had now set out to walk to the sacred river, in his forlorn plight, and under a burning sun.

As we rode along the summits of the cliffs that bound the Kedron defile near Mar Saba, we saw many animals, like the hedge-hog, scampering among the rocky ledges. This creature was, undoubtedly, the shaphan (translated "coney") of Scripture,* that makes its house in the rocks. This animal is the Daman of the Syrians, the Nabr of the Arabians, and the Ashkoko of the Abyssinians. We reached Mar Saba before five P. M. The convent is a curiosity of architecture, appearing to hang from the cliffs. Its walls and towers give it the air of a fortress. One of its towers is without the walls, and in this all ladytravellers are obliged to find shelter when they are overtaken by night at this point, the misogynist rules of the convent forbidding any female to cross its threshold. We wound along the walls and down a steep path to the little door. Here we were forced to wait until we had sent our letter of introduction (obtained from the Greek convent in Jerusalem) up in a window in the wall. After this application had been duly digested by the brethren, we were directed to descend the cliff to a lower door. This we soon did, and, entering, passed down a flight of stone stairs into this most wonderful of convents. Passing the church and other buildings, and glancing at the wee garden among these rocks, we found a detatched room, spread with divans, which was given up to our possession.

---

* Proverbs xxx. 26, &c.

We seated ourselves, and were soon visited by a venerable monk, who offered us araki and raisins, and then some refreshing coffee. Mounting the roof of our little room, we obtained a realizing sense of our odd position. We were on a mere ledge of the rock: directly opposite our door rose the precipitous cliff, full of hawks' nests, whose occupants were soaring over our heads. In this cliff, the monks had scooped out snug cells, and, by closing their fronts with mason-work, had formed most comfortable lodgings. Along the many ledges of the cliffs, various buildings and cells composed the *tout ensemble* of the convent. There was the church with its dome and huge buttresses, the little domed chapel of Saint Saba, and the little garden patch, a caricature of horticulture, where the gardener monk was playing his part admirably. The fortress walls of the convent climbed up the cliffs in the most impossible manner, and were increased in height by layers of loose stones, forming a parapet that a *high* wind might easily lay *low*. The whole convent resembled a gigantic set of book-shelves. With the company of a few monks, we visited the church—a poor affair, filled with wretched daubs of a long array of unheard-of saints, and boasting a tinselled pulpit and gaudily decorated screen, whose back was most pitiably deficient in ornament, and evidently not intended for the visiter's eyes. A frightful picture of the Last Judgment added to the interest of the interior, and under the front porch were several paintings of equal distinction, one a fearful representation of the massacre of 14,000 holy brethren by the Saracens in the twelfth century. The Saracens were performing the job with provoking coolness, and the friars' heads appeared perfectly good-natured even after separation from the bodies. The pavement between the church and the chapel of Mar Saba covers the vault for the dead. The chapel is ornamented in like style with the church, but is of so diminutive capacity, that three or four worshipers would form a full house,—an excellent size for the chapel of an unpopular preacher. Here the Saint Saba is buried, but whether this personage was a *he* or a *she*, where the same lived and when, are all questions that our heathen understandings could not answer. The monks looked the very ideal of laziness. They lounged in some quiet corner, or else slowly moved over their circumscribed promenades in more than oriental sluggishness. They were of far better appearance, however, than our quondam hosts of Mount Sinai, and treated us with most polite attention.

We spent a very comfortable night on the divans, and at 6½ o'clock in the morning, we left the brethren and their grotesque home. One of the friars, a fine looking old man, of skin wondrously fair, accompanied us. He had never seen the Jordan, and embraced this opportunity of a visit. We retraced our road for ten minutes, till we reached the end of the precipice, and then struck north-easterly towards the north shore of the Dead Sea, up and down and around hills utterly devoid of vegetation,—the dreary waste of the Judean desert.

Our first view of the Dead Sea (which the Arabs know as "the Sea of Lot") reminded us of the Hudson, its naked cliffs not being distinguishable in the hazy distance from green banks. As we approached the Pass of Kuneiterah (which leads from the high country of Judah to the Jordan valley), we caught sight of the minaret of the mosque of Neby Mousa, upon a height to our left. We found the pass steep, long, and tedious, and reached the sea-side at 11¼ A. M., four and three quarter hours from Mar Saba. There was stretched out the long quiet sea between lofty cliffs, not a ripple upon its surface, and not a sound of man or beast audible,—verily it was the "*Dead* Sea." Yet we were surprised to see vegetation on the very brink of the sulphurous sea, and even *in* the water itself. A great quantity of drift wood lined the shore, telling plainly of large trees upon its borders somewhere. The plain north of the sea, on which we stood, was covered with a saline incrustation, and the herbs were thickly coated with the same. A small peninsula jutted out into the sea, connected with the main shore by a very narrow neck. We passed out to its extreme end, in order to bathe, and were impressed with the belief that this was originally a T shaped wharf. It is highly probable that a town or settlement was placed at the head of this sea, as the port of Jericho and Beth-Hogla, by means of which port a commerce might have been carried on with Moab and Idumea. Keziz (mentioned in Joshua xviii. 21) seems to have been here situated, as we should judge from its name, which appears to signify "the end" (i. e. of the sea), and this wharf may be the relic of that port, or its successors, on the same site. Dr. Robinson passed too far from the border of the sea at this point to perceive this peninsular projection, and Lieut. Lynch thus notices the matter:

"At 6 25, P. M., passed a gravelly point, with many large stones upon it. It is a peninsula, connected with the main by a low, narrow isthmus. When the latter is overflowed, the peninsula must present the appearance of an island, and is doubtless the one to which Stephens, Warburton, and Dr. Wilson allude."

Our Arabs attempted to dissuade us from bathing, supposing us ignorant of the sea's peculiar qualities; but we nevertheless obtained the desired experimental proof of the reported characteristics of this strange expanse. The buoyancy of the water was as wonderful as we had anticipated. We threw ourselves on our backs, and lay as easily as on a sofa, our bodies utterly refusing to sink. From the very great specific gravity of the water, swimming was no easy matter, our extremities being thrown out of the water at every effort. Wherever the skin of our bodies was scratched the sting of the water was very great. Its taste was burning to the tongue, like caustic.* The stinging sensation continued a half hour after we had left the sea, and our bodies were slightly encrusted with salt. From the sea we started for the Jordan opposite Ain Hajla. It was a fearfully hot ride of an hour and a quarter, under a noonday sun in this northern Arabah. The ground appeared like ashes, and the horses' feet constantly sank in deeply. We descended two terraces before reaching the immediate banks of the river; these terraces were well stocked with bushes, but the very banks of the river were lined with fine forest trees, below which the stream ran dark and rapid towards the Sea of Sodom. The terraces of the Jordan were distinctly marked at the point where we visited the river, and almost wear the appearance of artificial formation.

PLAIN OF SAND | BUSHES | CHALK | JUNGLE TREES | RIVER

The current was more rapid than that of any river we had ever before seen. Its course was winding, and both banks were girt with the loveliest foliage. We were amazed at the river's beauty, for we had formed a far different idea of its appearance on our approach

---

* We brought home a stone jug of the water, and on opening it, eight months after taking it from the sea, the caustic taste had disappeared, and its buoyancy seemed to have been reduced.

over the hot ashy plain. We bathed by holding to the drooping branches, but several of the Arabs struck boldly across, reaching the opposite side far below, though the breadth of the stream was very inconsiderable.

After a bath, a luncheon, and a rest, we mounted the terraces, and struck westward to Ain Hajla, about two miles from the river, in the plain. It is a fine, clear, well enclosed fountain, in the midst of a jungle caused by its existence. Beyond, to the southwest, was the ruin of the convent of St. Gerasimus, called by the Arabs "Kusr Hajla." These names show the site of the scriptural "Bethhogla." On our right, near the Jordan, the ruined convent of St. John, " the Kusr el Yehud" of the Arabs, was visible. Before us, to the north-west, rose the Castle of Jericho, a dilapidated modern tower, and to this we directed our way, for we were to encamp near the tower for the night. The plain was here cultivated, and trees of various kinds grew plentifully. We encamped near a running stream, beneath a grove of figs, a situation surpassingly delightful. After shooting a few of the multitude of wild pigeons that surrounded us, and after eating such a dinner as Jericho might be expected to furnish, we walked to the field of ruins that lay a mile westward. In so doing, we followed up the pretty streamlet among luxuriant groves, and found the ground strewed with stones, such as we had seen at Milh. Turning northward, we passed by fertile fields, where men were harvesting the wheat, to Ain es-Sultan. This is the copious source of water that fills the plain with its fertility. It is enclosed by stone embankments, from which the water rushes impetuously through a stone-lined opening. There are the ruins of aqueducts and mills in the vicinity, and an immense amount of scattered and undistinguishable remains. A mile westward rises the gaunt cliffs of Quarantana, on whose summit appeared a building, and whose sides were full of grottoes, where the hermits of a former age had spent their lives, fondly imagining they were upon the mountain of our Lord's temptation. Between us and the mountain were several Saracen ruins.

The whole region near Ain es-Sultan was charming. The full-flowing streams, the waving grain, the busy reapers, the picturesque ruins of the Saracen edifices, the luxuriant groves, and the sombre mountain-wall beyond, composed an array of scenery of uncommon interest. The fountain is naturally supposed to be the same whose waters Elisha healed,[*] and from our experience we can testify to the permanency of the cure. Near the fountain we found a sculptured stone, the only one that we could discover on the plain. It was upon the side of a high mound, that seemed formed of accumulated rubbish. We looked anxiously to find one relic of the palm trees which had given a name to Jericho, and found but one, and that a dead and scorched stump—the mutilated fragment of the last of the palm trees. Here we were upon the remarkable site where the walls of Jericho had fallen before the trumpets of Israel, and here had Israel's leader denounced a fearful curse on him who afterwards should build the ruined city. Yet Hiel, the Bethelite, had dared the curse, and felt its anguish in his bosom. Ages after, the second Joshua passed through this fruitful region, and Bartimeus and Zaccheus bore witness to his glory.

We spent the night under our tent, closely inspected by straggling fellahin, from the dirty village of Eriha, that surrounds the tower; and the next morning we

---

[*] 2 Kings ii. 22.

started for Jerusalem. We struck westward to the mountains, passing the ruins of an aqueduct on our left. The way was extremely hot, through an inclined defile of the range. As we mounted the sides of the great valley, we saw a large square trench cut beneath us in the plain, of whose purpose and history we were utterly ignorant. If we had noticed it earlier, we should have examined it closely. The road was lonely and dreary, and well adapted to the story of the good Samaritan. We thought of the poor traveller's experience, as given in that parable, and had, moreover, the testimony of succeeding ages as to the danger of this route. It was not strange, then, that we viewed a mounted Bedouin with peculiar sensations of shyness, and were particularly sensitive in turning abrupt corners. Half-way between Jericho and Jerusalem are the ruins of two buildings, one on top of the right-hand hill, and one close to the road in the valley. They bear the name of Khan Hudrur, and are ruined inns, just where we may imagine the Samaritan deposited his wounded charge. The coincidence was pleasing, and seemed vividly to illustrate the parable.

A Bedouin Sheikh joined us as we passed on, and invited us to his encampment, presenting us with some saffron as a token of amity. We shortly came up to his black tents, but were too hurried to accept his hospitality. We passed through Bethany, and reached Jerusalem in 4¼ hours from Eriha, having put our horses to the run for much of the way.

We had appointed the 28th of May as the day of our departure from Jerusalem, intending to pass through the entire length of Palestine to the Sea of Galilee and Damascus, and thence to Beyroot. On the evening before our intended start, my fever and ague again recurred; but, by a due quantity of quinine,

I removed that obstacle, only, however, to find another in the trickery and impudence of our Muggries (or horse-keepers). All Jerusalem seemed to be filled with bad horses and broken contracts, and all the morning I was acting the ferry-boat between the British Consulate and our lodgings, ready to faint with the weakness left by my nocturnal shaking in the ague. We found, to our entire satisfaction, that a desert Bedawee is a nobleman when compared with a Syrian Muggry, and fairly sighed to have a Besharah or a Hossein to deal with for our tour in Palestine. After scenes of altercation, that completely beggar description, and such as, probably, couldn't happen out of Syria, we at length left at 1½ P. M., our truly kind host accompanying us without the Damascus gate. Our cavalcade consisted of twenty beasts, a patch-work of horses, donkeys, and mules. The human beings were only twelve,—four travellers, four servants, and four Muggries,—the surplus of quadrupeds carrying our inanimate household. Leaving the Damascus gate, we soon passed the so-called Tombs of the Kings, and crossed the bed of the Kedron. Under the olive groves that skirt the city at the north were gathered crowds of men, women, and children, amusing themselves in the grateful shade. Many were swinging on ropes suspended from the large branches, the children were gambolling, with all the careless joy of childhood, and happiness seemed to be marked on every countenance. We passed reluctantly from this delightful scene, and were soon on the high plain of Scopus, whence Titus made his first approach upon the doomed city. Here we obtained one of the finest views of its hills and dwellings, and took our latest look at the memorable spot.

The lofty height of Neby Samwil rose upon our

left,—a beacon for a vast extent of country. Beyond, we caught sight of the beautiful lands about Gibeon, (El-Jib,) and then passed, on a fine hill-summit to the right, the Ramah of Benjamin (Er-Ram). Near this, the walls and arches of a ruined Khan formed an appropriate monument for the whole country, where no provision is made for the stranger as he passes on his journey; and I fear the lack of hospitality that marked this very district, when a certain Levite of Mt. Ephraim sought rest in the neighbouring town of Gibeah, might now be experienced by the modern traveller.

Still further north, we reached the ruins of Ataroth (Atara) on a hill-side. A long wall, pierced by an arched doorway, was principally conspicuous. The next point of interest was a fountain, surmounted by a Mohammedan place of worship. This was one of the *Beers*, or wells, which gave name to the neighbouring town of Beeroth (*Wells.*) The village, on the ancient site, lay a short distance off the road, and thither our Muggries wished to go and pass the night, but we exercised our authority effectually in continuing our course. Shortly after leaving Beeroth, our way lay through a ravine, in whose side was a noble cavern whose roof was supported by pillars of rock, and from which a stream of water was flowing. The guides called it "Ain El Iksa." A little beyond was another fountain, Ain El Akabah, where our horses drank from a small pool, and our men from a small cup-like cavity in the rock. These running streams were such delightful companions by the way, and our route was in this respect so different from the arid desert to which we had lately been confined, that we magnified Palestine to the highest place in the ranks of earthly countries. We reached Bethel (Beitin) at six in the evening. It is situated, as most Syrian towns, upon a hill, and bears extensive marks of its former town. Broken walls and foundations are seen all over the hill-top, and in the valley on the S. W. is a large empty pool, resembling those near Bethlehem, and those of Gihon. To the S. E., on a high hill, the ruins of a church stood, relieved by the sky, probably on the spot where Abraham pitched his tent in the land of his new possession.* Bethel itself is rendered famous in the eye of all Christendom, for the vision that here Jacob saw; and from his exclamation of surprise at the astounding sight is derived the name, not only of this spot, but of a myriad edifices scattered throughout the world, whose walls are hallowed by the exhibitions of a love Divine. It was, no doubt, with special reference to the *pillar* which he erected here, that Paul used this language to Timothy—" That thou mayest know how thou oughtest to behave thyself in the house of God (Bethel), which is the church of the living God, the *pillar* and *ground* of the truth."† It was this holy vision that rendered Bethel famous, but it was Jeroboam's unholy division that rendered it *infamous*, for here his golden calf separated Israel from their worship at Jerusalem, and plunged the country into an abyss of ruin. Hiel, the rebuilder of Jericho, and unenviable recipient of the curse, was an inhabitant of this town, and was probably a fair specimen of the calf-worshippers.

The poor Bethelites collected around us as we encamped among their huts, as ignorant of us and our business as they were of the thrilling history of their town. They looked morosely on us as on intruders, but seemed to yield up their acerbity when they found us ready-money purchasers of their fowls and milk. The road from Jerusalem had been a stony mountain mule-path, winding among the hills of Benjamin. The

---

* Gen. xii. 8. † 1 Tim. iii. 15.

country was sparsely cultivated, but appeared capable, under good management, of yielding its ancient plenty. The hills were all terraced, either naturally or artificially, and girt by narrow vales, an open plain being a thing unseen. We had crossed Benjamin completely (for Bethel was a frontier city, sometimes appertaining to Benjamin and sometimes to Ephraim,) in four hours and a half, its width thus being about twelve miles, for our rate of travel was only three miles per hour, and our course *not direct* to Bethel.

The second morning we did not leave our place of encampment until nearly eight o'clock, our Muggries having spent more than two hours in loading. No coaxing or threatening had the slightest effect on these independent Syrians. To an obstinacy of no common sort they added an impudence unparalleled, so that a Syrian Muggry became at length in our minds the personification of those two easy qualities. In an hour northward from Bethel, we saw Yebrud, upon a hill. Further from the path lay Jufna and Ain Sinia. North of Yebrud stood Selwad, on the top of a high hill. We now descended a steep path into the ravine of Mezra, among noble vines and fig trees, Jibia standing upon a hill-top on our left. Notwithstanding the fertile beauty of this ravine, it was insufferably hot, the hills shutting it in so closely as to puzzle Æolus to effect an entrance in his most violent moods. Another ravine cut this at right angles, and here the figs gave way for olives, which grew luxuriantly in their retirement. Ascending hence by a third ravine, we passed a ruined fortress, said to have been formerly the head-quarters of banditti, near which was a cavern, that had doubtless been used by those gentry. We met some suspicious looking Arabs with guns hard by the ruined stronghold, admirable assistants in this blood-and-murder picture.

We continued for an hour with the sun's rays powerfully reflected upon us from the white rocks, when we reached a small and fertile plain, in the centre of which we saw upon our right Turmus Aya, well placed on a hillock, and shortly after upon our left looked back upon Sinjil, clinging to the rocks. Crossing the plain, that waved with grain, we saw, on a high elevation before us, the domed mosque of Abu el Auf. By the side of this we had a high pass to cross, reminding us of some of the Nukbs of the desert. The ascent was steep, and lay along the edge of a deep and pretty vale; but the descent was *excessively* steep and rocky, bringing us into the lovely Vale of Lubban, a small plain of grain and olives, hedged by beautiful and lofty hills. A ruined Khan lay at the foot of the pass, where was a copious supply of water. In and around the ruin were an immense number of black goats. On the hill-side, to the north-west of this little bowl of a valley, was Lebonah,[*] a small village, where the goat-herds dwelt. Passing diagonally over this peaceful plain, we turned down a side valley eastward, and on finding a goodly shade of olives, sat down and refreshed ourselves with food and rest. After leaving this, we crossed a large wady, and ascended the hill ridge upon its northern side. From the summit a noble prospect greeted us. The fine plain of Mukhna was at our feet, about two miles in width, and extending northward some six miles to the bases of Ebal and Gerizim. The reapers were in numbers at work among the yellow grain, and oxen were treading out the corn upon the threshing-floors. This strikingly brought to our minds the story of Boaz and Ruth, so fragrant with simple loveliness. The scene was one of those in which the

---

[*] Judges xxi. 19.

soul is fully satisfied; all our thoughts of the pastoral and agricultural that had rendered their pleasing hue to our ideas of oriental life, were here fully realized, and we needed no imagination to create the rural scenes of Scripture history. Nablous, (the ancient Shechem,) where we intended to lodge, was hidden from view by the mountains that skirted the plain upon the west; yet Ebal and Gerizim were both evident before us, between whose bases were concealed in its valley this ancient town.

Descending into the plain, we followed the track under the western hills, passing around their several projections. The large village of Howara seemed to have sent forth its whole population into the fields, and all the employments of agriculture were in full operation. We wound along the skirts of Gerizim by a path deeply worn in the limestone, at some elevation above the plain. Near the corner of the mountain, where the Vale of Nablous comes down to meet the plain, we left our horses and made our way down the steep declivities to the most interesting object of this vicinity—Jacob's well. It is in the plain, just at the extremity of the Vale of Nablous, and every way accords with the details of the Scripture narrative. The *plain*, over which we had come, I have no doubt, is "the plain of Moreh," near Sichem, to which Abraham came on his way to Bethel.[*] The *well* is only mentioned in the Gospel of St. John, and from its title of "Jacob's well," was probably dug by that patriarch, before the conduct of Simeon and Levi forced him to leave this part of the land. We were at first shown a small opening in the ground, nearly closed by three large stones overlapping its edge. This so little harmonized with our precon-

---

[*] Genesis xii. 6.

ceived ideas of the spot, that we doubted greatly the correctness of our information, and were not satisfied until, the next morning, we made a more complete examination. We then removed the stones with some effort, and descended through the hole, which was just large enough to admit our bodies, and which would be utterly impenetrable to a corpulent man. Before releasing our hold of the edge of the hole, our feet rested on an accumulation of rubbish beneath. Groping our way down this, we found ourselves in a small chamber, which had once, doubtless, been on a level with the ground, but which the accumulated soil of centuries had now rendered subterranean. In this apartment was the hole of the well proper, down which we cast pebbles, and so discovered the entire absence of water. Indeed, our Christian host at Nablous declared it had been dry to his knowledge for the last fifty years. Around the upper entrance-hole were the ruined relics of Helena's church visible. The well bore indisputable marks of its great antiquity, and is safely identified with that whereon the wearied Saviour sat in the heat of noon, and where, in asking drink from the woman who had come to draw, he took occasion to teach her concerning the value of the water of life. How beautiful the lesson to us! This water of Jacob's well has passed away, but still the living water of a grace divine runs copiously within our reach. In walking up to the town, which lies a mile removed to the westward, we made a short detour to visit the so-called tomb of Joseph, which is not far distant from the well. It is a plain white Santon's tomb, or Wely, such as is everywhere seen in Mohammedan countries, excepting that this one is roofless, and, consequently, lacks the usual white dome. In the interior, a vine grows from a corner, and spreads upon a trellis over the tomb, forming a pleasant bower. The branches climb over the walls, and illustrate beautifully the blessing which Joseph received from his dying father—" Joseph is a fruitful bough, even a fruitful bough *by a well*, whose branches run over the wall."*

---

* Gen. xlix. 22.

Samaria and Galilee.

SCHECHEM—SAMARIA—JENIN—ESDRAELON—NAZARETH—SEA OF TIBERIAS—TIBERIAS—CAPERNAUM—CANA.

From Joseph's tomb we struck up the vale of Nablous, passed the ruins of a village called Betal, to a fine flowing fountain, where our horses were in waiting. Remounting, we rode through a lovely olive grove, between the high sides of Ebal and Gerizim, until we suddenly came upon the town when at its very gates. We passed nearly through the whole length of Nablous, bazaars and all, with a hundred children hooting after us, and casting stones at the " Christian dogs," and then reached the house of a Greek Christian, who was known to entertain travellers. It was a sorry looking abode; but the old landlord was the very picture of kindness, and we ventured. We had two upper rooms lightened of their loads of dust and rubbish for our possession, while our servants bivouacked in a little court below. But no cleaning could keep out the plagues of vermin, and we underwent a torture all night such as might have been expected from Mohammedan fleas. However, we had enjoyed a day of delightful travel through a portion of the country of peculiar interest, and were now willing to suffer some annoyance. The flowers upon the way were plentiful. Anemones, convolvoli, and hollyhocks were conspicuous, and dotted the land with beauty. The red earth, over which we had travelled a part of the day, reminded us of the soil of northern Jersey, and brought up sighful thoughts of our distant home. Nablous is first heard of as Shechem, and plays a prominent part, under this name, in the Old Testament history. In the New Testament we hear of it as Sychar, a probable corruption of name by the Samaritans. In Roman days, and after the apostolic period, it took the name of Neapolis, the Latins always affecting Greek appellations. This Neapolis is still seen in the Arabic Nablous. The town is beautifully situated in the midst of gardens, between Ebal and Gerizim, and almost entirely fills up the width of the vale, a narrow passage only being left on the north, between Ebal and the city. Both of these mountains are sterile, though Ebal appears somewhat the most suitable for the mount of curses. We stood upon the flat roof of our house, and brought in review before our minds the scene of that day, when the ark of God was placed in the midst of the vale, by the stone altar of Jehovah, and all Israel appeared before it, the half upon the slope of either mountain, to speak the solemn blessings and cursings that should thereafter attend upon the obedience or rebellion of the nation. The curses of Ebal are yet sounding through the polluted land, and all the earth has caught the mournful echoes. While enjoying the evening breeze on the house-top, I unexpectedly surprised a numerous harem upon a retired terrace near my position. The females were indulging in a most unoriental freedom from reserve both in dress and manner, and were put to instant confusion at sight of the Christian intruder. There was a sudden seizure of veils and garments; but in one of the fair assemblage there was far more spite than modesty, for she spent the time wherein the others sought a hiding-place, in twisting her countenance into indescribable contortions, and cattishly ejecting saliva towards me. Finding the flat house-top thus exposing and exposed, I took a last look at the beautiful town and its green suburbs nestling in the vale, and descended to talk with our old host. Several of his acquaintances came to pay their respects to us, all of them Christians of the Greek church. In the morning we repeated our visit to Jacob's well and Joseph's tomb, returning to town by the fine gardens on the southern hill-side. Everywhere were running streams and fountains, by the side of which grew pomegranates, magnolias, figs, olives, oranges, and apricots, in the greatest luxuriance and profusion. We entered the Samaritan synagogue during the worship. Nablous contains about one hundred and fifty Samaritans, the last remnant of that mongrel people, whose history after the Babylonish captivity was so entangled with that of the Jews. The synagogue is a plain room, with an alcove. Slippers and shoes are removed on entering. There were about twenty persons present, fine looking men, of fair countenance, clothed each in a gown of white linen or cotton. One, with a noble black beard, wore a large kerchief over his head, and read from a large roll, five hundred years old, covered with red silk. To him the rest responded in mingled bass and alto, at full stretch of lungs. After the service, they showed us the famous old manuscript, which they assert was written by the son of Phinehas, grandson of Aaron! It is a large roll of parchment, in a tin gilt case, and written in the Samaritan text. This is covered with red silk, beautified with gold letters. A covering of green silk, with gold letters, is wrapped about the whole case when laid aside. A thousand years is the greatest antiquity I should like to venture for this reputed work of Abishua. The Samaritans still worship on their mountain (Gerizim) at stated periods of the year, and form a wonderful instance of continuance amid changes. But the remnant is now exceedingly small,—a slight matter will extinguish the spark; and the Samaritan people, a transplanted vine of aged growth, will only live on the pages of history. In conversation with the white-bearded, venerable Yusef, our Christian entertainer, I learned from him that there were a hundred families of Greek Christians in Nablous. There are many Jews also in the town, yet the bigoted Mussulmans form the great majority of the inhabitants. Probably in no part of Syria are the Mohammedans so tenacious of their faith, and so inimical to Christians.

In the morning, my room was suddenly transformed into a school, of which a young Greek Christian, who had been our guide to Jacob's well, was the instructor. Eleven tarbouched boys were squatted before their miniature tables and under full headway, bowing and vociferating their tasks, as if each were an independent school by himself. The teacher informed me, by means of an extremely elevated tone, that the full school numbered thirty, giving me to understand that Syrian boys were as prone to "playing truant" as any Anglo-Saxon youth. Of course, this school is confined to the Greek Christians, and its books are furnished by some English society.

It was nearly 9 o'clock when we left our lodgings to continue our journey. We passed down the narrow and filthy street, noticing in the ruins of a mosque and other buildings the effects of the earthquake which injured several cities of Syria a few years ago. Ten palm trees are seen in and near Nablous, a fact worthy of notice, as they are not often seen thus far north, except in the low valley of the Jordan, or the warm edge of the Mediterranean coast.

Nablous is situated on the water-shed of the vale, and in leaving the town by its western extremity, we began a very gradual descent past fine groves of olives and along the many streamlets that fill the valley with beauty. A weed-grown aqueduct of no great length excited our risibles by the ridiculously varying sizes and shapes of its pointed arches. Passing this, we climbed the western limb of Ebal, *en route* for Samaria, our baggage having gone on by a more direct route to Jenin, our intended resting place for the night. From the summit we enjoyed a noble view of the hill of Samaria, rising in graceful form four hundred feet above its surrounding valleys. The situation of this capital of Israel reminded us of that of Judah's metropolis, a grand elevation surrounded by yet higher hills or mountains. Descending into the broad basin, we passed two arches of an old aqueduct, climbed a portion of the hill of Samaria, and sat down to rest beneath the tempting shade of some aged olives. The modern village was above us, and by its side were the imposing remains of a Christian church. We mounted by a steep zigzag, among abundant relics of ancient structures, and examined this fine ruin. The east end is entire, beautifully arched and richly ornamented within and without. Within the enclosure of the church rises strangely a Mohammedan wely, and this is called the tomb of Neby Yehya ebn Zachariah, or John the Baptist. Beyond this ruin, on the summit of the extensive hill, grow figs and olives where formerly were the palaces and pleasure houses of Ahab and Jezebel. While in the enclosure of the ruined church, which is now a vegetable garden and a waste of prickly pears, we were prevented from further examinations by some sour-visaged villagers, who, by their rude speech, rendered it more prudent for us to quit the inhospitable spot and prosecute our journey before trouble should arise. Descending, therefore, whence we came, we remounted, and quitting the hill, crossed the northern valley to the range that bounds the basin of Samaria on that side.

Bonar has beautifully noticed the complete fulfillment of prophecy in relation to this city once so glorious. He quotes the prophecy of Micah,* "I will make Samaria as a heap of the field, and as plantings of a vineyard: and I will pour down the stones thereof into the valley, and I will discover the foundations thereof." He then illustrates these words by the actual condition of the spot. "Every clause reveals a new feature in the desolation of Samaria, differing in all its details from the desolation of Jerusalem, and every word has literally come to pass. We had found both on the summit and on the southern valley, at every little interval, heaps of ancient stones piled up, which had been gathered off the surface to clear it for cultivation. There can be no doubt that these stones once formed part of the temples, and palaces, and dwellings of Samaria, so that the word is fulfilled—'*I will make Samaria as an heap of the field.*' We had, also, seen how completely the hill has been cleared of all its edifices, the stones gathered off it as in the clearing of a vineyard, the only columns that remain standing bare without their capitols, so that, in all respects, the hill is left like *the plantings of a vineyard;* either like the bare vine-shoots of a newly planted vineyard, or like the well cleared terraces where vines might be planted. Still further, we had seen that the

---

* Micah i. 6.

ruins of the ancient city had not been left to moulder away on the hill where they were built, as is the case with other ruined cities, but had been cleared away to make room for the labours of the husbandman. The place where the buildings of the city stood has been tilled, sown, and reaped; and the buildings themselves rolled down over the brow of the hill. Of this the heaps in the valley, the loose dykes that run up the sides, and the broken columns on their way down into the valley, are witnesses; so that the destroyers of Samaria (whose very names are unknown), and the simple husbandman, have both unwittingly been fulfilling God's word—'*I will pour down the stones thereof into the valley.*' And last of all, we had noticed that many of the stones in the valley were large and massy, as if they had been foundation stones of a building, and that in many parts of the vast colonnade nothing more than the bases of the pillars remain. But, especially, we observed that the ruined church had been built upon foundations of a far older date than the church itself, the stones being of great size, and bevelled in a manner similar to the stones of the temple-wall at Jerusalem and those of the mosque at Hebron; and these foundations were now quite exposed. So that the last clause of the prophecy is fulfilled with the same awful minuteness—'*I will discover the foundations thereof.*'"

No apology is necessary for introducing this long extract, where is so clearly brought to view the accuracy of prophecy in its minutest particulars. We noticed all the points here produced, and found them fully to justify the words above quoted. As we ascended the northern mountains, we halted repeatedly to look back upon the unrivalled situation of the ancient city. How proudly must the heart of Ahab have beaten, as he gazed over these lovely valleys, and the magnificent hill of his capital rising from the centre of the scene! It was on the spot whence we regarded this noble view, that the inspired herdsman of Tekoah summoned, in his glorious imagery, the Philistine and Egyptian host to assemble, and look down upon the tumults and oppressions that were destroying their enemy's metropolis.* In this, how admirably precise is the Jewish prophet! for from these heights, if Samaria had still been a city, we could have clearly seen the whole movements of the inhabitants.

On the terraces of Samaria's hill, we could see many columns standing in desolation, almost the only upright relics of the city's grandeur. In the valleys Indian corn was growing, and appeared about two feet high, and cotton was about four inches above the ground. The villages were numerous, and situated, with picturesque effect, upon the declivities or summits of the mountains. We noticed very many piles of loose stones, resembling rude columns in shape, erected in the fields to mark the corner-limits of different ownerships. Sometimes a man's property would be only ten feet square! at each corner one of these rude pillars (such as Jacob must have erected at Bethel) rising as a sentry. The fields are thus divided and reckoned as lots in Wall street, by the feet and inches. In this region the men wear the tarbouch on one side of the head—probably a foppish fashion.

Beyond the summit of the road, we gained a view of the Mediterranean Sea, and the sandy hills that line its coast. Before us were the mountains of Galilee, and a giant among all rose the snow-capped Hermon, seventy miles away. A lovely valley, whose grain yielded a variety of agreeable hues, lay far below and before us. Slanting downward along the northern face of the mountain, we passed several villages, at one

---
* Amos iii. 9.

of which (Jeba) we regained the direct road from Nablous, by which our mules had passed. Beyond this we passed through a stony strait, and then came out into a beautiful broad valley, with the rocky height of Sanur in full view before us. The town appeared quite formidable. We passed under the height, and entered a fine large plain, holding a lake of rain-water, where were gathered myriads of white storks. This plain is called "Merj el-Ghuruk," or "Drowned Meadow," and is about three miles wide. The anemone, convolvolus, and many other flowers variegated the surface of the plain, over which we passed to gain the ridge beyond. Our course lay through a narrow vale, and then up a pass, from the top of which still new views of beauty were revealed. A basin of loveliest green lay below us on the left, and the mountains of Galilee rose beautifully in the clear atmosphere.

We soon passed Gabatiyeh and its immense groves of olives. This was the first village which we had passed *through* since leaving Jerusalem. Crossing another small plain, we entered a smooth narrow winding wady, which, in an hour and a half, brought us to Jenin, on the confines of the great plain of Esdraelon. Our tents were already pitched, and our men awaiting us. Beyond our tents was the encampment of a new governor of Jenin, who had just arrived at his station. The town was a few hundred yards upon the east of our camp, having nothing but a mosque, minaret, and a few palm trees, that possessed any attraction. Hedges of prickly pear abounded, and a running stream of some magnitude passed near. We were wearied with our day's ride, and gladly accepted the rest offered upon the sward. This part of the country possesses an unpleasant reputation, and we were rather uneasy in our position, in spite of the gubernatorial retinue that neighboured us, for a Turkish governor is generally but a licensed villain, and the fact of possessing a license gives but small comfort to the victim, who cares chiefly for results. We were now in Issachar, having come through Ephraim and Manasseh. He had been promised a pleasant land by Jacob,[*] and our first sight of the beautiful plain of Esdraelon or Jezreel amply proved the fulfilment of the patriarch's prophetic promise. We noticed the sheep here, as throughout Palestine, having tails as broad as their body at their roots, and thence tapering to a point. Grasshoppers were plentiful, and had a peculiar head-ornament of horns, which I had never seen elsewhere.

That night the moon shone in unusual beauty, and we smoked in admiration before the tent. The frogs were making music in the neighbouring ponds. A number of threshing-floors surrounded our position, on each of which a man sat watchman over the precious grain. On one, a watchman of higher rank, or greater industry, had erected a booth, under which he could mount guard with more comfort and, perhaps, less effect. Toads and ants were prevalent, and did not serve as agreeable additions to our moonlight enjoyments. We sat meditatively, and thought of the Canaanites, Issachar, and the Turkish sultan, till we felt our meditation gradually melting into sleep, when we pulled down the curtain of the tent, and encountered Morpheus in the usual manner.

In the morning, before starting, I took a hurried survey of Jenin. It was as dirty as Syrian towns generally. Its mosque, and palm trees, and a fine clear stream, with stone embankments and pebbly bottom, were all the lions of the ancient village of Ginaea. The people looked scowlingly upon me as I passed. Hurrying back, through the prickly pears and the burial-ground,

---

[*] Genesis xlix. 15.

we were soon off in the great plain. For 4¾ hours we were passing over the fertile expanse by the first good road we had seen in Palestine. The ground was cracked everywhere, deep crevices extending downward, and revealing the rich character of the soil. Flowers of every variety grew upon each side, but not a tree was visible in the whole extent of the plain. Crops of cotton, Indian corn, and wheat abounded, yet half the land was neglected and untilled—probably the mingled effect of an oppressive government and an indolent people. Gnats filled the air, and were as bothersome as they usually are.

The sites visible from the plain were of intense interest; Carmel, Elijah's abode, bounded Esdraelon upon the north-west, by the side of the Great Sea. Along the same range, and nearer to us, was Megiddo, where Ahaziah died of his wounds. Still nearer, on the hill-side, lay " Taanach with her towns."

On our right were the mountains of Gilboa, where Saul was slain; near our path was Jezreel, where dogs ate Jezebel. Beyond was the mountain of Ed-Duhy, at whose foot lay Shunem, where Elisha raised to life the son of the Shunemite. When we had passed Ed-Duhy, we looked back on Endor, where Saul had visited the witch, and Nain, at whose gate the widow had her son restored by the Incarnate God. Here the green and graceful Tabor recalled the triumph of Deborah and Barak, while the hills and mountains of Galilee before us encircled the earthly home of the Saviour. Surrounded by such stirring associations, our ride had all the excitement of romance, and we were wandering among the days of old.

We fell in with several horsemen exercising themselves in equestrian accomplishments, with the dashing recklessness of the Orientals. A Turk on foot shows as little animation as a zoophyte, but place him on a horse, and he is exuberant with life. There is a magic influence in the saddle which puts him to all the action of a mountebank; it is the only inspiration that can move a Turk. As we passed the little decayed village of Fuleh, that more resembled the mud settlement of beavers than the home of a human community, a horseman issued from its mounds of filth; he was splendidly mounted, and bore a formidable spear, at least twelve feet in length. A footman preceded him, and they directed their course across our path. We could easily imagine the knight an accoutred Saladin, and actually did fancy him a noble freebooter, prepared to pay his addresses to our luggage, for the plain was lonely and the neighbouring village would have made an admirable substitute for Ali Baba's cave, for concealment both of plunderers and property; but, on nearer inspection, the equestrian proved a Turkish soldier from Nazareth, and his avant-courier was an unfortunate peasant who had shown a dullness in comprehending the laws of ownership, and was therefore now about to enter the proper school for removing this deficiency of intellect. The poor Fulehite seemed to tremble at the very shadow of the long spear behind him, that utterly cut off his hopes of retreat, and he endeavoured to keep in advance beyond the reach of the military spit. This was a novel but effectual method of showing a culprit to prison, completely setting aside the necessity of musket or fetters.

After crossing the head waters of "that ancient river, the river Kishon," which had swept away the hosts of Sisera, and after long admiration of the graceful form of the green Tabor, we arrived at the northern limit of the plain at the foot of the mountains of Galilee. From this point, an hour of passage up a ravine and over intervening hills brought us to the Vale of Nazareth, a scene of sweet rural beauty.

The small cup-like valley is snugly sequestered among the heights; fields and gardens occupied its bed, the peasantry were busy in the yellow harvest, and the town of hallowed memories lay peacefully and pleasantly upon the western hill-side. The Latin convent was conspicuous among the neat buildings of the place; a mosque, with a girdle of cypresses, lent its picturesque effect; and the figs and olives, that add so much to the beauty of Palestine, were not wanting here. It was just such a view that we should wish to associate with " the child Jesus "—a natural frame of loveliness for that spiritual picture. We found rooms, neat and comfortable, in the guest-house of the convent, and experienced every attention from the monks.

After a substantial dinner, we ascended the hill behind the town, a height of about 500 feet. We passed several rows of houses that stand one above another on the acclivity, and then mounted by a steep path worn in the limestone through the fields of grass, in which numbers of children were at play, the swing being the most fruitful source of their merriment. On the summit is a Mohammedan wely, called " Neby Ismail." We seated ourselves beside the tomb, and enjoyed a glorious prospect. At the south was the green carpet of Esdraelon, terminated by Carmel and the glittering sea. On the north was the small and beautiful plain of El Buttauf, perhaps " the valley of Jiphthah-el."* In this plain the ruined castle of Sepphoris, or Dio Cæsarea, appeared upon its hill, resembling in shape a modern church with square tower. Beyond rose the mountains of northern Galilee and the snow-capped peak of Hermon. On the east, the mountains of Bashan bounded the view, between which and our position lay hidden the sacred sea of

---
* Joshua xix. 14.

Tiberias; and nearer by, the rounded summit of Tabor lifted itself above the intervening hills. No scene had excited such delightful emotion except the simultaneous view of Bethlehem and Jerusalem. There we gazed on the places of our Saviour's passion; here on the scenes of his action. As the Babe of Bethlehem and as the sacrifice of Calvary, he had exhibited himself mainly as the *passive* Saviour—he had been led either by his parents or his enemies; but in the vale of Nazareth, and among the hills of Galilee, he had been the powerful preacher, the energetic prophet, the untiring philanthropist, the *active* Saviour, " going about doing good." Judea, as it were, holds up to view the punished disobedience, and Galilee the rewarded obedience of man, represented in the suffering and performing Christ. And there is a correspondence in physical appearance to this spiritual consideration: Judea, which especially felt the force of Roman vengeance, is yet strewn with the wrecks of that awful storm, and the ruined towns and neglected tillage of the land are fearful mementos of the expended curse; while Galilee, in its fruitful plains and valleys, in its peaceful lake and green-clad hills, betokens aptly the rich blessings of God reconciled.

We sat in blameless enthusiasm, looking on the villages about us and the winding pathways, as once the frequent resort of the Nazarene. Perhaps the very hill-top where we sat had often been the retired spot where he had loved to pray, and whence in love and pity he had gazed upon the earth he came to save. Such moments of enjoyment as these would amply repay all labour taken in an Eastern journey; for, in comparison with such scenes, Europe has scarce a claim upon the traveller's steps. We could not wonder at the pilgrim's zeal, which would defy the combined powers of poverty, disease, and war, in order to feast upon such rich repast, and even the violence of the crusader received a momentary palliation.

The next morning we rode to Tiberias. Two hours' ride over the limestone hills brought us to the foot of Tabor. The village of Dabouriyeh (an evident corruption of the ancient name of *Daberath*) lay upon our right, upon the skirts of the noble mountain. The shape of Tabor is not conical, as we had presupposed, but rather that of a boat with its keel turned upwards. Its sides are covered with the dwarf-oak, among which a zig-zag path, rough, and even dangerous in some places, leads to the broad summit, which we reached in about an hour and a half from the base, having lost our way for about ten minutes of the time. A large field of wheat was growing upon the table-land of the summit over which we passed to reach the extensive ruins at the south-east extremity. These ruins mark the site of a large town, and some massive portions tell of an early date. There can be no doubt that, in the time of our Saviour, this height was crowned with an important fortress, which effectually overthrows the monkish legend of the site of the Transfiguration as connected with Tabor. The monks of early ages were professional site-makers, and one of their first rules of business seems to have run somewhat thus:— " Be sure to select a site so conspicuous, and so befitting the event in *one particular*, that posterity will hug the belief of its identity, in spite of its disagreement in *other particulars*." So *here* Christ is said to have been transfigured on a mountain *apart*, and the monkish college of illustration and adaptation immediately select Tabor, which rises *alone* upon the plain, as the incontrovertible spot, notwithstanding the almost certain fact of a town having occupied that summit at the time, and the strong evidence we have from the gospel narrative that the mount of Transfiguration was in the north of Galilee, near Cæsarea Philippi, whence to his city of Capernaum Jesus would have to pass " through Galilee."*

The view from Tabor is, as might be supposed from its isolated position, extremely fine, comprising most of the objects seen from the hill behind Nazareth, with the addition of a part of the Sea of Galilee. The majestic Hermon lifted its white head at the north, and reminded us of the Psalmist's words—" Tabor and Hermon shall rejoice in thy name."† We wandered for a time among the picturesque ruins hung with vines, among walls and vaults of great extent, and, having refreshed ourselves from the fine well of water that had formerly supplied the fortress and town, we descended by the same path by which we had mounted, until near the base, when we struck northward.

We were six minutes less than an hour in gaining the foot of the mountain, from which our course lay over low hills to Khan et-Tujjar, which, though a name in the singular, seems to be applied to two formidable looking Saracenic fortresses, one on either side the path, stationed in a retired wady. We were afterwards told, at Tiberias, that a great concourse from the neighbouring towns resorted every Monday to a fair held at this point. Leaving this, we passed Kefr Sabt on a hill, and then rode around the head of the depressed plain of Ard-el-Hamma, a beautiful expanse, variegated with all the shades of ripe and ripening grain, but possessing not one tree. On the left rose the two singular peaks, called the Horns of Hattin, which the site-makers have dubbed the Mount of Beatitudes. We

---

* See Mark viii. 27, ix. 30, and the corresponding passages in Matt. and Luke.
† Psalm lxxxix. 12.

could have been sure that so conspicuous a height would not have escaped a situation in the monkish nomenclature. But history has rendered it a surer memorial of another event—the famous battle of Hattin, which was gained by Saladin over the army of the crusaders on the ground over which lay our course back from Tiberias. It was this battle that practically overthrew the theory of "Christianity promoted by force," and sent the usurping Franks back to their more legitimate duties at home. Beyond this, we arrived upon the brink of the the heights that surround Gennesaret, and looked down upon the lake. It was a scene of rare beauty. The noble heights contrasted well with the peaceful surface of the water that had often borne the immortal body of the Son of God. We descended over a rough path, now gaining a view of the little plain of Gennesaret, that bordered the lake upon the north-west, and now obtaining sight of the town of Tiberias, that stood upon the very brink of the water beneath us. The town appeared forbiddingly dreary—its shattered walls were of sombre hue, and a few palm trees seemed to hang weeping over its desolation. We reached the gate in an hour from the summit of the hills, and on entering found the town a wretched skeleton. The earthquake had shaken it to fragments, and masses of ruins appeared on every side. The Jews' quarter only had been rebuilt, and thither, over the heaps of rubbish, we took our way. We stopped before the door of one Haiim Weissman, a German Jew, and were immediately waited upon by a bright faced, neatly dressed boy, who ushered us into a room that boasted of a cleanliness most out of place in Syria. Here we settled ourselves and our luggage, and were hospitably received by Mr. Weissman, who extended to us every civility in his power. The

Jews form almost all the inhabitants of Tiberias. This place, Saphet, Hebron, and Jerusalem, form the four sacred points of Palestine in Jewish eyes, and to these spots come all those whom religious zeal has attracted to the land of their ancient glory, the home of their fathers. They have five synagogues, all of them neat and clean buildings—but there are no traces of the celebrated academy of the School of Tiberias, where the compilers of the Mishna and Gemara prosecuted their task. Alas! the days of even that glory are passed away from Tiberias.

Shortly after our arrival, we heard of a wedding in the town, and hastened out to witness it. A great concourse had collected in the court of a synagogue. They kindly made way for us, and gave us a good stand by the door of the building. In the midst of the crowd was a canopy, but as yet no one stood beneath it. After waiting some time, at length the groom, a lad of fourteen, appeared, and stationed himself under the centre of the canopy. A procession then revolved about him, composed of two men with torches, the bride, in tinselled head-dress, and two old women, one of whom led and the other followed the bride. After several revolutions, this peculiar movement ended, and bride and groom each drank a glass of wine; then an old white-bearded Jew came forward and lifted up his voice in a prayer of deep solemnity, doubtless calling on the God of Israel to seal with His blessing the union that had there been proclaimed. This last scene was truly touching, and the whole assembly were evidently affected.

Tiberias has only a population of 1000 since the earthquake, of which the large majority are Jews. There are twenty families of Greek Christians, a few Mussulman families, and only *one* Latin Christian, besides a friar from Nazareth, who takes care of the old

Latin church. This church is some 600 years old, and purports to be built upon, or near, the site of the miraculous draught of fishes. It is now lately white-washed, and has a modern appearance. It is a long, narrow vault, with pointed-arch roof, without the slightest ornament, internal or external.

Beyond this, the town is almost wholly destitute of interest, besides its sacred associations. Columns and ruined friezes are seen about the lanes and in the sides of the houses, and the town in general, with its broken wall and mounds of ruins, is a shrunken body in a shattered frame— the saddest, most sombre place of abode our eyes had ever witnessed.

Early the next morning after our arrival, we hired the only boat upon the lake, as wretched and fragile a bark as ever rode the waves, and hoisted sail for Tell Hum, at the north end of the sea, but the wind proving very slight, we found our limited time would not permit so long a sail, and we accordingly steered for Ain et-Tin, or the Fount of the Fig, where Dr. Robinson has placed the site of Capernaum. This spot is about seven miles north of Tiberias, at the northern extremity of a small plain, formed by a recession of the mountains. A ruined khan (Khan Minyeh) lies above it, and from the rock a noble stream gushes forth, over which bends a beautiful cluster of fig trees, whence comes the fountain's name. The stream runs but a few rods, and then empties into the sea. The stream was full of small fish. Not far from this delicious fountain is a mound, on which are a few unimportant ruins, scarcely distinguishable, probably the all remaining of that exalted Capernaum which was to be thrust down to hell.* We pushed out into the lake opposite this, and fished where so often Peter and Andrew,

---

* Luke x. 15.

James and John, had cast their nets. A few peasants were gathering grain on the plain, but that and our own company was all of the human visible in this place, where a busy population had once beheld the Lord of Glory. In sailing back, we looked carefully at El-Mejdel, a miserable village at the southern extremity of the plain before mentioned. We looked carefully, for this is supposed to be the Magdala whence came Mary Magdalene, the faithful follower of Jesus. We reached Tiberias again, after an absence of six and a half hours. Our four boatmen, supposing we wished to be on the lake only half an hour, had gone breakfastless, a fact of which we had been ignorant; when it became necessary to row, they barely could summon strength, which had made our passage evidently slower than would have been under other circumstances. It was probably this unsatisfied condition of their stomachs that had induced them to urge us to give up our intended visit to Tell Hum, a loss which we afterwards greatly regretted.*

Opposite Tiberias is the land of the Gadarenes, and here the hills incline steeply towards the sea, almost appearing as cliffs. It was down one of these precipices the swine ran when the devils had entered into them. On a hill beyond the northern extremity of the lake, we saw the ruins of Bethsaida. South of Tiberias, about a mile distant, is the Emmaus of Josephus,† whose hot baths are famous, and where Ibrahim Pacha had erected a new building for the convenience of bathing. We left Tiberias at one in the afternoon,

---

* At 7 A. M. found the temperature of the air 71 deg., ditto of the water of the lake, 78 deg. (Fahr.)—*June* 2.

† Dr. Robinson thinks Emmaus but a Greek form of the Hebrew Hammath, signifying "warm baths;" and this Hammath he supposes the Hammath of Napthali.—Joshua xix. 35.

and mounted the steep hill-sides, towards the Horns of Hattin. On the way are shown the Hejar en Nusara, or stones where Christ sat when he fed the multitude. The monks have indeed been indefatigable in spreading a carpet of fanciful tradition over the Holy Land, which, however, the enlightened spirit of the age is fast wearing into shreds.

In two hours from Tiberias we arrived at a well, surrounded by stone troughs, where we halted to drink. Here we overtook an Egyptian, who interchanged cordial greetings with his countrymen, our servants. An Indian dervish and his two friends met us, whom we recognized as having before seen near Nablous. These were all, like ourselves, strangers in the land, and we felt a readiness to enter into a sympathizing conversation, but the waning day urged us onward. We passed the village of Lubieh, and then along the side of a fertile plain, over against the large and pretty town of Turan, to the hills that compose the region about Nazareth. Here we soon found the ugly hamlet of Kefr Kenna, at the foot of a limestone hill. This is the Cana of Galilee, according to the monks. Dr. Robinson has brought forward an array of testimony, which shows that there was formerly another place further north, that bore the name of Kana-el-Jelil, and which was regarded as the real Cana of Galilee. This place he was shown from the hill behind Nazareth, though he did not visit the spot. On our route from Nazareth to Akka, we passed within two miles and in full view of this supposed Kana-el-Jelil. I carefully inquired of the peasantry, and they assured me they had never heard the name. I then accosted a man apparently of some rank, and asked him concerning the desired spot. He told me that he had always lived in that neighbourhood, but had never heard that name before. He stated that there was a village called simply "Jelil," six hours north of our position, but no other of like title, to his knowledge. I then pointed him the ruined village east of Kefr Menda, which Abu Nasir had shown Dr. Robinson as Kana el-Jelil and asked him the name. He replied it was Deiduly,* and he knew it by no other name. From these facts, I would conclude that, while Kefr Kenna has been seized upon by the Latins as the true Cana, the Greeks have formerly used Deiduly for the same purpose; or if the Latins had also held the latter belief, they had changed the spot for one nearer at hand, as more convenient. As far then as evidence of name goes, Kefr Kenna seems to have the strongest claims, for manifestly the title of Kana el-Jelil is only known to the Christians, and from the total ignorance of this name exhibited by the natives, it has been the offspring rather than the parent of the tradition. Crossing another ridge of green hills, we descended into a sweet little valley, completely shut in by the beautiful heights. Here was the village of Er Reineh. A gushing fountain burst forth by the road-side, and by it stood a fine trough of white marble, with festoons in bas-relief upon its side, evidently a fragment of some important ancient building, hollowed out by modern hands for its present humble service. The peasants met us with a cheerful " Buon Sera," which they had derived from the monks of Nazareth—so different a reception from the customary scowl or indifference which the traveller in Syria learns to digest. Shepherds were watering their flocks at the stream, and girls of really beautiful countenance were bearing their water-jars to and from the fountain. The whole scene was eminently peaceful and pastoral, and realized our brightest fancies of the rural happiness of ancient

---

* This may be Idalah.—Joshua xix. 15.

Israel, when this very vale, "flowing with milk and honey," was the home of a people whose " God was the Lord." A ridge of hills divides this valley from that of Nazareth, over which we soon passed to our former lodgings, arriving in five hours from Tiberias.

Galilee and Syro-Phœnicia.

SUNDAY IN NAZARETH—LEAVE NAZARETH—SEFURIEH—VALE OF ABILIN—AKKA—TYRE—SIDON—BEIRUT.

The next day was Sunday, which we spent quietly in the town and its suburbs. The children, as before, were swinging merrily under the trees as we made a second visit to the hill-top, and we were confirmed in our former opinion that Nazareth and its vicinity exhibited more appearances of happiness and contentment than any portion of Syria we had seen. The women were decidedly pretty and affable, and this, too, was a strange fact for our eyes. In the afternoon, we went over to the Latin convent to attend vespers. The church is a fine edifice, with a raised centre, to which a staircase leads. The walls are hung with rich damask, and several altars adorn the sides. A number of the Christian inhabitants gathered in the church, and knelt upon the floor. We stationed ourselves by a side altar, and witnessed the apparent sincerity and earnestness of these Eastern Christians in their worship. The fine tones of the organ, and the solemn postures of the congregation in the town of our Saviour's abode, were affecting in the extreme. Yet we could not forget that that Saviour was robbed of his glory by these very worshippers that called themselves by his name. In ignorance, they did not view him as their *sole Saviour*, but the Romanist leaven had brought their *works* in rivalry with Him who "is made unto us wisdom, and righteousness, and sanctification, and redemption."[*]

Yet the scene was solemn, as is all sincere worship when its manner is subdued, even though error be a large ingredient; but I confess the solemnity fast diminished when the worthy cowled friar who presided at the organ gradually slid out of his psalmody, and showered upon us cotillons, waltzes, and polkas in most fertile variety. The organist in sackcloth was probably recalling his days of worldly folly by the enlivening influence of his youthful music, unaware that the critical ears of foreign amateurs were there to be confounded by these unseasonable sounds.

After the vesper service was concluded, Fra Benvenuto, the good-hearted brother who had acted as our special host, showed us the contents of this ecclesiastical museum. Several ordinary paintings helped to adorn the edifice, and one, the *large* picture of the Annunciation, possessed considerable merit. The *small* picture of the Annunciation (over the altar where the Annunciation took place!) we did not see, as we were unwilling to spend our time and money in a series of ceremonies that must needs preface its exposure to public gaze. Fra Benvenuto consoled us by declaring the picture to be of no great importance. This altar of the Annunciation is beneath the level of the floor, under the high altar. It bears a tablet, inscribed, "Hic verbum caro factum est." Here is shown the column, which, though severed from its base, and having its lower portion removed, yet miraculously hangs from the roof! Here, too, is the window through which

---

[*] 1 Cor. i. 30.

the announcing angel came! and here, most wondrous tale of all, formerly stood the house of the Virgin, which once grew weary of remaining in a land where it had so many rivals in the relic line, and flew over to Italy, where it could have the field more to itself!! On its way from Nazareth to Loretto, a goodly journey, and somewhat unusual for a house, it stopped to breathe awhile in Dalmatia, it may be, to plume itself and arrange its fair proportions, so that it could leap the Adriatic, and appear in its new home with greater effect. It is rather presuming on a man's verdancy to tell such a Munchausen story, nothwithstanding it be sprinkled with holy water by good Mother Church; and though the surprising legend had often excited our sense of the ridiculous, yet one might suppose that upon its sober enunciation at the alleged spot of the event, we would have considered ourselves insulted by the bare-foot friar. Not at all, good reader; we had become so accustomed to this tradition-diet, that the most spicy mouthfuls were taken without a murmur; and when we arrived in lands unblest by these valuable treasures, we found some time necessary to prepare our palates again for the plainer fare that the less imaginative cuisine of Protestantism prepares.

After Fra Benvenuto had duly expended his kindness and credulity upon us in the church, we were conducted to Joseph's carpenter shop! and to our Saviour's dining table! Then we visited the Maronite chapel, a small building of bare and unsightly interior. The old Maronite priest was ringing a big bell, like unto a boarding-school dinner-bell, to assemble his scattered flock, as primitive a method of summoning a congregation,—as the priest was primitive in his external appearance. Just over this little church the hill rises abruptly, forming a precipice, which may well be the point to which the crowd endeavored to bring our Lord in order to cast him therefrom. There is certainly no necessity, and little sense, in placing the spot at a distance of two miles from Nazareth, where the most sage and erudite traditionists affirm the site to be. The Maronites, though principally resident on Mount Lebanon, have many communities scattered about Syria. They were Monothelite heretics of the seventh century, supposed to have adopted the name of their first bishop Maro. In the twelfth century they became re-joined to Rome, and still own subjection to the pope, though they have rites, precepts, and opinions that Romanists would scarcely confirm. We saw but little of their worship, and that little was by no means favourable.

On Monday morning at seven o'clock, we rode out of Nazareth, expecting to reach the sea once more by evening, the very sight of which would seem to render home nearer. We passed the full fountain surrounded by the females of Nazareth, each waiting her turn to fill her jar; and leaving the Greek chapel on the outskirts of the town, we climbed the limestone path over the northern hills, from the summit of which we looked down on the lovely valley of Er Reineh, through which we had passed two days before. Before us rose the ruined castle of Sefurieh, or Sepphoris, towards which our path wound. In less than two hours from Nazareth, we reached that place. The hills clothed with pasture, the numerous flocks, the fields of grain, and the harvesters gayly singing at their work, were a living illustration of the description of the Psalmist—" The little hills rejoice on every side, the pastures are clothed with flocks, the valleys also are covered over with corn; they shout for joy, they also sing."* The village

---

* Psalm lxv. 12, 13.

of Sefurieh is a shabby, dilapidated collection of houses, at the foot and side of the hill which the ruined castle crowns. Our road lay in the valley before the village, but I turned off my horse, and struck upwards through the dirty lanes, over roofs of houses, and among threshing-floors and winnowing-grounds, to the consternation of the women and children of the village, until I came out behind the place, and reached the old ruin. The castle is exceedingly imposing when seen from afar, but has its grandeur greatly diminished by a close examination. It is evidently Saracenic, and partially built with stones of an older edifice. It is only about thirty feet square, its interior being one room, with roof and windows of pointed arch much smoked by fires made in it, when used, probably, as a dwelling by the natives. There seems to have been an upper story, but it is now destroyed. From Nazareth the building had appeared of great size, and if I had trusted to my view there had, I should have supposed the castle rather three hundred feet square than thirty, so wonderfully deceptive was the atmosphere, as we had seen, also, in previous instances. Below the castle, to the west, and almost in the village, is the ruined church of "Joachim and Anna," the reputed parents of the Virgin Mary, whose house is reported to have covered this site. There remain merely the extremities of the three aisles, and some fragments scattered about. Galloping down the uneven sides of the hill, I rejoined the party, and we proceeded north-west along the western side of the great plain of El-Buttauf. In an hour from Sefurieh, we passed a ruined Khan and well, where flocks were watering. This was called El-Bedawy.* Here commenced the Vale of Abilin, through which we were to pass to Akka. The opening was, at the junction, a

---

* Dr. Robinson marks it on his map as "Kaukab!"

mile broad. Opposite El-Bedawy, at the foot of the mountains on the north of the plain of El-Buttauf, was the village of Kefr Menda; and further eastward was the ruined Deiduly, whose supposed identity with Cana of Galilee has already been mentioned.

We now left the plain of El-Buttauf, which was a small likeness of Esdraelon, and turned westward through the Vale of Abilin. This was a pleasant, retired valley, between graceful hills, and offering an excellent natural road. It exhibited no cultivation for the most of its extent, but had a considerable wild growth of dwarf oak and butm. It was winding and narrow for an hour; it then widened, and presented patches of tillage, and here on the left we saw the imposing village of Abilin, perched on high, with its mosque and minaret. This is doubtless the town of Zebulun (Joshua xix. 27), and tends to prove my supposition that the plain of El-Buttauf is the valley of Jipthah-El. We here caught sight of the blue sea, with feelings of no common delight. Khaifa and its white walls appeared upon its brink, and beyond rose the "excellency of Carmel," with its formidable monastery, where the friars commemorate the abode of Elijah on the mountain, by living in a style the very antipodes of that which the frugal, eremitic prophet affected. Several villages appeared upon our right, and upon the left we looked back upon the lofty fortress of Shefa Amar, a most warlike looking object both in structure and position. We had passed Et-Tireh some distance before we obtained our first view of Akka about six miles in advance. In a few minutes more we were fairly on the plain of Akka, which extends from Carmel northward for twenty miles, and maintains an average breadth of five miles from the sea. On the plain, not far from the point where we entered, is a very curious large mound, shaped somewhat like a truncated cone, partly cultivated on its sides, but untilled on its flat summit. To the west of it is a well. Both mound and well bear the name of Bissan. We were an hour and forty minutes crossing the plain. As we approached the walls of Akka, we met many women carrying kettles full of bread and fruit, probably bought at the market of Akka, to carry to their homes in the neighbouring villages. They wore a profusion of coins around their faces,—a moneyed frame to their countenances. Each could truly tell her suitors that " her face was her fortune," and an heiress-hunter would be saved all the trouble of inspecting register offices, by carefully studying the visages of his female acquaintances,—a result that Lavater never dreamed of in his physiognomy.

We entered at length the gate of Akka, and were again in a large town. The usual sight of narrow lanes, rickety houses, bazaars, coffee-shops, and lazy Moslems, met our eyes, as we twisted through a score of labyrinthine passages to find the monastery, where we hoped to obtain lodgings. At length, we were conducted into the area of a large Khan, which afforded ocular evidence of serving as soldiers' barracks; for scattered about were the defenders of the Ottoman Empire, some rubbing up their bayonets, and others arranging their toilette. We could see no monastic appearance in anything here to justify our temporary settlement; so we retreated from the quadrangle, and started in search of the American Consul, for our eyes had been greeted, when entering the town, by a sight of the stars and stripes, which sufficiently indicated a consulate. Our search for the consul proved more entangled than our previous hunt after the convent. We were directed from one end of the town to the other, and then back to our original point of starting, but in vain. I climbed several houses, and endeavoured to catch a glimpse of the flag that had attracted our notice on the plain, but, as an ignis fatuus, it had disappeared. Persevering, we at length stumbled upon the desired consulate. We found the Consul a Syrian, most anxious to oblige, and, under his escort, we were shown to the convent, which proved to be a portion of the identical Khan we had before visited. Here we found that the good monks were taking a siesta, and must not be disturbed, and, moreover, we were informed that an Arab family were occupying the rooms which the convent set apart for ladies, and our occupation of those rooms would consequently turn out-of-doors the present tenants. In this emergency we were about forsaking Akka, and encamping somewhere on the plain, when our Consul begged us to accept his rooms for the night, and an Italian friend of the Consul, who resided in the Khan, also tendered his apartments for our use. As we were already near the latter, we accepted the Italian's offer, and had our baggage brought up to a terrace or gallery that ran beneath the rooms. The Khan was ornamented by a fountain, overhung with willows, in the centre of the open quadrangle, and about this were soldiers and others loitering in the oriental bliss of inactivity. Along the stone corridors of the interior, where were the barracks, the soldiers had raised small patches of Indian corn, which reminded me of the crops of oats children often cultivate in tumblers, there being a great similarity in the extent of *rurality* and *profit* of the agricultural schemes.

Akka did not exhibit as much of interest in its interior as we had been led to anticipate by its formidable aspect from without. It has a goodly gate, but there end its virtues. The point of land on which it stands forms the side of its only harbour, and there we counted its extensive marine, numbering in all *four* small fishing boats! We rowed out to an isolated fortification that had been well riddled by English shot, and thence along the outer sea-wall, partially repaired, but still exhibiting huge gashes and rents formed by British cannon. The next morning, the Consul, in company with the Pacha's janissary, called upon us, and invited us to view the fortifications. We set out, and made the complete circuit of the town upon the walls, as far as was practicable. The old janissary strutted before us, as proud as a pacha, and at every guard-house half a dozen ragged looking soldiers, in faded regimentals, and commanded by a corporal in corresponding habiliments, turned out, and did their Frank visiters honour by presenting arms, in this case as warlike a manœuvre as is seen in the old nurse, when she *presents arms* to an infant. From the walls we had an excellent view of the dilapidated condition of the town, and saw the wrecks of the powder-house, which had done such havoc by its explosion during the siege. In the ruined walls on the sea-side there remained many cannon-balls imbedded, which we attributed to the English, but which the Akkaites refer to Ibrahim Pacha.

At eight o'clock we left Akka by its single gate, and struck northward along the sea. The plain contained many villages before us and upon the right. We soon passed the country palace of the Pacha, surrounded by oranges, pomegranates, and cypresses. Beyond this, we were opposite the hundred arches of the Akka aqueduct. Wherever this aqueduct crosses a hollow, it is supported on weed-grown arches of picturesque effect; near the town it passes almost on a level with the ground, and, instead of the roads being built over it, it is strangely elevated above the roads by an arch, under which the passing traveller receives a copious shower-bath from the numerous leaks. These arches, seen at various points on the plain, have a very peculiar appearance.

We continued along the sea, though not upon the beach, over several dry beds of streams. Three hours north of Akka, Ez-Zib (the *Achzib* of Scripture) resembled an Egyptian village with its palm trees. An hour beyond this we reached the bold promontory of Nakoura, (pronounced *Na 'ura*), the village of El-Bussah, beautifully embosomed in olives, lying at its foot, upon our right. A regular pass conducted over the high rocky promontory which bounds the plain of Akka on the north. As we ascended, we had a fine view of the extensive plain we had left, and the fortress of Akka formidable in the distance. At the summit of the pass was a small ruined fort. The declivities about us were covered with green shrubs and bushes, but the rock permitted no cultivation. Before us appeared Tyre, fifteen miles away, jutting out into the sea, and far beyond rose the snow-clad heights of Lebanon, while the vast expanse of the Mediterranean stretched out limitless upon our left. With such a grand prospect before our eyes, we descended the north side of the promontory, and reached the village, khan, and fort of Nakoura, having been an hour and a quarter in passing the Cape. Two noble cedars spread their foliage near the Khan, and drew us willingly be beneath their shade; a running stream furnished our beverage, and we rested in this delicious spot for a half hour, reluctant to leave its attractions.

Twenty minutes further north, we discovered some columns on a hill some distance to the right. Turning our horses' heads thitherward, we galloped over the plain, and up the steep acclivity to the site. Among entangled bushes one column stood erect and complete, another broken at the middle, while multitudes of others lay prostrate, scattered over an area of half a mile in extent. They were of late Roman date, but on no map is this site denoted, and since arriving at home, I have been wholly unable to identify the ruins with any ancient town. The only notice I have seen of the spot, besides our own, is a drawing of the ruins by Cassas, shedding however no light on their history.

Another small promontory was passed, by a road evidently of old Roman date, formed with the same sort of large stone as are seen in the Via Appia, and other Roman roads in Italy. Beyond this a quarter of an hour, were the slender remains of Alexandroschenæ, now bearing the name of Iscanderoon. Here a copious supply of water bursts out, in two full jets, from beneath a Saracenic arch, and runs down a fine stream into the sea. Another quarter of an hour brought us to the celebrated Ras-el-Abiad, or Promontorium Album, a high headland, which, on the northern side, exposes a precipitous wall of chalk, whence its name is derived. This we crossed by a rock-worn and rock-hewn pathway, said to be the work of Alexander the Great. It is the Scalæ Tyriorum of antiquity. In many places, the path overhangs the sea, to the terror of weak nerves; and on the northern side of the promontory, the steps are cut out regularly from the white rock, while a natural parapet remains on the outer side, as a bulwark for the traveller. The precipitous cliffs above and below, and the surf dashing against them, rendered this pass wild and picturesque in the highest degree. We were twenty minutes in reaching the beach beyond, and twenty minutes more brought us to the ruins of Sheberieh, an unimportant fragmentary collection of modern remains. Near by, and close to the sea, was a fine old well, approached by descending steps, by the side of which I noticed an old marble well-curb, grooved by the friction of ropes. In another twenty minutes the ruins of a massive bridge over a wady appeared upon our left. From this point we looked back on the apparently formidable castle of Shemmon, prominently situated on the summit of Ras-el-Abiad, back from the sea. Observing what appeared to be ruins a half mile to the right of the road, I galloped over to them, and found immense stones, resembling those in Stonehenge, though smaller, morticed for some purpose, which baffled my conjectures. They probably were relics of Palea Tyrus, the old Tyre of Nebuchadnezzar's demolition.

We now arrived at Ras-el-Ain, where were four reservoirs of solid masonry, and three dripping aqueducts, the latter Saracenic, with one Roman exception. Of course, there was a grateful foliage around, that yielded a welcome resting place. This site is, with great probability, supposed to have been included in Old Tyre. Quitting this pleasant spot, we left the prominent rocky hill of Ma'shuk upon the east, turned westward, along the sandy isthmus, and entered the gate of New Tyre at six o'clock in the evening. A young Syrian met us in the street, and addressed us in French, inviting us to his house. We followed him through the forlorn lanes of the wretched town, and reached his house upon the brink of the sea, where we could have the very best prospect of the ignominious state of that once mighty capital, whose merchants were princes. The rooms were tolerably comfortable, but the entrance to the house was by a dark and dirty cellar-like passage and yard. The young man introduced us to his father and stepmother, the former a venerable old Greek Christian, and the latter a blooming young woman, with an infant attaché. She wore the usual costume of the Tyrians, which exposes rather more of the bosom than Frank propriety would allow. With her child in her arms, and mounted on high wooden pattens, she busied herself strenuously in preparing our accommodations. Our young guide was the only one in the family, or (according to his own account) even in the town, who could speak French. He was therefore in general demand by the native consular agents, and by all the travellers who stopped at Tyre. He proved very obliging and efficient, and would have made our stay at Tyre one of unalloyed pleasure, if the fleas had permitted him. His father represented himself as in slender circumstances, and designed to undertake a journey to Egypt soon, in order to repair his finances. The interpreter son was to remain with his "belle-mère," and keep the house of entertainment for Frank pilgrims, such as we were. He gave us his name as "Michel Farrah."

In Tyre there is but little to see, and that little is of melancholy interest. The modern town only partially covers the "Island," or extremity of the Peninsula, leaving on the west and south a large space of fine pasture-land between the houses and the sea. At the north are the remains of an artificial harbour, nearly enclosed by a wall, a little port, and well filled with sand; beyond this were several small fishing-craft, eight or ten schooners, and one good sized ship, a better representation than at Akka, but yet what a fleet for the proud city, in whose harbour were once "all the ships of the sea, with their mariners!"[*] The people of the town were cheerful and unreserved in their manner towards us, having been more conversant with Franks than had been the inhabitants of Lower

---

[*] Ezekiel xxvii. 9.

RUINS OF TYRE.

Palestine. The bazaars had a ragged, picturesque appearance, suggestive of a decline in Tyrian trade. North and west of the town are very many prostrate columns upon the low flat rocks, over which we walked, though the sea often covers them. They were plain, but massive. I searched in vain for a fluted pillar or an ornamented capital. From the summit of a ruined light-house we obtained a good view of the desolation that has passed upon this mistress of the seas, and yielded our minds to the natural reflections upon so sad a scene. At the south-east corner of the town we found the fragments of the cathedral, a noble relic of Christian architecture, resembling the wrecked hull of a fine vessel with barnacles clinging to its sides, for, both within and without, the huts of the town are fastened to its walls, and greatly hinder a correct idea of the original structure. The ruin was somewhat like that of the church in Samaria. The large round end of the nave still stood, the most conspicuous portion of the building, and the form of the cross was clearly discernible. Some immense prostrate columns of red granite, in one of which we found a single block of twenty-eight feet in length, attracted our notice among the numerous hovels.

Such is the modern Tyre; for an idea of its ancient splendour, it is only necessary to read the 27th chapter of Ezekiel, where the most brilliant picture of earthly prosperity ever drawn forms the contrast to the above description of Tyre's abject condition as now beheld.

The next morning we received a kind farewell from our host and his family. In passing through the bazaar, we noticed snow exposed for sale, but it was sadly spoiled, and could scarcely be supposed an article used in figure as the emblem of purity. It had been brought from the mountains of Lebanon, on whose summits we could see happier specimens of the injured element. The day was very hot until the sea-breeze rose. Each day that we were on this coast, we found the sea-breeze commenced about ten in the morning, without which the ride would have been intolerable.

Leaving Tyre, and the few palm trees that lend a beauty to its sadness, we passed over the sandy isthmus and renewed our journey northward. The plain is smaller and less flat than that of Akka, but, for those reasons, and the fact of Lebanon's proximity, is more picturesque and agreeable to the traveller. We crossed the Leontes, (the modern Kasimiyeh,) a fine full stream, by a noble bridge of a single arch. At its southern extremity, above the bank, is the partially ruined Khan el Kasimiyeh. A multitude of sheep and goats (for in Syria the flocks are always intermingled) were drinking at the stream, which was the largest and swiftest we had seen in Palestine, excepting the Jordan. Passing a ruined bridge upon our left, over a dry water-course, we reached, in one hour and three-quarters from the Leontes, the supposed site of " the City of Birds," the Ornithonpolis, which Strabo mentions as " a little city (πολχνιον) between Sidon and Tyre." Here the low rocky cliff on the right was penetrated by numerous tombs. Beyond this we bathed in the sea, and sought out a pleasant spot, beneath some mulberries, by the side of a running brook, for our noon repast. An hour further, Sidon came in sight, in situation much resembling Tyre, though possessed of a more imposing appearance and a greater beauty. The ugly village of Sarafend crowned a hill on our right, opposite which, between us and the sea, were the almost untraceable remains of Sarepta or Zarephath, where Elijah raised to life the widow's son.* A little mosque is now erected over the spot that tradition marks as the site of the widow's house. We soon after reached the beautiful fountain of Kanterah, with its little pool, its fir trees, its gardens of mulberries, and a mammoth oak,—one of those exquisite little retreats from town and sun which so dot the traveller's course in Syria with pecuculiar charms. Then came successively a brook lined with oleanders, and boasting a ruined bridge; a sorry looking Khan; the little river Zaherany, with its bridge severed as by an earthquake; and a broad torrent-bed, of winter importance. The village of El-Ghazieh was very prominent on the hill-side at our right. By the side of the road lay prostrate a plain granite column, with this inscription, which I copied, as others had done before me:

```
        IMPERATORES
         CAESARES
       L. SEPTIMIUS SE
       VERUS-PIUS PER
       TINAX,-AUG:-ARA
       BICUS AD + + + + +
       PARTHICUS MAXI
       MUS TRIBUNIC + + P.
       OTES VII IMP. XI Cos.
```

Passing numerous gardens, and under a beautiful *berceau* of trees, we entered Sidon at forty minutes after four, in seven hours and forty minutes (travelling time) from Tyre. At the entrance of the town is a Moslem cemetery, the first we had seen beneath a grove. Women in white were moving like spirits among the tombs, and could be easily fancied the ghosts of the dead that lay below the sod. Sidon is finely situated on a hill projecting into the sea, and is fortified on the land side by a high wall,† through which we entered by

---

* 1 Kings xvii. 9–24.

† On this wall are built very high houses, the only lofty dwellings we had seen in the East.

the gate, and, passing through the attractive bazaars, reached the Khan el Frangee, a large quadrangular building, enclosing a fine open court, in the centre of which was a pool of water, surrounded by trees and overhung with vines. A small part of this Khan (as is the case with that of Akka) is used as a convent, and there we applied for admission; but a rude monk gruffly told us he expected a bishop that evening to arrive, and occupy all the rooms they could spare, and we must hunt elsewhere for our lodging. Thus rebuffed, we found plenty of offers from the holders of rooms along the corridor of the Khan, and were soon comfortably fixed in a small suite of apartments. A number of fine looking, intelligent, and well dressed boys were playing about the corridor, who attracted our attention. Finding they could talk French, I entered into conversation with the youngsters, and found they were the sons of Sidonian gentlemen, and members of a school in the Khan, whose teacher was a Frenchman. This was the dawning to us of a higher state of civilization in our route. The whole appearance of Sidon formed an epoch in our journey. We suddenly lost sight of the lazy, dilapidated Orient, in the life and bustle of a large and busy town, as is Sidon, and saw in its inhabitants a tone of rank and intelligence that we had not witnessed since leaving Cairo. We felt for the moment that we had exchanged Syria for France, for both European dress and manners now greeted our eyes, so long accustomed to the robes and sedateness of the Shemitic races. True, the Khan was the principal seat of this Frankish semblance, yet even in the remote corners of the town there could be seen a different spirit at work than in Hebron, Jerusalem, Nablous, or any of the towns of Syria we had previously visited.

The harbour of Sidon is in as bad case as that of its sister Tyre; if one of the old Sidonian or Tyrian fleets should return to its native port, it would find a sorry welcome, for sand and rubbish have effectually established themselves as exclusive tenants of the greater part of these famous harbours. Enough room, however, was left in that of Sidon to allow a few fishing boats to anchor within the ruined walls, as a burlesque on " Great Sidon." In the harbour is a fortress of the crusade period, built on a rock, and connected with the town by a bridge of nine arches. On the south side of Sidon, the hill on which it is built exhibits a green declivity down to the sea-beach, adding greatly to the view of the town taken from the Tyre road.

The summit of our khan was a delightful promenade, commanding a fine view of the entire vicinity. Eastward from Sidon were the beautiful mountains of Southern Lebanon, and between them and the town groves and gardens added a remarkable loveliness to the scene. Northward, southward, and eastward, was the Great Sea—the classic sea of Poetry and History, yielding to our ears the same murmur that had stirred the souls of David and of Homer. When night arrived, and moonlight bathed every object in its peculiar charms, the scene was as a vision—the enchantments of dream-land seemed to surround us, for there was an unearthly softness and purity in the moonlit landscape.

Hearing there was an American Consul in Sidon, and hoping to find a like character with our kind Akka friend, I started in pursuit. Following several crooked lanes, I came to the house pointed out as the consulate, and knocked at the inner door of the divan. I heard a hurried scrambling and confusion ensue within, as of rats disturbed in their festival, and thereupon made bold to enter. Here was a fine scene for an American consulate. A crowd of servants occupied the divan-hall, evidently met in blissful saturnalia, thankfully to commemorate their master's absence. Not knowing the rank that the Sidonian representative of the American government might hold in his native town, I imagined at first that he might be an individual member of this merry-making company, and accordingly inquired of one of the worthies, if he or any of his companions in enjoyment were the American Consul. This seemed to put them all into renewed glee, and I left them to continue their fun undisturbed by outside barbarians. I suspect the servant, or servants, of the absent Consul had seized the favourable opportunity to collect all the domestics of Sidon in the master's hall, not anticipating such an ill-timed official visit as ours. My search after Mr. Carr, our minister at Constantinople, who was reported to be in Sidon, was attended with a like success as my consular hunt. I afterwards found him in Beirut.

The next morning we left Sidon before eight o'clock. Winding along its narrow streets, looking at the present representatives of the skilful artists (Σιδόνες πολυδαίδαλοι of Homer) of the ancient city, and issuing by the town-gate, we passed northward, along the beach, striking a short distance easterly to cross the Nahr el Auly, a fine stream that comes down from Lebanon. Fording this, near the old stone bridge of the famous Fakhr ed Din, four of us left the remainder of the party, and hurried onward to Beirut. The mountains of Lebanon grew loftier and more grandly picturesque, and the sea-plain was reduced to a mere beach, and even that at times was crossed by a projecting headland. The road was either rocky or sandy the whole distance to Beirut, and scarce a furlong would permit a gallop. On the promontory of Jajunieh, we had our last look at the beauties of Sidon behind us, and further on, we passed over the remains of an old Roman road. Coves of large extent succeeded one another along our course. These we crossed upon the curved beach, and then would come the boundary promontories, which presented a mile or two of rocky path. Such was the character of the road until we crossed the peninsula of Beirut. In the centre of one of these coves is the Wely Neby Yunas, with its little white dome marking the spot where Jonah and the whale parted company, and near it is a khan, also bearing the name of the prophet. This is supposed by Pococke and Dr. Robinson to be the site of Porphyreon. We should also find the site of the Leontonpolis of Strabo in this neighbourhood. Still further north, we crossed the fine river Damur, evidently the ancient Tamyras or Damouras; the stream was lined with oleanders, and northward stretched away miles of beautiful groves of mulberry, which suggested the position of Strabo's Æsculapian Grove ('Ασκληπιοῦ ἄλσος). The valleys and defiles running down from Lebanon presented scenes of a decided Swiss character, and formed a continual feast of delight to the eye. We passed several khans, all of them as if made in the same mould, low square structures, inviting only because of the cool water we knew could be found within. Near one of these khans (el Khulda) are quantities of sarcophagi strewed upon the ground, but no ruins appear. Probably, in ancient times, an undertaker had his manufactory on this spot. The empty coffins were not bad emblems of the poor fellow's resurrection, each one serving in this place of his occupation as good purpose as the "Resurgam" of the hatchments.

The Cape of Beirut is about seven miles wide at its neck, where we crossed, and is almost wholly composed of hills and hollows of red sand. East of our route, between us and the mountains, extended for miles the immense olive groves of Beirut, the largest in Syria, and probably in the world. Among these trees, and all over the sides of the mountains, perched like pigeons on the ledges of a house, were the villages of this populous region. Near Beirut we came among villas, a strange sight in the East, where the habitations of the land are generally clustered in towns and villages. Here, and at Sidon, were the only country villas seen hitherto on our entire route. The road now became narrow, between high hedges of prickly pear, and intersected by cross roads of the same nature, that led to the numberless villages in the neighbourhood. We rode for miles through these ways, doubting if Beirut would ever appear, till at last our perseverance was rewarded by the sight of the sea at the north of the cape, and a view of the neat dwellings of the town. We reached Beirut in $7\frac{3}{4}$ hours from Sidon, but the rest of the party arrived three hours after us.

Lebanon.

BEIRUT—EXCURSION TO BALBEK—THE GOODLY MOUNTAIN—ZAHLEH-BALBEK, AND ITS VAST RUINS—RETURN TO BEIRUT.

BEIRUT is beautifully situated on the northern slope of the cape, and almost surrounded by gardens, groves, and orchards, of richest verdure. The sea washes the foot of the town, and a few rent fortifications remain to testify to the bombardment. We found good quarters upon the quay, in the inn that bears the high sounding title of "Hotel d'Europe," and from the balcony enjoyed a grand view of the magnificent towering Lebanon, rising majestically from the very brink of the sparkling sea. On the morrow we exchanged visits with several residents and fellow-travellers, and were assailed by numbers of salesmen proffering articles of Druse manufacture.

We discovered that the steamer for Smyrna sailed on the following Wednesday, and this was Friday, so that our projected trip to Damascus was out of the question. But Baalbec was only two days off, and there we determined to go. Peparations were made to start that day, and we had mounted our horses before the hotel, when the rascally chief Muggry who had brought us from Jerusalem seized my horse's rein, and effectually stopped my progress. I had reduced his pay, owing to his failure to comply with several requisitions of our contract, and he was now determined on revenge. In vain I attempted to push him off or pull him along with the horse. I struck his turban from his head, but he still held on. I then leaped from the horse, and administered some striking remedies. He removed his hands, but before I had remounted he was again fast. This never would do. Time was passing, and we were losing our only chance of Baalbec. I sprang from the horse again, and ordered the scamp to follow me to the Pacha. A troop of Arabs accompanied us, and I found myself at the head of a procession composed of all the loafers of Beirut. Arrived at the palace, a forlorn building of considerable pretension to style, we found the divan occupied by some underling, to whom I stated the case. The Muggry then gave his emended version, and the Sub-Pacha thereupon most blandly requested me to give up my scruples and pay the full price. This sort of judicial lop-sidedness, though exceedingly oriental, was extremely offensive, and I stoutly refused his demand. Finding I was not easily overcome by his speech, he sent a messenger to the Pacha, stating that he had a hard case before him in the shape of an American infidel, and desired His Excellency's will on the subject. His Excellency's will suited me exactly, as it referred the whole case to Mr. Chasseaud, the American Consul, and left the matter to Mr. C.'s decision. So the procession formed again, and off we marched to the consulate. Mr. Carr, the American Minister, and Mr. Porter, the Consul at Constantinople, were both present at the important trial, which resulted in the Muggry's occupation of a room in the prison for that night, with the privilege of having his feet supported in a board admirably adapted to them.

All this had detained us for two hours, so that the day was fast waning, when we at length sallied out of Beirut. We had gone but a short distance beyond the gate when we discovered that our guide knew nothing of the way. Here was another delay while we sent him back and waited for a substitute. By 4¼ P. M. we were fairly off and passing through the paths lined with hedges of prickly pear. The fragrance of the jessamine perfumed the air, and the landscape was one of unrivalled beauty. On all sides we heard the buzzing sound of the innumerable silk wheels in operation, and we saw, half hid among the mulberries, the neat little houses where the process was conducted. After crossing the extensive plain, and mounting a short distance up the foot of the immense range of Lebanon, I felt my old fever and ague returning—the chills creeping over me more and more perceptibly, until, though my horse was walking, I shook with all the effectiveness of a brisk trot. I could not think of returning, for that would have forever shut Baalbec from my eyes, and therefore I shook myself on, in rather bad case to enjoy the remarkable scenery about me. The horses mounted the steep path with the facility of cats. In passing a rude khan, I was sorely tempted to stop, and even wheeled my horse to return to Beirut; but I checked the intention, and pushed on. The view at every step increased in interest. We looked down over the sandy promontory of Beirut upon the sea glowing in the rays of sunset. Beirut itself, with its shipping, lay upon the right; west and south of the town the country was studded with villas, and nearer to our position spread the vast plain of olives, while the mighty Lebanon itself, in its lovely valleys and terraced declivities, clothed in fairest green, and glittering with a hundred villages, gave the highest glory to the view. At 7½ another khan was reached, and here we inquired the distance to the next. "An hour and a half," was the reply. I summoned all my energies, and still cried "onward." Darkness now came on, concealing the heights and dells, the cliffs and gorges from view, and rendering us uncertain of the path. We were compelled to dismount and lead our horses over the wretched stony road. My chills had been succeeded by fever, and I nearly fainted with fatigue as we toiled up the dark and rocky pass. The hour and a half seemed interminable, and my despondency was verging on despair, when a light was seen before us, close at hand, and we arrived at the doorway of Khan el Hussein, nearly five hours from Beirut. We entered a little stall-like room behind the porch, and, after spreading some matting over the ground (which is the sole floor of a khan) I quickly prostrated myself in feverish exhaustion. The gaunt stone walls of the forlorn building afforded poor accommodation for an invalid, yet, after pouring down my throat a large bowl of strong coffee, and wrapping myself in my blanket, I fell asleep and slept soundly until morning, when, to my agreeable surprise, chills and fever had both forsaken me, and I was ready for the continuance of the journey.

At a quarter of five we set off and ascended among tracts less green and more wild, but commanding views of astonishing grandeur and beauty, that fully justified the noble mention repeatedly made of this lofty range in the pages of Scripture. "That goodly mountain Lebanon" was the object of desire to the aged Moses; both Solomon and Hosea refer to the sweet "smell of Lebanon,"[*] arising from its

---

[*] Sol. Song iii. 11; Hosea xiv. 6.

flowers; Isaiah represents the rich foliage of the mountain as "the glory of Lebanon,"* and David often referred to this unrivalled range in his lyrical compositions. Nor can any one look upon these glorious mountains, abounding in all the essentials of the sublime and beautiful, without echoing in ecstacy the epithets of the Hebrew penman. Certainly no mountains that I have ever seen can vie with these Syrian heights. In form, colour, and magnitude, they are perfect, these three elements so harmoniously combining as to leave no room for improvement in their united effect.

We reached the summit at a quarter past eight o'clock, three hours and a half from the khan. This makes the distance from Beirut eight and a half hours of travel, and the ascent of the mountain about six and three quarter hours, or sixteen miles. The air was fresh and invigorating; wreaths of mist encircled the various peaks and projections of the mountain, and lay in the hollows like little lakes, but the view of the sea and magnificent slopes of Lebanon was unobstructed and unspeakably grand. On every hand we could see the picturesque villages sitting on apparently inaccessible heights, whose very situation must give their inhabitants a poetical cast of mind.

Abandoning this gorgeous panorama, we crossed the summit, amid higher peaks, and where vegetation was but slight. Then the south part of Coele-Syria (El-Bekaa) was spread out as a carpeted floor before and below us.† Anti-Lebanon formed its eastern wall, among whose noble heights Hermon lifted his snowy head pre-eminent. The scene was grand, yet totally

---

* Isaiah lx. 13.
† Strabo is rather out in his calculations when he puts the Jordan and the Lake of Gennesaret in Coele Syria. L. 16, cap. 2.

different from that we had gazed upon at the western side of the range. There was no endless sea here, no frequent villages studded the mountain-side, and the valley was far less deep than was the Mediterranean coast; but we had a mighty ridge of mountains rising before us, and a plain of surpassing beauty at our feet.

The projecting mountains at the north hid Baalbec from our view, which was still distant at least twenty-seven miles. The mountain is so much steeper, and its height from the plain so much less on this side, that we had completed the descent in one hour and a half from the summit, leaving the little ruined village of Mekseh among the crags on our right. Continuing along the foot of the range, and around the hills that form its outworks, we reached the large and flourishing village or town of Zahleh at 11 o'clock. This was the finest village we had seen in the East. The houses were well built of crude brick, whitewashed in front, and set each separate from the other,—an instance entirely unique in Syria, as far as our knowledge extended. Everything betokened thrift and industry, and it is almost useless to state that the inhabitants are Greek Christians. Turn out the Christians, and fill the place with Mussulmans, and Zahleh would soon find a level with Jenin, Sefurieh, and the other hovel collections of Palestine.

Beautiful groves of poplars and willows surround this interesting town, through which we rode a quarter of an hour before we reached its northern circuit. A gay wedding procession was passing along the road—men on fine horses practising all the equestrian pranks conceivable, and shouting in unchecked mirth. They saluted us, and challenged us to a race, but our nags were in poor condition for any such operation, and we let the Zahlehites seek for other competitors. Just beyond the town was a full flowing brook, and by its border grew an inviting tree. We could not resist, but alighted and rested in the welcome shade, to indulge in our noonday meal. An extensive apple orchard grew beside us, the kind old proprietor of which immediately brought us an offering of the tempting fruit. He joined our party, and chatted with us pleasantly during our stay. He added to our delightful impressions of Zahley, a place we shall never forget for its beauty, thrift, and friendly population.

An hour beyond Zahleh, we caught sight of Baalbec —then it disappeared from view, and again, at three o'clock, it re-appeared permanently. It seemed a large village, or town, with a high scaffolding, supporting a watch-tower, as its most conspicuous item. This, on closer approach, we found to be the gigantic columns of the great temple. The plain seemed interminable as we galloped on towards tho deceitful town, which appeared to defy a close proximity. Crossing the head waters of the Leontes, we at length put our horses to full run, and stayed not till we dashed among the huts of Baalbec, throwing the entire community into trepidation and alarm. We had passed an old ruin a mile or two from the town, but were too hurried to regard it, and we now sped past the mammoth remains of the ancient Heliopolis, with barbarian indifference to the wrecks of magnificence that were there existing. The truth was, we had been riding twelve hours, excepting our stoppage at Zahleh of three-quarters of an hour, and were both wearied and hungry. If Balbek had invited Thebes and Palmyra to assist in our reception, we would have equally slighted the trio, and sought, as we now did, the locanda and its kitchen. Alas! we found the locanda had no existence, at least in that capacity, for the Italian adventurers who had boldly erected a hostel in the shadow of the Temple of the Sun, had, as was to have been anticipated, not succeeded in keeping a crowded house, and therefore had sold out their building (decidedly the best in Balbek) to a Syrian gentleman, while the unsuccessful speculators had wandered elsewhere on the world's wide surface, to seek a better investment of their capital. The Syrian, however, kindly received us, and gave us beds in a comfortable room, where gaudy pictures of Leonora and Beatrice hung as mementoes of its former possessors. The house was built solidly, and with considerable taste, and had a little shaded courtyard before it, where coursed a fine stream of water between banks of stone, all showing that the establishment had been started on an extensive plan—and witnessing, moreover, the extreme folly of the attempt to make a Cheltenham or Saratoga in the remote vale of Coele-Syria.

Our host, though he furnished us with room and bedding, apologized for his inability to provide the still greater necessaries of life, stating that he was a bachelor, and therefore had no kitchen, but trusted, I suppose, to the liberality of his neighbours. This was exceedingly bad news to us, for so certain were we, when we left Beirut, of the existence of a loconda at Balbek, that we had come unprovided with either pantry or kitchen. Yunas and Haleefy, our two Fridays, were immediately despatched to seek material for a repast, and after an uncommonly long absence, they returned with one chicken and an armful of Balbek bread, the circular loaves of which have the disproportioned dimensions of eighteen inches in diameter, and a quarter of an inch in thickness. This was all the provision Balbek could make for our fierce appetites. We devoured the old hen (for such it was) half cooked, and finished our meal of compulsory frugality with sundry square-yards of the blanket-like bread, washing all down with copious draughts of coffee, the only actual enjoyment in the entire feast.

Balbek is a straggling ugly village, situated in an alcove of Anti Lebanon, on the side of the great plain of Coele-Syria, and only interesting for its antiquities, unless we except a beautiful sward, shaded by magnificent walnuts, and watered by delicious streams, which lies behind the town against the mountain, and bears the name of Ran el-Ain, or the " fountain-head." This is the source of the Leontes, whose mouth we had seen near Tyre, some seventy miles distant. On the green grass of this place the inhabitants of Balbek collect and lounge, enjoying life in that listless laziness characteristic of oriental taste. South of this spot is a hill, or spur of the mountain, on which, beside the ruins of Saracen walls, are seen a little quarry of undoubted antiquity, the ruins of a large monumental column, and a finely carved block, formerly connected either with the column or some neighbouring building. Moreover, within the quarry are some carved stones, which the workmen had wrought upon in their original position, from which they had never been removed. A larger quarry (the most important quarry near Balbek) is south of this a considerable distance, where one immense block of seventy feet in length and fourteen feet in breadth and thickness, lies where it was originally hewn. Some distance west of Balbek, on the plain, is a mound, containing a third quarry, but in which we found nothing of great interest. Several miles north rises a Corinthian monumental column, which we only viewed in the distance.

The great ruins of Balbek lie just westward of the town, and compose a vast area of magnificent remains of art and masses of undistinguishable rubbish. Between these and the town, almost among the houses, is the beautiful little Corinthian " Temple of the Winds." This is a circular edifice, of thirty-two feet in diameter, and surrounded by eight columns, which support projections of the cornice, or, I should say, *did* support, for four only are now standing upon the east side, the western portion of the building being very greatly ruined. This little temple is an exquisite gem of art, and perhaps as it appears now, overhung with usurping verdure, it wears a greater beauty than in its days of pristine glory. Behind each column is a Corinthian pilaster against the circular body of the edifice, from capital to capital of which hang sculptured garlands, and beneath these are ornamental niches with vacant pedestals. On the north-west side are the remains of the huge doorway. The two door-posts are standing, each about twenty feet in height, and five feet in breadth and thickness. All the stones of the temple are about three or four feet square, their large size rendering the building apparently smaller than the reality. A dome formerly covered its now roofless area. Leaving this interesting introduction to ruined Balbek, we cross several fields, and reach the Great cluster.

Of this it is utterly impossible to convey a correct idea by description. Imagine a vast raised area of nearly a thousand feet in length, with a width varying from one hundred and fifty to four hundred feet. On one extremity of this area is a gigantic temple of two hundred and eighty-five by one hundred and fifty-seven feet, and the rest is occupied by enclosed courts and approaches to the magnificent fane. Underneath all are immense vaults supporting the entire mass. Attached to the east side of this extensive pile is a

THE GREAT TEMPLE GROUP. 347

smaller raised area and temple; its remains are more complete than those of the other; and if it had not its greater neighbour as a rival, it would be called a mighty structure, its two dimensions being two hundred and twenty-two and one hundred and fourteen feet. Never having seen a ground plan of the temples of Balbek, from which I might copy, I shall have the presumption to place before my readers a general sketch of their outline, as rude as a child's delineation of a horse that requires the name to be underwritten, yet sufficiently correct to give an approximate idea of the matter. I beg the good reader not to quote my plan for authority, as my eyes were all the theodolite I possessed, and my guessing power had to serve for a measuring tape.

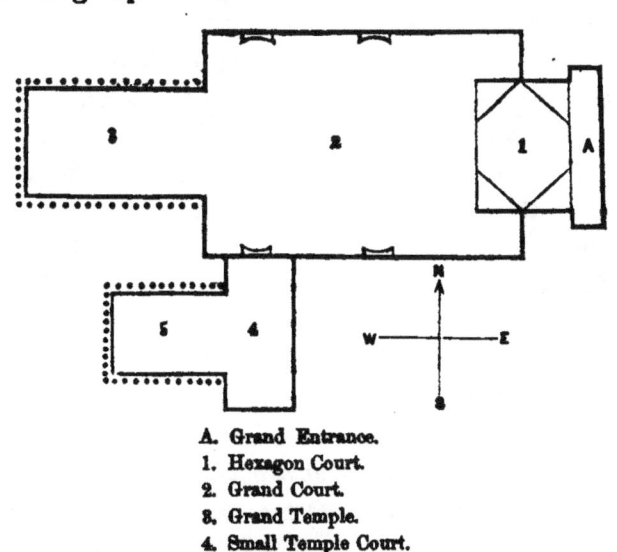

A. Grand Entrance.
1. Hexagon Court.
2. Grand Court.
3. Grand Temple.
4. Small Temple Court.
5. Small Temple.

The hexagonal court of the Great Temple shows marks of great architectural beauty in itself and the chambers around it. Leaving this, you enter the mighty area immediately before the temple; when the building stood complete (if it ever did), the coup d'oeil from this point must have been one of the most magnificent architectural feasts ever enjoyed. But alas! now only six columns of the temple remain standing, supporting the shattered architrave, yet these remaining pillars are nearly seventy feet in height. What must have been the imposing effect of fifty-six such columns! Large alcoves, as it were chapels, are built around the grand court, and these are ornamented with niches. In the side of the raised area, at the west end of the temple, are seen three huge blocks of stone, each sixty-three feet in length, and of proportioned width and thickness. From these stones, which are evidently out of place, and those in the quarry unremoved, it is reasonably supposed that this vast structure was never completed.

But the side temple has been complete, and even now is well preserved. It originally had eight columns on the west end, and thirteen along either side. Of these, three columns remain standing with a portion of the architrave on the west, nine remain on the north side, and five on the south. These columns are Corinthian and not fluted, and support a portico carved most skilfully and exquisitely upon the under side, with arabesque work and heads interspersed. Much of this roof had fallen, and we could closely examine its beauties. One stone in the south wall we found to be twenty-eight feet in length. At the east are two *fluted* Corinthian columns, with architrave at the *south* side of the great entrance; only a fragment of one of the corresponding two *north* of the entrance is visible. There are no traces of any other *fluted* columns. An ugly Saracen wall has been built up before the front of the edifice, under which we crept by a small aperture, and entered the little space intervening between the front and this wall. Here is the large doorway, elaborately carved; the huge stone of its lintel has partially fallen, and seems ready to crush the visitor as he enters. On the suffit of this stone is sculptured an eagle and thunderbolts. Entering the temple, now roofless, seven Corinthian fluted half columns are seen against either side wall, with two rows of ornamented niches interspersed, the lower row arched and the upper pointed. Beyond these, at the west end, are traces of an enclosed sanctum, and here are three pilasters on either side, in lieu of the half columns. The west end exhibits a plain wall, excepting two pilasters, one near either side wall. The nave of the temple has been divided from its aisles, and probably was hypaethral, the aisles and sanctum only being roofed. A square turning staircase ascends on either side the entrance to the top of the edifice. The doorways of these staircases are now probably buried in the rubbish, but we found an entrance through a hole cut in the side, just large enough to admit the body. The southern stairway is completely ruined. We ascended the other and found unsightly fortifications around the summit, erected by the Arabs in their wars.

Such is a brief and very incomplete account of this remarkable cluster of ruins, probably excelled in magnitude and interest by no other in the world, except the unequalled Karnac. In Karnac, the grandeur of design is in perfect harmony with the massive style of Egyptian architecture; but here is the strange yet pleasing contrast of grandeur in design, and the graceful lightness of Corinthian art.

The ruins of Balbek are sadly disfigured by a Saracen wall that surrounds them, and numerous erections of the same period scattered among and *on* the ruins, when the whole area was turned into a fortress by the utilitarian Arabs. It has been these rough tenants of the place to whom we are to attribute much of the ruined state of the Balbek temples, for the elements seem to have done nought or little of harm to their fair proportions.

It is now generally conceded that these magnificent edifices were the work of Antoninus Pius; perhaps they were designed and commenced by the architect-emperor Adrian. Mr. Wood, an early visiter of Balbek, quotes thus from John of Antioch: "Ælius Antoninus Pius built a great temple at Heliopolis, near Libanus in Phœnicia, which was one of the wonders of the world." They are evidently ruins of a period later than the Augustan age. The quantity of ornament and other peculiarities prove this, and if these stupendous structures had been here at the beginning of the Christian era, Strabo would never have mentioned Heliopolis without noticing them.

The history of Balbek is enshrouded in mystery. Some suppose it the Baal-Gad of Scripture;[*] but we must look much further south, near Hermon, for Baal-Gad. Others suggest its identity with Baalath, as Tadmor with Palmyra,[†] but Baalath seems rather to have been a city south-west of Jerusalem, in the tribe Dan.[‡] More sure is our knowledge of the identity of the Greek Heliopolis with Balbek.

Here, Macrobius relates, the Assyrians worshipped sun under the name of the Heliopolitan Jove. It was not, probably, until under the Roman sway, that Balbek became aught else than a petty village. Then it gradually increased in importance until Adrian, in his extensive designs, determined to make it a Syrian seat of luxury. He failing to complete his intentions, Antoninus Pius

---

[*] Josh xi. 17, and xii. 7.   [†] 1 Kings ix. 18.   [‡] Joshua xix. 44.

followed out the original design, and Balbek became and continued a dignified city, until the Eastern hordes overthrew its glory simultaneously with the Roman power.

Such is the most consistent history we can derive of the rise and fall of this remarkable place, which is so little mentioned by ancient authors, and I might add, so little known to the modern world.*

We spent two nights at Balbek on poor diet, and then galloped over the plain towards Beirut. We crossed the expanse of Coele-Syria, passed its brooks and streams,—reached Zahleh, and ate a meal again by the apple orchard, and chatted with the good old Christian,—ascended Lebanon, resting a brief while at two khans,—and then descended the other side to Beirut, losing our way in the dark, and getting into innumerable difficulties, yet arriving finally at Beirut, under a late risen but glorious moon, at one o'clock in the morning, having mounted our horses at five the preceding morning, and having been seventeen hours of the twenty in the saddle.†

---

* The little odd-shaped ruin which we passed before entering Balbek, was a wretched heaping together of materials from old temples, evidently set up by the Arabs or Turks as a guard-house.

† In going to Balbek we were 15½ hours of travel,—in returning 17 hours. The distance cannot be less than fifty miles.

The Mediterranean.

DEPARTURE FROM BEIRUT—LAODICEA—ALEXANDRIA AD ISSUM—TARSUS—RHODES—THE ISLANDS—SMYRNA—QUARANTINE—THE HELLESPONT—SEA OF MARMORA—CONSTANTINOPLE—ADIEU TO MOSLEM LANDS.

On the 13th of June we rowed out to the English steamer "Grand Turk," that lay upon the glassy surface of the sea before the town. Lebanon was radiant with more than usual majesty, and the sunlight streamed upon minaret and grove with all the glory of its beams. A thrill of regret was ours to leave this scene of almost unearthly beauty, and the tear was scarce suppressed as we gazed long and steadfastly on every feature in the view. Our Egyptian retinue bade us an affectionate farewell, the boats were hoisted, the anchor weighed, and the paddles of the "Grand Turk" commenced their revolutions. We could do nothing but enjoy the charming prospect of the Lebanon, its groves and villages, and the town which we had left, with its old shattered castle, until darkness compelled us to desist, and urged us to the examination of our passenger-list. Six of our number had crossed the Arabian desert together; two others (Americans) had been companions in Egypt and Syria; and our English friend and his wife, who had so kindly arranged a quasi treaty with old Sheikh Hossein of Akabah, with a view to benefit future travellers, were also of the party; a German professor who had passed some time in Egypt accompanied the latter, and four other gentlemen, English, Scotch, French, and Italian respectively, completed the number of our co-occupants of the first cabin. I except a lady and her two children, who remained aboard only one night, having left us at Latakiyeh. She was the daughter of the English Consul-General, who was now residing at the mouth of the Orontes. And I except also a Turkish Bey and his suite, who, though probably booked as cabin passengers, bivouacked principally upon the quarter-deck, the dignified Bey alone seeking his night quarters below, when his method of getting into a berth was a constant source of amusement to our pitiless company.

We left Beirut on Wednesday, and arrived in Smyrna the ensuing Tuesday, and during the entire trip the sea was as smooth as a mountain lake. This calm serenity of Neptune, combined with a cloudless sky and an oriental climate, rendered the voyage the most delightful we had ever taken. Every day we stopped at some port, where an agreeable variety presented itself in costume, scenery, and interesting associations. Our captain was a gentleman of unaffected kindness and careful attention to his duties, the boat itself was unexceptionable in cabin and kitchen, and (perhaps the greatest delight of all) the crew talked nothing but plain, comprehensible Saxon.

On the morning of Thursday, we found ourselves passing pleasantly along the Syrian coast, where the snow-capped mountains still formed the prominent feature of the view. A ruined Saracenic castle of considerable magnitude, crowning a hill near the shore, drew our attention, beyond which we passed the town of Jebili, the Gabala of Strabo, which he mentions as a neighbouring little city to Laodicea. At ten o'clock we anchored before this Laodicea, now Latakiyeh, famous through the East for its delightfully flavoured tobacco. The town lies a mile away from the sea, among groves of loveliest green. Its little port is now almost inaccessible by reason of the rubbish and sand that have filled it. A ruined castle stands at its entrance, serving more the picturesque than the useful. We rowed past this battered structure, and landed at the little village which calls itself the port of Latakiyeh. We noticed many old columns built in the walls of the castle and scattered around its base,—ruins doubtless of the ancient harbour. Strabo thus speaks of this place in his day: " Then comes Laodicea-on-sea,* an admirably built city, possessed of a fine harbour, and surrounded by a country which, in addition to its general fertility, produces a large quantity of wine. It affords the most of the wine for Alexandrian consumption, for the whole mountain behind the city is one vast vineyard almost to the summit. * * * * * Dolabella injured the place greatly by flying to it and suffering here a siege from Cassius, whereby the better part of the city was destroyed with the fugitive." The place had been originally a Phœnician settlement, but Seleucus Nicator, about 300 B. C., induced by the fruitfulness of the country and its capabilities for trade, founded it anew, under the name of Laodicea, after his mother, the wife of Antiochus. After Cassius had nearly destroyed the place, Antony conferred on it important privileges, as a compensation. More than 200 years after, Pescennius Niger injured its prosperity, and Septimius Severus, his succcessful rival, acted as

---

* So called to distinguish it from five other places called Laodicea.

its physician. Under Moslem rule, it has followed the usual system of decay common to things Mohammedan, and in 1797 an earthquake almost shook it out of existence. Yet its beautiful situation and its eventful history render it a place of no ordinary interest.

The day was very warm, as we walked along the narrow road that led to the town. In the stone walls that bounded the path were many fragments of ancient columns, others lay half buried in the road, all indications of a site of importance in a former age. A native in Frank dress met us; he proved to be the English Consul, and furnished us with a guide, inviting us kindly to come to his house after we had made our examinations of the town. The modern Latakiyeh we found of no great interest in itself, differing little from other Syrian towns, exhibiting the same narrow streets, low houses, semi-picturesque bazaars, and ornamental mosques and minaret. The ruins of ancient Laodicea were, however, more attractive. At the further end of the town we found eight plain columns built in a wall, six of which were complete, and near by one column of the same sort standing out from any other building. Beyond these, we reached an imposing gateway, now converted into a mosque. It is double, having archways through each diameter, the side arches being much the smaller. Its columns, of which there are four, two on either side, are plain shafts with Corinthian capitals. In front, and also in the rear, are plain pilasters instead of columns. An ornamented cornice runs above the arches, and a carved work of greaves, breastplates, helmets, and other armour surround the top. The whole is surmounted by a dome of stone, well constructed. The general effect of the structure is heavy and clumsy. We were convinced it had been a quadrivium, and its date is probably contemporaneous with that of the arch of Janus Quadrifrons in Rome, which it resembles in general heaviness of design, though its detail is more elaborate than the Roman arch. Septimius Severus, who restored Laodicea in a measure, was probably the builder of both.

Not far from this antiquity we found another. This was four Corinthian columns (*three* of the side and *one* of the front) supporting a frieze, the *interior* of which was ornamented by carved work of a grape-vine and clusters,—an appropriate sculpture for this then vine-growing region. This ruin is also built around, and forms part of a little mosque, over whose low door is a long Arabic inscription from the Koran. We sat in a little adjoining garden, while one of our party sketched the ruins. These were all of ancient Laodicea we were able to discover, and I doubt if aught of these could boast of an earlier date than the days of Septimius Severus. In the noble divan-hall of the English Consul, where the breeze could enter unobstructed, and the hot rays of the sun were entirely excluded, we spent the remainder of the visit ashore, smooking sheeshas and drinking the inimitable coffee of the Orient.

At 5¼ P. M. we weighed anchor, and continued our voyage. Before dark we passed the lofty and graceful shaped "Mons Casius," that rises by the entrance of the Bay of Antioch, the mouth of the Orontes. Pliny had such a *high* idea of this mountain, that he states the rising sun could be seen from its top at the fourth watch (3 A. M.), while darkness enveloped the base.

At 4 o'clock the next morning we cast anchor off Iscànderoon, known generally as Alexandretta, the ancient "Alexandria ad Issum," so called from its situation on the Sinus Issicus, or Gulf of Issus, the north-eastern corner of the Mediterranean. The village was utterly unlike anything we had seen, and more resembled an American frontier settlement than an Eastern town. It is situated on marshy ground, and is therefore very unhealthy; but high hills of loveliest green rise close behind it, recalling the verdant Highlands of the Hudson, and forming a landscape of uncommon beauty. Across the gulf towered the snowy heights of Taurus, beyond the confines of Syria.

As arrivals from the lower Syrian coast were here counted as subjects for quarantine, we could not land, but contented ourselves with obtaining the ship's boat and taking up a position near the beach, where we enjoyed a delightful swim. We remained all day anchored before the little village, which seemed to slumber noiselessly in the extreme heat, the sea maintaining its profound calm, everything thus wearing the appearance of rest. In such a situation sleep was inevitable, and much of the day was dozed away beneath the awnings. Now and then we would wistfully glance at the white snow on Taurus, but soon turn away in despair, and compose ourselves for another nap.

By evening we left the peaceful roadstead of Iscanderoon (for harbour there was none), and started westward towards the snowy mountains. At six o'clock Saturday morning, our anchor was again dropped off Mersyn, the port of Tarsus. Here we noticed the same American looking houses we had seen at Iscanderoon, and concluded we had left the Syrian style of house architecture behind, and entered upon a new order, peculiar to Western Turkey. Such, in truth, was the case; and often afterwards we remarked the resemblance to transatlantic villages in the external appearance of the villages of Asia Minor and European Turkey; the wood material for edifices being a prominent feature of the resemblance. Mersyn is a trifling hamlet of five or six houses, situate on a small bay, destitute of harbour, but surrounded by magnificent scenery. Tarsus is, according to Strabo, only five stadia or furlongs from the port, and presents a host of historical memories. As capital of Cilicia it was a famous city, and the rival of Athens for learning and refinement; it was here where Alexander nearly lost his life by bathing in the cold waters of the Cydnus, and here Cleopatra captivated the heart of Antony.

> "The barge she sat in, like a burnished throne
> Burned on the water; the poop was beaten gold,
> Purple the sails, and so perfumed that
> The winds were love-sick with them; the oars were silver,
> Which to the tune of flutes kept stroke, and made
> The water, which they beat, to follow faster,
> As amorous of their strokes."

This place is probably the Tarshish to which Jonah attempted to flee; but its crowning glory, in the eyes of Christendom, is the fact of its being the birth-place of the great apostle of the Gentiles.

We left Mersyn at 10 o'clock in the morning, and sailed along the bold and beautiful coast of Cilicia, passing here and there a green islet close to the shore. Sunday morning found us off the deep bay of Adalia; the land at the head of which was too distant to be visible. Crossing its broad mouth, we arrived before its western cape, the Ἱερα Ακρα, or "Sacrum Promontorium" of Strabo. Here are the Khelidonian Isles, which the same author correctly describes as "three rugged islands, of equal size, some five stadia apart from one another, and six stadia from the main shore." Along the eastern front of the Sacred Promontory, we could see, in the various crevices of the rocky face, the ruins of Phaselis and other towns.

We were astonished at the remarkably blue colour of the water, that resembled a vast expanse of liquid turquoise, comparing well with the gaunt cliffs that here rose from its surface. The temperature was indicated by the mercury at 95° at noon in the shade,— the average temperature of that hour on the whole trip from Beirut to Smyrna.

We finished our view of the bold coast on Sunday with Castelorizo or Mais, the ancient Antiphellus, over whose harbour stood a ruined castle. The mountains here came down to the very brink of the sea, in magnificent groups, which, tinted with the rays of the setting sun, formed a scene of remarkable splendour.

At half-past four on Monday morning we entered the miniature harbour of Rhodes, at the northern extremity of the island of the same name. Neither Knight nor Colossus welcomed our arrival, and the laws of quarantine forbade our landing. During the six or seven hours we spent in the harbour, we could only look upon the exterior of the really pretty town, that sits imposingly beside the water, and behind which rise hills covered with villas, among which that of Sir Sydney Smith was prominent. There are in reality two harbours to Rhodes, each of lilliputian dimensions, the larger being about a quarter of a mile square. The Colossus stood, probably, across the entrance of the smaller harbour,—a very inconsiderable width. A castle stands on each projection of the two harbours, ornamental, though not formidable.

The people of Rhodes are great bigots, and not a Christian lives within the walls. The Bey, our fellow-passenger, was a commissioner of quarantines, and Rhodes was his destination, where he expected to meet several brother Beys, to confer on the subject of quarantine regulations. He accordingly went ashore, and found, to his chagrin, that his colleagues had come and gone, having transacted their business without his presence. Poor fellow! he had to take up his abode in the Rhodes lazaretto, and await the return of our steamer. Leaving the city of the Knights, we entered the Ægean Sea, and now our voyage was a continual feast.

First came Karki, Piscopi, and Nisan, the rocky sponge islands; then we passed between Cos and the main land. Cos lies in the jaws of the Ceramicus Sinus, and is an island of extreme beauty. The town is embosomed in groves, and partially surrounded by a strong looking wall. Behind it, the mountains rise in grandeur, shutting in the gulf, and making it an apparent lake. In Cos, the painter Apelles and the physician Hippocrates were born. Opposite the island, and snugly situate among the mountains of Caria, was Boodroom, the ancient Halicarnassus, the native city of Herodotus and Dionysius, the historians. We passed two or three crowded brigs in this lake-like bay, the only vessels we had seen since leaving Beirut. Night again fell over our vision as we were passing among the Kalydnae Islands, one of which is the "fæcunda Calynda" of Ovid. Near these a low rock, with some masonry upon it, projecting from the sea, was pointed out as the "Pacha's Rock," but wherefore we could not discover.

On Tuesday morning, we looked back on the lofty mountains of Samos, among which Pythagoras had first seen the light. By its side were the less elevated heights of the Fournis and Nicaria, the latter being the ancient Icaria, named after the unfortunate youngster, who, being drowned in his attempt to fly, was washed up by the waves on the shores of this island. Soon after, we entered the Straits of Scio, that separate that island from the main. Scio is the ancient Chios, but is rendered more famous for the awful massacre of its population by the Turks, than for any passage in its *ancient* history. The town is beautifully situated at the foot of the rocky mountains of the island, in the midst of extensive groves. White villas, scattered along the side of the straits, glittered in the sun, as we passed northward. Rounding the promontory of Melœna, we entered the spacious and beautiful bay of Smyrna; on the north of the bay appeared the ancient Phocæa, which was a colony formed from Phocis. Herodotus gives a detailed account of the Phocæans, giving them the credit of being the first explorers of the Adriatic, Tyrrhene, and Western Mediterranean Seas. They were driven from their city by the army of Cyrus under Harpagus, and while many sought refuge in Chios, Corsica, and Italy, some returned again to their old town. The place is now a village. *Marseilles* was founded by a colony of Phocæans, a fact sufficient of itself to render their history worthy of preservation. Beyond Phocæa, the Sarabat emptied its waters in the gulf; this river is the ancient Hermus, which received the golden sands of Pactolus, and by its side were the white hills which marked the site of Leucæ, where Andronicus, the pretender to the crown of Pergamus, was defeated by Crassus. Passing the long, green, but uninhabited island of Chustan, the bay became narrow toward its western end, and we ran along the graceful verdant hills that skirt the southern shore. A fine group of these, that wear a family likeness, bear the title of the "Brothers and Sisters." The low white castle, that seems to mark the division between Smyrna bay and Smyrna harbour, was now behind us, and in full view ahead was Smyrna and its shipping, decidedly the most important looking place we had seen since Cairo. It is finely located, nearly at the head of the long horn-shaped gulf, with all the ornament of water and green mountain scenery that could be desired. Our "Grand Turk" most tantalizingly stopped two miles short of the town, and deposited us before a huge, ugly, yellow building, which needed no sign-board to tell its quality. The sickly colour of the edifice, its dreary and retired situation under a precipitous stony hill, its high walls and barred windows, all declared it that which is at once the traveller's rest and disquiet—the Quarantine. Twelve long days were appointed as the term of our durance within those sombre limits. Protestations were useless, and we meekly moved ashore with our luggage. The captain accompanied us to our lodgings, and a malicious smile was on his features as he turned to leave, after congratulating us on our new abode. There can be little said in praise of the Smyrna lazaretto. A large enclosure, bounded by a high wall, and divided into two parts by a partition-wall, formed the area in which was the yellow edifice, and, removed from it, a miniature structure of like colour, where *Spoglio* is performed, that is, where one endures an atmosphere of smoke for a half hour, in order to obtain the atmosphere of freedom three days earlier. In this enclosure the grass wore a quarantine hue, and a few orange, pomegranate, and pride-of-India trees supplied us with slender materials for rural enjoyment. Although the sea came up almost to the base of the building, all bathing was *taboo*. We were, moreover, informed by a ponderous Bey, who was Supreme Governor of the Hygeian territory, that our linen could only be sent out to wash after seven days' airing and forty-eight hours' soaking! As this would seriously interfere with our ideas of personal cleanliness, we preferred importing a washerwoman from Smyrna, and succeeded in obtaining an old hag, whose very face rendered more intolerable the woes of quarantine. The Bey was unbendingly strict in the enforcement of the regulations, which seemed to grow in number and severity exactly as his despotic soul desired, and we therefore determined to be revenged, big with indignation at the tyranny of his High Mightiness.

We had just been sitting under the orange trees, when the pompous officer, with a suite of attachés, approached, and sat down upon the chairs we had left the moment before. This was our signal. We all crowded around, and informed him the chairs had just been vacated by us, and, therefore, he was our companion in quarantine. He sprang up as bitten by a serpent, and, dashing the chair ten feet from him, profusely vociferated the only two Frank words he knew, "No quarantine." We laughed loudly, and ridiculed his consternation. He was completely thrown off his dignity, while we persecuted him with shouts of merriment, when he took to his heels and bolted out of the yard, in order to escape our laughter. We had frightened him not a little, and if we had desired, could have enforced his quarantine; but we were satisfied with his discomfiture, and troubled him him no further. The mortified Bey never showed his face again while we were occupants of his dominions.

Our rooms comprised the whole upper story of the building, and were furnished by the hotel keeper at Smyrna, who duly sent down a company of domestics and all things else necessary for our comfort. But the sinks of the building were out of order, probably never having been *in order*, and a nauseous stench continually filled our apartments. For this reason several of our party were taken severely sick, and I doubt not that this effluvium was a chief cause of the death of a Turkish boy, who had been one of the steerage passengers in the "Grand Turk." He was laid out and buried before our windows, in the enclosure.

We were driven to every device for pastime during our sojourn. We read and smoked, wrote and chatted, till aweary—the quoits were introduced, and vigorously pitched—at length, a horizontal bar was erected, and a series of gymnastic performances ensued. One of the most brilliant passages of fun, however, which we experienced, was a grand game of leap-frog after this wise:

Some forty Turks were in quarantine with us, who were close imitators of our Frankish sports, at once novelties and amusements to these true believers. We were aware that the Turkish costume was not designed for the laudable game of leap-frog, and arranged matters accordingly. Our positions were duly taken, and we infidels ran bounding over one another's backs with a rapidity and oddity perfectly marvellous in the eyes of Islamism. After losing breath, we withdrew our forces, and sat quietly beneath the trees. As expected, the Turks immediately took the field, and a dozen bent backs were presented to the neophyte leapers. A young Moslem, proud of his prowess, opened the scene. A short run, a bold leap, and two Turks were sprawling upon the ground. Another daring youngster followed, and down came two more turbaned sons of the Prophet. Cursing the clumsiness of their predecessors, a third and a fourth attempted the leap, but again and again the loose trowsers sent a new couple to the ground, while Turk and Frank alike were nearly convulsed with laughter.

At length our days of incarceration expired, the physician (a good-natured Italian) pronounced us wholesome members of the community, and informed us that we could give up looking out of our windows at the bay, and take a closer view of its beauties. On the last day of June we left the melancholy spot, and were rowed to Smyrna in the noble row-boats that are peculiar to that region, and which, for grace, speed, and capacity united, have not their equals in the world. Our quarantine had been so situated as to shut out all view of the city, and it was not till the day of our escape that we indulged in a protracted examination of its external appearance. It lies chiefly along the edge of the water, though at its southern extremity it covers some hill-sides, where groves of tapering cypress mark the place of graves. Behind the southern part of the town rises Mount Pagus, a rocky height on which is a Genoese castle, built around the site of the ancient Stadium. A number of vessels were anchored in the harbour, one of which bore the colours of our own republic.

We had a busy day in Smyrna, seeing nothing but bankers and consuls, and at 4 P. M. we were aboard the "Mentor," a French steamer, *en route* for Constantinople. Retracing our way along the beautiful bay, we reached the island of Mytilene, the ancient Lesbos, where Sappho's muse first sang, and passed between this large island and the main. On rising in the morning, we were beyond Tenedos, behind which the Grecian fleet had lain concealed from the sight of the Trojans. The great plain of Troy was stretched out beside us, bounded by the range of Ida. Imbros was far on our left, and before us was the Thracian Chersonese.

Passing the Sigæan promontory, where Achilles and Patroclus were entombed, now covered with windmills, and the mouth of the Scamander, by which the

Grecian host encamped, we entered the Hellespont, Europe on our left and Asia on our right. On either side, a Turkish castle guards the straits. The Asiatic castle is termed Chanak-Kalessi, and here is a forlorn wooden town of the same name, also known as the town of Dardanelles, the ancient Dardanus. A dozen flags were flying from as many houses, each denoting a Frank consulate, and before the town was a fleet of shipping. This place is a sort of outpost to Constantinople. We remained three hours, for some commercial or quarantine reason which I could not fathom. Opposite, was the castle on the hill-side, bearing the modest title of "The Lock of the Sea." A village surrounds it, and by its side is the mound which is said to cover the remains of Hecuba. Further north, we passed the point of Abydos and its white castle,— then the supposed site of Xerxes' bridge, where the straits are narrowest (perhaps one and a half miles broad),—and then Sestos was upon the left. Lord Byron has connected his name indissolubly with this vicinity. At length we passed the pleasant looking town of Gallipolis, and entered the Sea of Marmora. The Hellespont was pretty, and that's all. Its banks were surmounted by low hills, neither cultivated nor inhabited for the most part, and it was impossible to excite much enthusiasm. We paddled by the Island of Marmora in the moonlight, and in the morning we were in sight of the minarets of St. Sophia. But that was almost all we could see of the Metropolis of Turkey, for a dense fog veiled the city from our view. Our steamer paced the waters like a sentinel, backward and forward, for two or three hours, afraid to enter the port during the fog, when at last the mist was dissipated, and one of the most gorgeous visions ever seen was ours to behold. Palaces, domes, and minarets rose rank on rank from the water's edge; the Bosphorus was alive with gay caiques; and beyond the imperial city, as far as the eye could discern, the green banks of this unequalled water was lined with noble mansions and smiling villas. Much as we had heard of the magnificence of Constantinople, we were astonished at the scene. The ideal of beauty is here realized, and the imagination has no cause for employment.

In an hour more, our feet again trod the soil of Europe. I do not intend a notice of our twelve days' sojourn in the environs of Stamboul. The city of the Sultan is almost as well known to the Western World as the capitals of France or England. Authors have thoroughly described its beauties and its filth, its population and their customs, and have left no fragments for me to gather. Artists, too, have brought away every street and house in all Stamboul for our minute inspection, and we realize the Arabian story of the invisible man, in looking unseen upon the wonders of the Turkish metropolis. Suffice it, then, that our twelve days were spent in busy enjoyment of Stamboul, Pera, Galata, Scutari, and the unparalleled suburban scenery of the Bosphorus, while the kind attentions of the American missionaries and our legation at the Turkish Court were such as shall ever be gratefully remembered.

On the 15th of July we were again in Smyrna, and had time, during the two days of our sojourn, to enter more largely into its comprehension. The caravan bridge, the great rendezvous of the camels and their owners, was visited; and Mount Pagus was climbed, where we saw the remains of the stadium in which Polycarp suffered martyrdom. Hence was a splendid view of Smyrna and its noble bay. From such positions as this the world looks all happiness below, for we see little else but the glassy water, the lofty mountains, the green groves, and the wild valleys—the works of God; but descend the height, and, in inseparable union, misery and the works of man arrest your eye.

On the calm, lovely evening of the 17th of July we were upon the deck of the French steamer "Tancréde," watching the rocky summits of Scio, that were fast fading from view behind us. The shades of night were gathering over the peaceful Ægean, and the perfect tranquillity of nature conduced to meditation not unmixed with sadness. While thus gazing towards the land from which we were hastening, and bringing in review the enchantments of the Past, darkness enveloped the heights of Scio, and the curtain fell forever between us and the *Lands of the Moslem*.

Appendix.

HINTS FOR TRAVELLERS ON THE NILE.

BOAT.

IF a person goes *solus*, take a "cangia"—if there are more, a "dahabiyeh." Not more than four travellers can go in one boat. If a dahabiyeh is taken, by no means have less than ten sailors, including rais and pilot, and make the rais take a boy besides to cook for the crew. See that the boat is new, and that it has not been used as a grain-boat—else you will be overrun with vermin. Sinking the boat before using it is sometimes practised, but unless the vessel is alive with vermin it is poor policy, and if the boat *is* alive with vermin, you would do better to obtain another less inhabited. Examine the hold and see if it leaks, for if a leaky boat is taken, much valuable time is lost on the voyage in baling out. Do your examinations personally. If ladies go, oblige the crew to wear drawers. Make the contract by the *trip*, and not by the *month*, allowing yourself (if the voyage is only to Thebes) ten days for stoppages to see ruins, &c. You track or sail *up*, and row or sail *down* the river.

MANAGEMENT OF CREW.

Never let the rais get the upper hand for a moment; if you threaten him, by no means avoid putting the threat into execution, when he continues his misconduct. Give the crew (excluding pilot and rais) for "backsheesh" *a spanish dollar among all*, (*not to each*,) three times on the trip, say, at

Minyeh, at Syoot, and at Thebes, and treat them (pilot and rais included) to a sheep *twice* at least on the voyage. Then to the pilot give two Spanish dollars, and to the rais three Spanish dollars as "backsheesh," for the whole trip, if you are satisfied with them. If you give more, you spoil them and render travelling the more expensive to your successors on the Nile.

You can generally avoid flogging any of the crew, though *in some cases* it is absolutely necessary.

Be firm, yet mild, and Egyptians or Nubians are easily managed. If the rais is troublesome, don't scold, but threaten him with a visit to some governor of a neighboring village, and make no hesitation in conducting him thither if he does not alter his behaviour. Above all, treat rais and crew with uniform kindness.

If the rais has conducted himself badly on the whole trip, do *not* by any means, from carelessness or mistaken notions of forgiveness, give him any backsheesh. If you do, he has no motive for future good behaviour.

Have your contract drawn up at your consulate in due form. Allow the crew one day's stoppage at Syoot to bake their bread.

PROVISION AND UTENSILS FOR NILE VOYAGE.

You can procure all your eatables and drinkables, and kitchen articles, at Cairo, unless you are very fastidious. Go with your dragoman, if you have time, and get what you can at the *native* stores, for the Franks are extortionate. The following was my list, with the prices, for four persons.

Bought in Cairo.		Piastres.	Bought in Cairo.		Piastres.
Rice	20 okas	. 50	Spoons	6 .	. 9
Flour	4 okas	. 16	Furnaces (by wt.) 4 3-7 .		. 31
Maccaroni	10 okas	. 40	Cups and saucers 6 pair		. 30
Sugar	25 okas	. 112½	Glasses	6 .	. 6
Vinegar	2 okas	. 6	Metal tumbler	1 .	. 5
Salt	1 package	. 5	Rat trap	1 .	. 12
Coffee	4 okas	. 36	Gridiron	1 .	. 12
Soap	6 okas	. 42	Table	1 .	. 50
Knives and forks	6 pairs	. 24	Ladles	2 .	. 10

APPENDIX.

Bought in Cairo.			Piastres.
Ale	12 bottles	.	72
Tin plates	4	.	20
China plates	8	.	6
Smoothing iron	1	.	10
Candles	16	.	16
Canteens	2	.	44
Brick	1	.	5
Match-box	1	.	0½
Frying-pan	1	.	5
Salt-cellar	1	.	2
Wooden spoons		.	2
Filter	1	.	50
Hooks	4	.	2
Carving knife and fork	1 pair	.	15
Fire-tongs	1	.	6
Meat knife	1	.	8
Ale basket	1	.	2
Oval plates, small,	2	.	10
" large,	1	.	10
Rice sacks	2	.	7
Dish	1	.	20
Shovel	1	.	4
Stew-pan	1	.	15
Blacking		.	8
Brushes	2	.	6
Cheese		.	26
Potatoes	50 okas	.	125
Sauce-pans	4	.	166
Earthen dish		.	4
Broom		.	2
Copper polish		.	6
Fruits		.	70
Mustard		.	9
Beans		.	12
Tobacco-bag		.	8
Butter jar		.	4½
Basket		.	1½
Bread and 2 baskets		.	42
Butter, fine and common		.	43
Honey		.	14
Wood		.	12
Mashgal		.	13
Oil		.	39
Two large candles		.	16
Table cloth		.	15
Kitchen table		.	12

Bought in Cairo			Piastres.
Tub		.	18
Bason, kettle, sieve, &c.		.	33
Oil kettles	2	.	6
Lanterns	2	.	10
15 fowls and 2 pair pigeons	.	33½
Eggs		.	13
Cafasses		.	7
Wooden mortar		.	8
Building of kitchen		.	15
Spices		.	3½
Alum, flint, and sulphur		.	8
Two chairs		.	30
String, nails, &c.		.	5½
Bottle		.	2½
Tobacco	3 okas	.	60
Pipes		.	51½
Wire		.	1½
Copper basin		.	85
Skin for tobacco		.	2½
Paper		.	10
Vegetables		.	20
Meat		.	16
Plates		.	10
Brandy		.	50
Tea	½ oka	.	20
Curry		.	7
Mats		.	10
Sewing silk		.	3
Egg cups		.	7½
Milk-pot		.	3
Biscuit		.	3
Blower		.	3
Charcoal		.	72
Candles (again)		.	24
Food for fowls		.	1
Soup-ladle		.	5
Tureen		.	6
Milk		.	4½
Screws		.	7
Jug	:	.	1½
Sundries		.	6
			2095
Bought on the Nile, fowls, &c.		667
			2762
		or	$124 00

Total expense of trip from Cairo to Thebes and back—for *four* persons:

Dahabiyeh	$125 00
Backsheesh	12 00
Provision and outfit	124 00
Dragoman's wages (6 weeks)	37 50
Cook's wages (6 weeks)	15 00
Sight seeing	16 50
	$330 00

Thus $330 is the total expense of a six weeks trip to Thebes and back for four persons. That is $82 50 for each individual, or $1 96 (say $2) per day apiece.

GENERAL DIRECTIONS.

As in Upper Egypt it is difficult to find change for large coins, it is necessary to take a large large quantity of copper five-para pieces ($\frac{1}{4}$ of a cent). They can be put in a matting-basket.

For *our* trip, we found $25 worth just a right amount.

Don't fail to take crackers or biscuit with you, as bread is only to be found at a few places, and the biscuit soaked in cold water is the best substitute. Twice-baked rolls left to dry, are also excellent when soaked.

Remember future travellers, and don't lavish your money needlessly on guides and donkey-boys. Don't stop the songs of your crew,—you might as well prohibit steam from an engine. Singing is the "sine quâ non" of their work.

HINTS TO TRAVELERS ON THE DESERT.

EXPENSES OF JOURNEY FROM CAIRO TO HEBRON, VIA MOUNT SINAI, AKABAH, AND PETRA.

I premise, by stating that one traveller cannot go comfortably with less than *four Camels*, one for himself, one for his sheikh, one for his servant, and one for his luggage.

APPENDIX.

	Piastres.
Four camels	2120
Petra taxes	120
Backsheesh	100
Three days at Sinai	100
Stay at Akabah	80
Outfit and way expenses	1475
Dragoman's wages, (he acts as cook too)	500
Food purchased on the route	80
Dress to the Sheikh	150
Sundries	100

Total expenses of one person — Piastres 4925, or $221. or $7 36 per day.

The particulars of the *camel-price* are thus:

From Cairo to Sinai,	each camel	150 piastres.
Sinai to Akabah,	"	100 "
Akabah to Hebron	"	280 "

Petra taxes are 100 piastres a person for entrance into the valley, and 20 piastres a person for ascending Mount Hor.

The particulars regarding *outfit* and *way expenses*, I give, by presenting our own for *four* persons, as follows:—

DESERT OUTFIT.

	Piastres.		Piastres.
Four water-skins	61	Vinegar	6
Two water-casks	41	Blacking	2
Four Zemzemias	41	Two lanterns	7
Candles	70	Three okas good tobacco	60
Bags and carpets for tent	77½	Seven okas common tobacco	49
Irons for kitchen	20	Leather bags for do.	7
Irons for tent	11	Copper polish	8
Wood for tent	15	Cutting tobacco	2
Four mallets	6	Lantern sticks	5
Sago	20	Tins	15
Rice	10	Cheese	24
Maccaroni	16	Oil	7
Camel bags	46	Kitchen towels	15
Dried fruits	62	Cords and ropes	19
Two cook's knives	5	Camel nets (4)	65
Broom	2	Kitchen sundries	19
Fly brush	3	Books	232
Two locks	2	Bags	18
Seven okas flour	35	Levinge	125

APPENDIX.

	Piastres		Piastres
Figs	10	Box	22
Tent	700	Dates	14
Small kitchen tent	70	Fowls	52
Private tent	35	Pigeons	8
Potatoes	100	Eggs	10
Oil	22	Padlocks	5¼
Honey	59	Candlestick	7½
Pipes	2½	Extra camel nets	22½
Hammer	6	Bread	30
Fans	10	Biscuit (again)	47½
Mirrors	11	Water	11
Cups, saucers, knives, forks, &c.	30	Contract drawn	60
Three large boxes	130	Calico for mattresses	8
Cooking butter	26	Meat	14
Mats for skins	12	Fowls, (again)	8¼
Tin for honey	6	Milk	13
Cord	2	Tongues	28
Charcoal	56	Wood	3
Fresh butter	23	Vegetables	9
Jar for same	4½	Stools	70
Salt	1	Basin	4
Needles	1	Oranges, (again)	8
Cafasses	2	Fan	2
Oranges and lemons	16½	Iron pins for tent	8
Sewing the bags	8	Tomato sauce	18
Paper	10	Bedsteads	180
Sugar	13½	Rolls	65
Coffee	49	Pillows	48
Mattresses, &c.	65	Arrow root	15
Washing the same	25	Pistols	185
Sherbet	60	Powder and shot	20
Preserved roses	82	Cartridges	26
Biscuit	107½	Bullets	7
Baskets	2½	Lantern	4
Maccaroni	15	Twine	5
Tea	12		
Sundries from Frank store	470		4486

EXPENSES ON THE ROUTE.

	Piastres
Bill at Suez Hotel	166
Sight seeing	36
Provision on route	700
Sundries	517
	1419
Total outfit &c., for four	Piastres 5905

The trip across the desert is thus seen to be nearly four times as expensive (per day) as that upon the Nile.

GENERAL DIRECTIONS.

You take camels at Cairo from the Towarah Arabs, to go to Akabah. *There* you take camels from the Alawin Arabs, to go to Hebron.

Pay at Cairo in advance for the route as far as Sinai; but leave the portion of the route from Sinai to Akabah to be paid at Akabah, when you dismiss the Towarah.

Pay at Akabah two-thirds the price to Hebron, and at Hebron pay the remainder.

Take *gold*, (Turkish guineas), as the money for the desert, and a *little silver* for incidental expenses, but *not* copper.

Procure a well-known Sheikh at Cairo, to conduct you. I can recommend Besharah and Mousa, of the Waled Said, and Nassar ebn Mansur, of the Owarmy.

For dragoman, Ibrahim Vyse, a Cairene, is incomparable, being honest and economical, two rare and valuable traits in a dragoman.

At Akabah don't let your Towarah go until you are safely off with your Alawin, or the latter will be extortionate, seeing you completely in their power. For stoppage the Towarah will expect five piastres per day for each camel.

Take water-*casks* as well as skins, and let both be soaked *two weeks* or more before starting, to remove any unpleasant taste.

Take bread baked repeatedly and well dried; when about to use it, soak it slightly in water; it is admirable. Take abundance of coffee and tobacco for the Arabs. Keep the keys of your water-casks yourself. Have stirrups for your dromedaries. For a lady, let a saddle be made like an easy-chair, with high back and sides.

After leaving Cairo, *good* water is found—

First, at Wady Feiran,	10	days' journey.
Secondly, at Sinai,	1	" "
Thirdly, at Petra, (the Akabah water being only tolerable),	9	" "
Lastly, at Hebron,	5	" "

The expenses of travelling in Palestine are a medium between those in Egypt and those on the Desert.

Each person ought to have four horses at least. From Jerusalem to Beirut via Tiberias and Akka each horse costs one hundred and fifty piastres, or more than six dollars. If you go from Jerusalem to Beirut via Damascus, the price is two hundred and twenty piastres for each horse.

In making the excursion from Beirut to Balbek and back, we paid ten piastres for each horse for the first day, and sixteen piastres for every other day absent.

The whole trip from Alexandria to Thebes, Cairo, Mount Sinai, Petra, Jerusalem, and Beirut, may be made by a single person for *five hundred dollars*, the time being *four months*. Of course some economy must be practised in this case. It can be done the easier if the traveller goes in company with others.

TEMPERATURE AS INDICATED BY THE THERMOMETER, IN THE SHADE.

EGYPT.

	Degrees.		Degrees.
March 14, 6 A. M. Syoot,	55		
" 15, 3 P. M. Gebel Aboofoda,	80	Nile water,	68
" 16, Noon. Sheikh Abadeh,	94	" "	70
" 18, 9 A. M. Gebel e' Tayr,	64	" "	68
" 19, 7 A. M. Aboo-Girgeh,	48	" "	65
" 20, 7 A. M. Aboo-Girgeh,	53	" "	64
" 21, 6½ A. M. Aboo-Girgeh,	51	" "	62
" 22, 8 A. M. Beni Sooef,	59	" "	63
" 23, 7½ A. M. Beni Sooef,	53	" "	63
" 25, 8 A. M. Rigga,	56	" "	62
" 25, 2 P. M. Rigga,	80	" "	64

This short list is inserted to show that the equable temperature of the Egyptian climate is greatly exaggerated. I add some observations of the temperature in the Desert and Syria, for comparison:—

APPENDIX.

THE DESERT.

				Degrees
April 9, 9 P. M.	Between Cairo and Suez,			60
" 10, 6 A. M.	" "			55
" 10, 1 P. M.	" "			87
" 10, 9 P. M.	" "			64
" 11, 6 A. M.	" "			60
" 11, 1 P. M.	" "			86
" 11, 7 P. M.	" "			71
" 13, 6 A. M.	Peninsula of Sinai,			70
" 13, 2 P. M.	" "			98
" 14, 6 A. M.	" "			70
" 14, 1 P. M.	" "			100
" 15, 6 A. M.	" "			66
" 15, 2 P. M.	" "			101
" 16, 3 P. M.	" "			102
" 17, 5½ A. M.	" "			83
" 17, 2 P. M.	" "			97
" 18, 9 A. M.	" "		(in sun.)	125
" 18, 2 P. M.	" "		(?)	102
" 24, 2 P. M.	" "			83
" 25, 6 A. M.	" "			73
" 25, 3 P. M.	" "			81
" 26, 6 A. M.	" "			67
" 26, 2 P. M.	" "			92
" 27, 6 A. M.	" "			67
" 27, 2 P. M.	" "			82
" 28, 6 A. M.	" "			63
" 28, 2 P. M.	" "			85
May 1, 6 A. M.	Akabah,			75
" 1, 2 P. M.	"			100
" 1, 6 P. M.	"			82
" 2, 6 A. M.	Arabah,			77
" 2, 2 P. M.	"			87
" 3, 6 A. M.	"			62
" 3, 2 P. M.	"			91
" 3, 6 P. M.	"		(?)	82
" 5, 6 A. M.	Petra,			61
" 5, 3 P. M.	"			71
" 7, 6 A. M.	West of the Arabah,			68
" 7, 2 P. M.	" "			96
" 8, 6 A. M.	" "			76
" 8, 2 P. M.	" "			97
" 9, 6 A. M.	" "			74
" 9, 2 P. M.	" "			92
" 10, 6 A. M.	" "			73
" 10, 2 P. M.	" "			85

It will be observed that, on April 15, a change of thirty-five degrees took place in eight hours.

PALESTINE.

	Degrees.		Degrees.
May 28, 6 P. M. Bethel,	58		
" 29, 6 A. M. "	52		
" 30, 7 P. M. Jenin,	66		
" 31, 6 A. M. "	65		
June 2, 7 A. M. Tiberias,	71	(Water of Lake),	72
" 5, 2 P. M. Tyre,	80		

VALUABLE BOOKS

PUBLISHED BY

ROBERT CARTER & BROTHERS, 285 BROADWAY.

NEW YORK.

Abeel's (Rev. David) Life. By his Nephew,	$ 50
Abercrombie's Contest and The Armor. 32mo.	25
Adam's Three Divine Sisters—Faith, Hope, &c.	60
Advice to a Young Christian. By a Village Pastor. With an Introduction by Rev. Dr. Alexander. 18mo.	30
Alleine's Gospel Promises. 18mo.	30
———— Life and Letters. 12mo.	60
Alexander's Counsels to the Young. 32mo. gilt,	25
Ancient History of the Egyptians, Assyrians, Chaldeans, Medes, Lydians, Carthaginians, Persians, Macedonians, &c. 4 vols. 12mo.	2 00
Anderson—The Annals of the English Bible. By Christopher Anderson. Revised, abridged, and continued by Rev. S. I. Prime. 8vo.	1 75
———— The Family Book; or, The Genius and Design of the Domestic Constitution. 12mo.	75
Australia, the Loss of the Brig, by Fire. 18mo.	25
Bagster—The Genuineness, Authenticity, and Inspiration of the Sacred Volume. 12mo.	60
Baxter's Saint's Rest. Large type. 12mo.	60
———— Call to the Unconverted. 18mo.	30
———— Choice Works. 12mo.	60
Bible Expositor. 18mo.	50
Bickersteth's Treatise on Prayer. 18mo.	40
———— Treatise on the Lord's Supper. 18mo.	30
Blunt's Undesigned Coincidences in the Writings both of the Old and New Testaments, an Argument of their Veracity. 8vo.	1 25
Bogatzky's Golden Treasury. 18mo.	50
Bolton (Miss) Memoir, or the Lighted Valley.	75
Bonar's Night of Weeping. 18mo.	30
———— Story of Grace. 18mo.	30
———— Morning of Joy,	40
Bonnet's Family of Bethany. 18mo.	40
———— Meditations on the Lord's Prayer,	40
Borrow's Bible and Gypsies of Spain. 8vo.	75
Boston's Four-fold State. 18mo.	50
———— Crook in the Lot. 18mo.	30
Brown's Explication of the Assem. Catechism,	60
Bridges on the Christian Ministry. 8vo.	1 50
———— On the Proverbs. 8vo.	2 00
———— On the cxix. Psalm. New ed. 8vo.	1 00
———— Memoir of Mary Jane Graham. 8vo.	1 00
———— Works. 3 vols., containing the above,	5 00
Brown's Concordance. New and neat ed. 24mo.	20
Do. gilt edge,	30
Buchanan's Comfort in Affliction. 18mo.	40
———— On the Holy Spirit. 18 mo. 2d ed.	50
Bunbury's Glory, and other Narratives,	25
Bunyan's Pilgrim's Progress. Fine edition, large type, with eight illustrations by Howland. 12mo.	1 00
Do. do. gilt,	1 50
Do. do. close type. 18mo.	50
———— Jerusalem Sinner Saved. 18mo.	50
———— Greatness of the Soul. 18mo.	50
Butler's Complete Works. 8vo.	$1 50
———— Sermons, alone. 8vo.	1 00
———— Analogy, alone. 8vo.	75
———— and Wilson's Analogy. 8vo.	1 25
Burn's Christian Fragments. 18mo.	40
Calvin on Secret Providence. 18mo.	25
Cameron's Farmer's Daughter. 18mo.	30
Catechisms—The Assembly's. Per hundred,	1 25
Do. with Proofs,	3 00
———— Brown's Short Catechism. Per hund.	1 25
———— Smyth's Ecclesiastical Catechism. 18mo.	25
———— Willison's Communicant's. 18mo.	10
———— Key to the Assembly's Catechism. 18mo.	20
Cecil's Works; comprising his Sermons, Original Thoughts on Scripture, Miscellanies, and Remains. 3 vols. 12mo. with portrait,	3 00
———— Original Thoughts on Scripture, separate,	1 00
Charnock's Choice Works. 12mo.	60
Chalmers' Sermons, enlarged by the addition of his Posthumous Sermons. 2 vols. 8vo. with a fine Portrait,	3 00
———— Lectures on Romans. 8vo.	1 50
———— Miscellanies. 8vo.	1 50
———— Select Works; comprising the above. 4 vols. 8vo. with portrait,	6 00
———— Evidences of Christian Revelation. 2 v.	1 25
———— Natural Theology. 2 vols.	1 25
———— Moral Philosophy,	60
———— Commercial Discourses,	60
———— Astronomical Discourses,	60
Christian Retirement. 12mo.	75
Clarke's Daily Scripture Promises. 32mo. gilt,	30
Clark's Walk about Zion. 12mo.	75
———— Pastor's Testimony,	75
———— Awake, Thou Sleeper,	75
———— Young Disciple,	88
———— Gathered Fragments,	1 00
———— Experience. By the same author. 18mo.	50
Colquhoun's World's Religion. 18mo.	30
Commandment with Promise. By the author of "The First Day of the Week," "Guilty Tongue," &c. With beautiful illustrations by Howland. 16mo.	75
Cowper—The Works of William Cowper; comprising his Life, Letters, and Poems, now first collected by the introduction of Cowper's Private Correspondence. Edited by the Rev. T. S. Grimshaw. With numerous illustrations on steel, and a fine portrait by Ritchie. 1 vol. royal 8vo.	3 00
———— Do. do. sheep,	3 50
———— Do. do. half mor.	4 00
———— Do. do. cloth extra gilt,	4 00
———— Do. do. mor. extra,	5 00
———— Poetical Works, separate. 2 vols.	1 00
Cumming's Message from God. 18mo.	30
———— Christ Receiving Sinners,	30

CARTERS' PUBLICATIONS.

Cunningham's World without Souls. 18mo.	$ 30
Dale—The Golden Psalm; an Exposition of the 16th Psalm. By Rev. Thos. Dale, M.A.	60
Davies' Sermons. 3 vols. 12mo.	2 00
Davidson's Connections. New ed. 8vo.	1 50
David's Psalms, in metre. Large type, 12mo.	75
— Do. do. gilt edge,	1 00
— Do. do. Turkey mor.	2 00
— Do. 18mo., good type. plain sheep,	38
— Do. " do. Turkey mor.	1 25
— Do. 48mo., very neat pocket ed. mor.	25
— Do. " " " gilt edge,	31
— Do. " " " tucks,	50
D'Aubigné's History of the Reformation. Carefully revised, with various additions not hitherto published. 4 vols. 12mo. half cloth,	1 50
— Do. " " full cloth,	1 75
— Do. " " 4th vol. half cloth,	35
— Do. " " full cloth,	50
— Do. " " Complete in 1 vol.	1 60
— Life of Cromwell. 12mo.	50
— Germany, England, and Scotland,	75
— Luther and Calvin. 18mo.	25
Dick's Lectures on Acts. 8vo.	1 50
Dickinson's Scenes from Sacred History. 3d ed.	1 00
Doddridge's Rise and Progress. 18mo.	40
— Life of Colonel Gardiner. 18mo.	30
Duncan's Sacred Philosophy of Seasons. 4 v.	3 00
— Life by his Son. With portrait. 12mo.	75
— Tales of the Scottish Peasantry. 18mo.	50
— Cottage Fireside. 18mo.	40
— (Mrs.) Life of Mary Lundie Duncan,	50
— — Life of George A. Lundie. 18mo.	50
— — Memoir of George B. Phillips,	25
Erskine's Gospel Sonnets. New edition,	1 00
English Pulpit; a collection of Sermons by the most eminent English Divines. 8vo.	1 50
Farr's History of the Egyptians. 12mo.	75
— History of the Persians. 12mo.	75
— History of the Assyrians, Chaldeans, Medes, Lydians, and Carthaginians. 12mo.	75
— History of the Macedonians, the Seleucidæ in Syria, and Parthians. 12mo.	75
Ferguson's Roman Republic. 8vo.	1 50
Fisk's Memorial of the Holy Land. With steel plates,	1 00
Fleury's Life of David. 12mo.	60
Foster's Essays, on Decision of Character, &c. Large type, fine edition, 12mo.	75
— Do. Close type, 18mo.	50
— Essay on the Evils of Popular Ignorance	75
Ford's Decapolis. 18mo.	25
Free Church Pulpit; consisting of Discourses by the most eminent Divines of the Free Church of Scotland. 3 vols. 8vo.	5 00
Fry (Caroline) The Listener. 2 vols. in one,	1 00
— Christ our Law. 12mo.	60
— Sabbath Musings. 18mo.	40
— The Scripture Reader's Guide. 18mo.	30
Geological Cosmogony. By a Layman. 18mo.	30
God in the Storm. 18mo.	25
Graham's (Miss Mary J.) Life and Works. 8vo.	1 00
— Test of Truth, separate. 18mo.	30
Green—The Life of the Rev. Ashbel Green, D.D., by the Rev. Dr. Jones, of Philadelphia,	2 00
Griffith's Live while you Live. 18mo.	30
Haldane's Exposition of Romans. 8vo.	$2 50
Hall (Jos. Bishop of Exeter,) Select Works,	75
Hamilton's Life in Earnest,	30
— Mount of Olives,	30
— Harp on the Willows,	30
— Thankfulness,	30
— Life of Bishop Hall,	30
— The Happy Home. Illustrated,	30
— Life of Lady Colquhoun. With portrait.	75
Hawker's Poor Man's Morning Portion. 12mo.	60
— " Evening Portion,	60
Zion's Pilgrim. 18mo.	30
Hervey's Meditations,	
Hetherington's Hist. of the Church of Scotland,	1 50
Hengstenberg's Egypt and the Books of Moses, or the Books of Moses Illustrated by the Monuments of Egypt. 12mo.	75
Henry's (Matth.) Method for Prayer,	40
— Communicant's Companion,	40
— Daily Communion with God,	30
— Pleasantness of a Religious Life,	30
— Choice Works. 12mo.	60
Henry (Philip) Life of. 18mo.	50
Hill's (George) Lectures on Divinity. 8vo.	2 00
— (Rowland) Life. By Sidney. 12mo.	75
History of the Puritans in England, and the Pilgrim Fathers. By the Rev. W. H. Stowell and D. Wilson, F.S.A. With 2 steel plates,	1 00
History of the Reformation in Europe. 18mo.	40
Housman's Life and Remains. 12mo.	75
Horne's Introduction. 2 v. royal 8vo. half cloth.	3 50
— Do. 1 vol. sheep,	4 00
— Do. 2 vols. cloth,	4 00
— Do. 2 vols. library style,	5 00
— (Bishop) Commentary on the Psalms.	1 50
Howard (John) or the Prison World of Europe.	1 00
Howell's Life—Perfect Peace. 18mo.	30
Howe's Redeemer's Tears, and other Essays.	50
Huss' (John) Life. Transl. from the German,	25
Jacobus on Matthew. With a Harmony,	75
— Questions on do. 18mo.	15
— On Mark, Luke, and John,	
James' Anxious Inquirer. 18mo.	30
— True Christian. 18mo.	30
— Widow Directed. 18mo.	30
Janeway's Heaven upon Earth. 12mo.	60
— Token for Children 18mo.	30
Jay's Morning Exercises. 12mo.	75
— Evening " 12mo.	75
— Christian Contemplated. 18mo.	40
— Jubilee Memorial. 18mo.	30
Jerram's Tribute to a beloved only Daughter,	30
Johnson's Rasselas. Elegant edition,	50
Key to the Shorter Catechism. 18mo.	30
Kennedy's (Grace) Profession is not Principle,	30
— Jessy Allan, the Lame Girl. 18mo.	25
Kitto's Daily Bible Illustrations. 4 vols. 12mo.	4 00
Krummacher's Martyr Lamb. 18mo.	40
— Elijah the Tishbite. 18mo.	40
— Last Days of Elisha. 12mo.	75
Life in New York. 18mo.	40
Lowrie's Letters to Sabbath School Children,	25
— (Rev. W. M.) Life. Edited by his Father.	1 50
Lockwood's Memoir. By his Father. 18mo.	40
Luther's Commentary on Galatians. 8vo.	1 50
Martin's (Sarah) Life. 18mo.	30

CARTERS' PUBLICATIONS.

Mackay—The Wycklifites; or, England in the 15th Century,	$ 75
Martyn's (Henry) Life. 18mo.	60
Mason's Essays on the Church. 12mo.	60
" " on Episcopacy. 12mo.	60
Marshall on Sanctification,	50
Martyrs and Covenanters of Scotland. 18mo.	40
Malcolm on the Atonement. 18mo.	30
McCrindell—The Convent, a Narrative,	50
McGilvray's Peace in Believing. 18mo.	25
McGhee on the Ephesians,	2 00
McLeod's Life and Power of True Godliness,	60
McCheyne's (Rev. Robert Murray) Works. 2 v.	3 00
—— Life, Lectures, and Letters, separate,	1 50
—— Sermons, separate,	2 00
—— Familiar Letters from the Holy Land,	50
McFarlane—The Mountains of the Bible, their Scenes and their Lessons. With four Illustrations on steel. 12mo.	75
—— Do. do. extra gilt,	1 25
Meikle's Solitude Sweetened. 12mo.	60
Miller's (Rev. Dr. S.) Memoir of Rev. Dr. Nisbet	75
—— (Rev. John) Design of the Church,	60
Michael Kemp, the Farmer's Lad. 18mo.	40
Missions, The Origin and History of. By Choules and Smith. With 25 steel plates,	3 50
Moffat's Southern Africa. 12mo.	75
Monod's Lucilla; or, the Reading of the Bible,	40
More (Hannah)—The Book of Private Devotion. Large type, elegant edition, 18mo.	50
—— Do. do. do. gilt,	75
—— Do. do. small ed. 32mo.	20
—— Do. do. " gilt.	30
Morell's Historical and Critical View of the Speculative Philosophy of Europe in the 19th Century,	3 00
Murphy—The Bible Consistent with Geology,	
My School Boy Days. 18mo.	30
My Youthful Companions. 18mo.	30
The above two bound in 1 vol.	50
Newton's (Rev. John) Works. 2 vols. 8vo.	3 00
—— Life, separate. 18mo.	30
—— Memoir of M. Magdalen Jasper.	30
Noel's Infant Piety. 18mo.	25
North American Indians. Illustrated. 18mo.	50
Olmsted's Counsels for the Impenitent,	50
Old White Meeting-House. 18mo.	40
Old Humphrey's Observations,	40
—— Addresses,	40
—— Thoughts for the Thoughtful,	40
—— Homely Hints,	40
—— Walks in London,	40
—— Country Strolls,	40
—— Old Sea Captain,	40
—— Grandparents,	40
—— Isle of Wight,	40
—— Pithy Papers,	40
—— Pleasant Tales,	40
Opie on Lying. New edition, 18mo.	40
Owen on Spiritual Mindedness. 12mo.	60
Paley's Horæ Paulinæ. 12mo.	75
Pascal's Provincial Letters. Edited by M'Crie,	1 00
—— Thoughts on Religion. 12mo.	1 00
Paterson on the Assemb. Shorter Catechism.	50
Pike's True Happiness. 18mo.	30
—— Religion and Eternal Life. 18mo.	30
Pike's Divine Origin of Christianity. 18mo.	$ 30
Philip's Devotional Guides, 2 vols. 12mo.	1 50
—— Marys,	40
—— Marthas,	40
—— Lydias,	40
—— Hannahs,	40
—— Love of the Spirit,	40
—— Young Man's Closet Library,	75
Pollok's Course of Time. The most elegant edition ever published; printed on superfine paper. 18mo. with portrait, cloth,	1 00
—— —— gilt, cloth, extra,	1 50
—— —— Turkey morocco, gilt,	2 00
—— —— Small copy, close type, 18mo.	40
—— Life, Letters, and Remains. By the Rev. James Scott, D.D. With Portrait, 16mo.	1 00
—— Tales of the Scottish Covenanters. Printed on large paper, uniform with the above. With portrait,	75
—— Do. do. small copy, 18mo.	50
—— Helen of the Glen. 18mo.	25
—— Persecuted Family. 18mo.	25
—— Ralph Gemmell. 18mo.	25
Porteus' Lectures on Matthew. 12mo.	60
Psalms in Hebrew. Neat miniature edition,	50
Reign of Grace. By Booth,	75
Retrospect, The. By Aliquis. 18mo.	40
Richmond's Domestic Portraiture. Edited by Bickersteth. New and elegant edition,	75
—— Annals of the Poor. 18mo.	40
Rogers' Jacob's Well. 18mo.	40
Romaine on Faith. 12mo.	60
—— Letters. 12mo.	60
Rowland's Common Maxims of Infidelity,	75
Rutherford's Letters. New edition, 8vo.	1 50
Scott's Force of Truth. 18mo.	25
Scougal's Works. 18mo.	40
Scripture Narratives. By Dr. Belcher. 12mo.	60
Select Works of James, Venn, Wilson, Philip and Jay. Eight complete works in 1 vol.	1 50
Select Christian Authors; comprising Doddridge, Wilberforce, Adams, Halyburton, à Kempis, &c. With Introductory Essays by Dr. Chalmers, Bishop Wilson, &c. 2 v.	2 00
Serle's Christian Remembrancer,	50
Sinner's Friend. 18mo.	25
Sigourney (Mrs. L. H.) Water Drops. 2d edit.	75
—— The Girl's Book. 18mo. illustrated,	40
—— The Boy's Book. " "	40
—— Child's Book. Square, "	35
Sinclair's Modern Accomplishments,	75
—— Modern Society.	75
—— Charlie Seymour. 18mo.	30
—— Hill and Valley. 12mo.	75
Simeon's Life, by Carus. With Introductory Essay by Bishop McIlvaine. With portrait,	2 00
Sir Roland Ashton. By Lady Catharine Long,	75
Sketches of Sermons on the Parables and Miracles of Christ. By the author of the Pulpit Cyclopædia. 12mo.	75
Smyth's Bereaved Parents Consoled. 12mo.	75
Sorrowing Yet Rejoicing. 18mo.	30
—— Do. do. 32mo. gilt.	30
Spring (Rev. Gardiner, D.D.)—A Pastor's Tribute to one of his Flock, or Memoirs of the late Hannah L. Murray. With a portrait,	1 50

CARTERS' PUBLICATIONS.

Stevenson's Christ on the Cross. 12mo.	$ 75
—— Lord our Shepherd. 12mo.	60
Sumner's Exposition of Matthew and Mark.	75
Stoddard's British Pulpit. 2 vols. 8vo.	3 01
Symington on the Atonement. 12mo.	75
Tacitus' Works translated. Edited by Murphy.	2 00
Tennent's Life. 18mo.	25
Tuplock's Circle of Human Life. 18mo.	30
Taylor's (Jane) Life and Correspondence.	40
—— Contributions of Q. Q. New edition, with fine illustrations by Howland. 2 vols. in one.	1 00
—— Original Poems. 18mo.	30
—— Display, a Tale. 18mo.	30
—— Mother and Daughter.	30
—— Essays in Rhyme. 18mo.	30
—— Original Poems and Poetical Remains. With 12 fine illustrations by Howland.	40
—— (Isaac) Loyola ; or, Jesuitism in its Rudiments.	1 00
—— Natural History of Enthusiasm. 12mo.	75
—— (Jeremy) Sermons. Complete in 1 vol.	1 50
Turretine's Complete Works, in original Latin, The Theological Sketch Book ; or, Skeletons of Sermons, so arranged as to constitute a complete body of Divinity. From Simeon, Hannam, Benson, &c. 2 vols.	3 00
Tyng's Lectures on the Law and Gospel. New edition, large type, with a fine portrait, 8vo.	1 50
—— Christ is All. 8vo. with portrait.	1 50
—— Israel of God. 8vo. enlarged edition.	1 50
—— Recollections of England. 12mo.	1 00
Thucydides' History of the Peloponnesian War. Translated by William Smith. 8vo.	1 25
Turnbull's Genius of Scotland ; or Sketches of Scottish Scenery, Literature, and Religion. New ed. with 8 fine illustrations. 16mo.	1 00
—— Pulpit Orators of France and Switzerland, with Sketches of their Character and Specimens of their Eloquence. With portrait of Feneion,	$1 00
Waterbury's Book for the Sabbath. 18mo.	40
Whately's Kingdom of Christ and Errors of Romanism.	75
Whitecross' Anecdotes on Assem. Catechism.	30
White's (Hugh) Meditation on Prayer. 18mo.	40
—— Believer ; a Series of Discourses. 12mo.	40
—— Practical Reflections on the Second Advent. 18mo.	40
—— (Henry Kirke) Complete Works. With Life by Southey. 8vo.	1 50
—— Do. extra gilt.	2 50
Wilson's Lights and Shadows of Scottish Life.	50
—— Do. on large paper, 16mo. with 8 illustrations, from original drawings, by Croome, Billings, &c., engraved by Howland.	75
—— Do. do. extra gilt.	1 25
Williams (Rev. John), Memoir of. Missionary to Polynesia. By Eb. Prout. With two illustrations, 12mo.	1 00
Winslow on Personal Declension and Revival.	60
Wylie's Journey over the Region of Fulfilled Prophecy.	30
Xenophon's Whole Works. Translated.	2 00
Young's Night Thoughts. Elegant edition. 16mo. with portrait,	1 00
—— Do. do. extra gilt.	1 50

NEW BOOKS.

Blunt's Coincidences and Paley's Horæ Paulinæ. 2 vols. in one. 8vo.	$2 00
Brown's, Rev. John, D.D., Exposition of the First Epistle of Peter. 8vo.	
Broken Bud, or Reminiscences of a Bereaved Mother. 16mo.	
Cecil's, Cath., Memoir of Mrs. Hawker. 12mo.	
Cheever, Rev Dr., Lectures on the Pilgrim's Progress. New edition, 12mo.	1 00
David's Psalms, with Brown's Notes. 18mo. sheep.	0 50
Dickinson's, R. W., D.D., Responses from the Sacred Oracles. 12mo.	
Duncan, Mrs., Children of the Manse. 16mo.	1 00
Do do. Gilt.	1 25
——, Mary Lundie. Rhymes for my Children.	
Hooker, Rev. Herm., Uses of Adversity. 18mo.	0 50
——, Philosophy of Unbelief. 12mo.	0 75
James, J. A., Young Man from Home. 18mo.	0 30
—— Christian Professor. 12mo.	0 75
Kennedy, Grace, Anna Ross. With six fine illustrations. 18mo.	0 30
Leyburn's, Rev. John, Soldier of the Cross, 12mo.	
Line upon Line. 18mo.	0 30
Lowrie, Rev. John C., Two Years in Upper India. 12mo.	0 75
Matthews, Rev. James, D.D., The Bible and Civil Government. 12mo.	$1 00
M'Cosh, Rev. J., The Divine Government, Physical and Moral. 8vo.	
M'Lelland, Prof. Alex, on the Canon and Interpretation of Scripture. 12mo.	0 75
New Cobwebs to catch Little Flies. Illustrated.	
Pastor's Daughter, by Louisa P. Hopkins.	0 40
Peep of Day. New edition. 18mo.	0 30
Pollok's Tales of the Covenanters. Illustrated edition. 16mo.	0 75
Do. do. Gilt.	1 00
Powerscourt's, Lady, Letters and Papers. 12mo.	0 75
Precept on Precept. 18mo.	0 30
Smith, Rev. James. The Believer's Daily Remembrancer, or Green Pastures for the Lord's Flock.	
Taylor, Jane, Hymns for Infant Minds. Illustrated. Square.	
Waugh, Rev. Alex., D.D., Memoir of, with Selections from his Correspondence, &c , by Dr. Hay and Dr. Belfrage. 12mo. Portrait.	
Wilberforce's Practical View. Large type, fine edition. 12mo.	
Wimer's Idioms of the Language of the New Testament. 8vo.	2 50

R. Carter & Brothers have nearly ready the first volume of the "WORKS OF JOHN OWEN," to be completed in sixteen volumes octavo. It is their intention to issue a volume every three months till the whole are issued.

CPSIA information can be obtained
at www.ICGtesting.com
Printed in the USA
BVHW041647120820
586242BV00008B/78

9 781165 433988